Templer
and the Road
to Malayan
Independence

The **Institute of Southeast Asian Studies (ISEAS)** was established as an autonomous organization in 1968. It is a regional centre dedicated to the study of socio-political, security and economic trends and developments in Southeast Asia and its wider geostrategic and economic environment. The Institute's research programmes are the Regional Economic Studies (RES, including ASEAN and APEC), Regional Strategic and Political Studies (RSPS), and Regional Social and Cultural Studies (RSCS).

ISEAS Publishing, an established academic press, has issued more than 2,000 books and journals. It is the largest scholarly publisher of research about Southeast Asia from within the region. ISEAS Publishing works with many other academic and trade publishers and distributors to disseminate important research and analyses from and about Southeast Asia to the rest of the world.

Templer

and the Road to Malayan Independence

The Man and His Time

LEON COMBER

INSTITUTE OF SOUTHEAST ASIAN STUDIES

Singapore

First published in Singapore in 2015 by
ISEAS Publishing
Institute of Southeast Asian Studies
30 Heng Mui Keng Terrace
Pasir Panjang
Singapore 119614

E-mail: publish@iseas.edu.sg
Website: <http://bookshop.iseas.edu.sg>

The responsibility for facts and opinions in this publication rests exclusively with the authors and their interpretations do not necessarily reflect the views or the policy of the publishers or their supporters.

ISEAS Library Cataloguing-in-Publication Data

Comber, Leon, 1921–
   Templer and the road to Malayan independence : the man and his time.
   1. Templer, Gerald, Sir, 1898–1979.
   2. Marshals—Great Britain—Biography.
   3. Malaysia—Politics and government—20th century.
   4. Malaya—History—Malayan Emergency, 1948–1960.
   I. Title.
DS597 C72   2015

ISBN 978-981-4620-10-9 (soft cover)
ISBN 978-981-4620-11-6 (e-book, PDF)

Typeset by Superskill Graphics Pte Ltd
Printed in Singapore by Markono Print Media Pte Ltd

CONTENTS

LIST OF TABLES

FOREWORD

This book presents a fresh look at General Templer, whose brief presence in Malaya (1952–54) played a significant and pivotal role in the making of self-rule in the colony, which subsequently led to the first General Elections in 1955 and then the all-important independence in 1957. It highlights the political and socio-economic aspects of his governance which were underpinned by a military model, principle and discipline.

Templer's "political philosophy" was deceptively simple and was captured well in the following statement of his that he made regarding his strategy to defeat the Communists forward movement in Malaya during the Emergency period (1948–60): "The answer (to the uprising) lies not in pouring more troops into the jungle, but in the hearts and minds of the Malayan people" (Brian Lapping, *End of Empire*, 1985, p. 224). The words "hearts and minds" have since become a mantra in Malaysian realpolitik with only a handful knowing of their origin, but Dr Comber explains the origin of this phrase, which was actually first used in 1818 by John Adams (second U.S. President).

It is generally known that even though he was well qualified to deal with the military aspects of fighting the Chinese-dominated Malayan Communist Party during the Emergency, Templer, however, did not have the same kind of expertise to deal with the "complex and complicated" ethnic relations in Malaya. His opinion on and attitude towards the leadership of UMNO and MCA was not entirely favourable and at best only civil. In spite of that Templer successfully fought to grant Malayan citizenship to 2.6 million non-Malayan residents, a majority of whom were Chinese. He also sought political and social equality of all Malayans long before the idea became fashionable among NGOs and civil society groups in Malaysia in the 1980s.

Dr Comber, through his sharp scholarly lens and the rich analytical skills he acquired while in the intelligence service, takes us on a journey many Malaysians have never taken before, that is, looking closely at the short but highly impactful life of a high-ranking British officer in shaping Malayan, and eventually Malaysian, ethnic politics and governance.

Many Malaysianists recognize the role of "colonial knowledge", a theory developed by Bernard Cohn, in the making of the history, territory, rule-of-law and society in Malaya (Malaysia). However, in this important book, Dr Comber has successfully "put a face to a theory", as it were, by introducing Templer and his brief and extremely influential presence in colonial Malaya in the creation of "colonial knowledge" of the Malayan variety. This is an achievement of Dr Comber that deserves accolades.

Dr Comber's study also reflects the reservations that were often felt about Templer's authoritarian style. Relying for the most part on primary and other first-hand sources, he also notes that while Templer was no doubt a good general and had an excellent military record, his skill as a diplomat did not measure up to his military skills, and his proconsulship in Malaya was often marred by his well-known abrasiveness and sharp tongue, and his lack of understanding of the nuances of Malaya's cultural background and history.

Written with sensitivity and insight towards past and present socio-political realm in Malaysia, this book is an outstanding contribution to a history of inter-ethnic understanding, to ethnic studies in general, and colonial knowledge in particular. For Malaysian Studies enthusiasts and those interested in post-colonial studies, this is a must-read.

Shamsul, A.B.
Distinguished Professor and Founding Director
Institute of Ethnic Studies,
Universiti Kebangsaan Malaysia

Member, International Advisory Board
Institute of Southeast Asian Studies,
Singapore

ACKNOWLEDGEMENTS

My grateful thanks are due to the following persons:

Ambassador K. Kesavapany, the former Director of ISEAS, who suggested I should write the book.

The former President of Singapore, S.R. Nathan, for his great encouragement and help throughout the writing of the book and his support for the research without which the book could not have been written.

ISEAS Director, Tan Chin Tiong, Singapore's former distinguished Ambassador to Japan, for encouragement and continuing support in so many ways.

The late and never forgotten Tunku Abdul Rahman Putra Al-Haj, Malaysia's first Prime Minister, and the godfather of my daughter, who suggested many years ago that I should write this book, and who now appears in it many times.

Pitt Kuan Wah, Head, ISEAS Library, who has gone out of his way to obtain primary source material for me, and Ng Kok Kiong, Head, ISEAS Publications Unit, and Senior Editor Rahilah Yusuf for their technical assistance in preparing the book for publication.

Puan Mahani binti Muhamad, Head, Reference and Access Section, National Archives of Malaysia, for her help in obtaining photographs.

I am greatly indebted to Lee Su Yin, an outstanding educator, and an author and historian in her own right, who was a tower of strength, support and encouragement throughout the research and writing of the book.

My friends of many years, Professor George Bishop and Chan Chow Wah who allowed me to stay at their house in Singapore.

The anonymous readers of the manuscript of my book who gave of their time and expertise in providing helpful comments for improving the text.

Both my wife, Takako, and my daughter Dr Akii, who was completing her Fellowships in Radiology and Nuclear Medicine, for holding the fort in Melbourne.

ABBREVIATIONS

ADC	Aide-de-Camp
ASEAN	Association of Southeast Asian Nations
BAOR	British Army on the Rhine
CCP	Chinese Communist Party
CIGS	Chief of the Imperial General Staff
CLC	Communities Liaison Committee
CPM	Communist Party of Malaya
DWEC	District War Executive Committee
IIL	Indian Independence League
IMP	Independence of Malaya Party
INA	Indian National Army
IRD	Secret Information Research Department, British Foreign Office
ISEAS	Institute of Southeast Asian Studies, Singapore
JIC	Joint Intelligence Committee
KMT	*Kuomintang*
KVHG	Kinta Valley Home Guard
MCA	Malayan Chinese Association
MCS	Malayan Civil Service
MIC	Malayan Indian Congress
MI5	Security Service (U.K. Internal Security Service)
MI6	Secret Intelligence Service (SIS) (foreign section of U.K. Security Service)
MFU	Malayan Film Unit
MNLA	Malayan National Liberation Army
MPAJA	Malayan People's Anti-Japanese Army
MRLA	Malayan Races Liberation Army

MSS   Malayan Security Service
MP   Member of Parliament
NATO   North Atlantic Treaty Organization
PCTMA   Perak Chinese Tin Mining Association
PN   Parti Negara (National Party)
RIDA   Rural and Industrial Development Authority
SB   Special Branch
SEP   surrendered enemy personnel
SEIO   State Emergency Information Officer
SIFE   Security Intelligence Far East
SWEC   State or Settlement War Executive Committee
UMNO   United Malays National Organisation
UCSCA   United Chinese School Committees Association
UCSTA   United Chinese School Teachers Association
USIS   United States Information Services
VCIGS   Vice-Chief of the Imperial General Staff

Map of Malaya (1952–54)

Map©Monash Asia Institute

Map of Malaya (1956): Locations of Communist Terrorists by State

Map©Monash Asia Institute
Source: Adapted from CO 1030/10 DOPS. Secret Appendix 'C' Review of Emergency Situation 1956.

PROLOGUE

This book came about as a result of a conversation I had with Ambassador K. Kesavapany, then Director of the Institute of Southeast Asian Studies (ISEAS), Singapore, in May 2010, when he asked me whether I thought there would be a place for a new book on General Sir Gerald Templer, High Commissioner and Director of Operations, Malaya, 1952–54. I replied that I thought there would be, provided it focused on General Templer's time in Malaya and the implementation of the political and socio-economic sides of the Directive he had been given by the British Government rather than the military side, which has already been adequately covered, though there might be some overlapping at times of the two sides.[1]

On the political side of his Directive, the British Government instructed him to "assist the peoples of Malaya in due course to become a fully self-governing nation within the British Commonwealth" and "to promote such political progress of the country as will, without prejudicing the campaign against the terrorists, further our democratic aim in Malaya."[2] On the military side, he was instructed to restore law and order and defeat the Communist Party of Malaya's uprising, which has become known as the Malayan Emergency.

Templer never wrote his memoirs and the only full-scale biography of him is John Cloake's *Templer, Tiger of Malaya: The Life of Field Marshal Sir Gerald Templer* which was published several decades ago.[3] John Cloake, an old family friend, was commissioned to write it by Lady Peggie Templer, General Templer's widow. It is well written but much new material has become available since then. There is, too, a short thirty-nine-page monograph, *Templer in Malaya*, by C. Northcote Parkinson, then Professor of History at the University of Malaya in Singapore, which is brief and insightful, but it was published rather hastily in Singapore to coincide with Templer's departure from Malaya in 1954.[4]

The part played by Templer in his short but important two-year Malayan proconsulship at a vital time in Malaya's history undoubtedly helped to shape the beginning of the road to self-government leading to independence, although both came about after he left Malaya in 1954.

While General Templer left Malaya at the end of May 1954, some six years before the Emergency was brought to an end, there is no doubt that during his two years in Malaya he revitalized with his drive, military determination, and energy the counterinsurgency operations against the Communists which were beginning to run out of energy following the murder by Communist terrorists in October 1951 of Sir Henry Gurney, the previous High Commissioner.

However, when General Templer became High Commissioner and Director of Operations in February 1952, he was fortunate in inheriting the ready-made "Briggs Plan" originated by General Sir Harold Briggs, the Director of Operations before his arrival, which provided the road map and the winning strategy for defeating the Communist uprising.[5] The plan had been approved by Sir Henry Gurney, then Malaya's High Commissioner, and the British Government before Templer's arrival. It was the Briggs Plan which Templer followed with his customary determination and vigour, with some minor adjustments that eventually led to the defeat of the Communist insurrection in 1960.

Meanwhile, General Briggs, who had retired to Cyprus in ill health a few months before Templer's arrival, did not live to see the success of his efforts and he died of cancer in the following year.

Templer arrived in Malaya from London on 7 February 1952 accompanied by Donald MacGillivray (later Sir Donald), who had been appointed Deputy High Commissioner. This was the first time in Malaya's history that a Deputy High Commissioner had been appointed. His task was to look after the more routine side of government administration so as to leave General Templer free to concentrate on policy and political socio-economic matters while directing the military campaign against the Communists.[6]

Four days before his departure from London for Malaya, Templer told his Military Assistant, Major (afterwards Major General) Lloyd Owen, that he considered his main priorities on arrival were threefold: to coordinate intelligence under one person; reorganize and retrain the Police; and ensure that the Government's information services told the people what the Government was doing.[7] He did not refer at this stage to his political plans, presumably because he wanted to see the situation for himself on the ground. But he did outline his political programme in his inaugural address to the Legislative Council on 19 March 1952, some six weeks after his arrival at Kuala Lumpur, which was referred to by the *Malay Mail* as "The Templer Plan" and will be examined later in this book.[8]

This account will focus largely on Templer's relations with the leading Malayan political leaders of the time, such as, Tunku Abdul Rahman, Tan Cheng Lock, Colonel H.S. Lee, Dato' Onn bin Ja'afar, Tun Dr Ismail, Tan Siew Sin, and others, all of whom played important and vital roles in the struggle for Malayan self-government and independence, although evidently, as will be brought out, he did not always have an easy relationship with them. Cloake, Templer's biographer, for instance, refers to Templer's distrust of Tunku Abdul Rahman's policies when the Tunku was the leader of UMNO (United Malays National Organisation), and his relations with Tan Cheng Lock, the President of the MCA (Malayan Chinese Association), the Malayan-Chinese organization representing the Chinese in the country, were not particularly close either.[9] Tan was quite outspoken in his criticism of Templer's administration in a speech made on 27 December 1953, some five months before Templer left Malaya, which is worth quoting in part:

> In the second half of the twentieth century, we are in Malaya, which is an integral part of the most ancient, most civilised, most populous and largest continent in the World, almost alone in Asia still living in a state of subservience under a purely and essentially autocratic form of government, despite the oft-declared policy and promise of the powers-that-be to guide the citizens of the Federation [of Malaya] and Singapore to responsible self-government within the Commonwealth.
>
> This country since the conclusion of the last World War has been at almost at a standstill politically, economically and socially ....
>
> Though there has been much talk of fighting for the hearts and minds of the people,[10] in actual practice we Malayans are not permitted to cooperate with Government on equal terms, so that there is a lack of confidence and contact between Government and people, and the Government has struck no root in the life of the people.
>
> Our Legislature is impotent and unrepresentative of the people... .
>
> ... It is obvious that Malaya to all intents and purposes has made no appreciable advance toward responsible self-government and political democracy ... .[11]

These are rather strong words and a trenchant criticism of Templer's administration but they are probably written from Tan Cheng Lock's own rather bold point of view at the time and the political differences he had with Templer over the visit of Dr Victor Purcell and Francis Carnell to Malaya at the invitation of the MCA in August 1952 as honorary political advisers, which will be examined later in this book. Even so, it is clear from the records that General Templer did not have a high regard for the MCA of which Tan Cheng Lock was the President, and his relations with the Chinese were never easy. He clearly found it difficult to win over their hearts and minds, as witness for instance, their reluctance to join the Federation of Malaya Army and the uniformed branch of the Malayan Police. There was an improvement in the situation, however, when he worked with the assistance of Colonel H.S. Lee, Leong Yew Koh, Lau Pak Kuan, and other Perak MCA leaders, to establish the Kinta Valley Chinese Home Guard for the defence of Chinese tin mines in the Kinta Valley of Perak, for which he provided Government funding and support (see Chapter 5).[12] Most of the Perak MCA leaders had a close connection with the Kuomintang (KMT) and Colonel Lee had been a Colonel and Leong a Major General in the Kuomintang Army during World War II. Nevertheless, in one of the speeches Templer made before he left Malaya, he still thought it necessary to refute an allegation made by Purcell that he was anti-Chinese.

As stated, the focus of this book will be on General Templer's implementation of the political and socio-economic sides of his Directive and his dealings with local Malayan political leaders rather than waging war against the Malayan Communist insurgents. There is no doubt he was well qualified to deal with the military aspects of the Emergency as he had an outstanding record as an infantry officer and commander in the British Army during his service in Europe, Iran, Iraq and Palestine, but not in the Far East. His unfamiliarity with Malaya and its history, politics, and the nuances of its culture, no doubt placed him at some disadvantage in dealing with the complicated and involved socio-political situation with which he was faced when he arrived in Malaya, especially as in the early 1950s when the population was more or less evenly distributed between the Malays and Chinese, with the Indians making up a small minority, each with its own dreams and ambitions.[13] The relationship between the three main ethnic groups in Malaya, in fact, still exercises the minds of the present-day Malaysian Government although many decades have since passed.

The main political parties on the political stage in Templer's time were UMNO, MCA, and the Malayan Indian Congress (MIC) and briefly to a lesser extent Independence of Malaya Party (IMP) and Parti Negara (National Party). The latter two parties were formed by Dato' Onn after he resigned as President of UMNO in 1951, which left the way open for Tunku Abdul Rahman to take over as President of UMNO. IMP and PN were both non-communal political parties but contrary to what Onn expected, they did not receive widespread support as there were very few Malays, Chinese, and Indians who were ready to join non-communal parties at that juncture.

It should not be forgotten, too, that Malayan politics were played out against the background of the Communist Party of Malaya's (CPM) determined uprising to overthrow the Government of Malaya, which affected literally every aspect of Malayan economic and socio-political life, and was never very far away in the background at a time when colonial Malaya was just recovering from the effects of WWII and the Japanese Occupation.[14]

Some of the more inviting questions that will be examined in this book are:

- What steps did General Templer take to implement the instructions he had been given to lead Malaya to self-government?
- What was the response from the public and local politicians to his policies?
- What steps did he take to deal with Malaya's cultural pluralism and harmonize ethnic relations between the Malaya, Chinese, and Indians to bring about a united Malayan nation?
- How did he respond to such issues as the political, economic, and social development of Malaya?

The first chapter will examine the circumstances of General Templer's appointment as High Commissioner and Director of Operations. Chapters 2 and 3 will deal with Templer's arrival at Kuala Lumpur and discuss what has been called "The Templer Plan", that is, his political programme for dealing with the situation; Chapters 4 focuses on the visit of Dr Victor Purcell and Francis Carnell as honorary political advisers to the MCA and the problems that arose; Chapter 5 is a case study of the establishment of the Kinta Valley Chinese Home Guard and Templer's involvement; Chapter 6 highlights the disturbing features of the Lee Meng case and the system of justice during Templer's time, which was to lead to the introduction of the jury system after he left; Chapter 7 is concerned with the struggle for self-government in which Templer, the UMNO/MCA Alliance, and other political actors were involved; and Chapter 8, the Conclusion, deals with Templer's departure from Malaya at the end of his two-year proconsulship in 1954 which was unfortunately overcast by his involvement at the end of World War II, when as Director of Military Government in the British sector of occupied Germany he had summarily dismissed for obstruction and inefficiency Dr Konrad Adenauer, who was then the *Oberbürgermeister* (Mayor) of Cologne. Adenauer never forgave Templer for the way in which he had been treated. By 1954, Adenauer had become the first Chancellor of the Federal Republic of Germany and Supreme Commander of the new German Army, and when Templer was about to leave Malaya to take up his new appointment in Germany as Commander of the 80,000 strong British Army on the Rhine and Commander of the Northern Army Group, Allied Forces, Central Europe, Adenauer vetoed it.

Although this matter came up on the eve of his departure from Malaya, Templer specifically asked the British Chief of the Imperial General Staff (CIGS) not to announce that his posting had been barred by Adenauer, and it was not until after he had left Malaya that it became publicly known. This dealt a serious and embarrassing blow to Templer's military career and had unfortunate consequences resulting in his being unemployed and sent on long leave after he left Malaya stretching into 1955, before he fully resumed his army career. A full account of this unpleasant incident is given in Chapter 8.[15]

As the Bibliography suggests, the methodology followed has been to conduct research in the official archives in Britain, Malaysia, Singapore, and Australia; the ISEAS Library, Singapore, where the private papers of Tun Dato Sir Cheng Lock Tan, Tun Sir Henry H.S. Lee, P.G. Lim and Tun Dr Ismail have been deposited; the Singapore National Library; the National University of Singapore Library; the University of Malaya Library, Kuala Lumpur; the National Army Museum, Chelsea, London, which was established by General Templer after his retirement from the Army and where his papers are deposited; and conduct interviews or correspondence with persons who had information to bear on the subject. The author has been in communication, too, with Lieutenant Colonel Miles Templer, General Templer's son but no new leads were provided by him.

Unlike his predecessors as High Commissioners, Templer did not send "official despatches" as such to the Secretary of State but preferred to communicate with him by informal, private, and confidential letters which provided his own record of what he was thinking and doing, usually on a monthly basis.[16] Not all copies of these rather informal letters appear to have survived or have been regularly placed on Public Record Office (PRO) files, and copies of them, if they were deposited in the National Army Museum that Templer established after his retirement from the Army, may have been subsequently withdrawn. He left most of the routine, official correspondence with officials in the Colonial Office to be dealt with by his deputy, Donald (later Sir) MacGillivray.[17]

The author was able to make use in this study of his personal knowledge at a subaltern level of many of the Malayan politicians referred to whom he first met in 1951 while he was honorary Aide-de-Camp to the ill-fated Sir Henry Gurney, Templer's predecessor as High Commissioner of Malaya, who were still actors in the political drama being played out when Templer arrived, as well as his experiences as a Special Branch officer during the Malayan Emergency. It is possible that his views and recollections of events and the main players may have coloured this study though he has tried not to allow this to happen or to distort his view of the Malayan ecumene.

Notes

1. For the military side, see Anthony Short, *The Communist Insurrection in Malaya 1948–60* (London: Frederick Muller Ltd, 1975). Reprinted in 2000 by Cultural Lotus Press, Singapore, under the title *In Pursuit of Mountain Rats*; Richard Clutterbuck, *The Long Long War. The Emergency in Malaya 1948–1960* (London: Cassell, 1967); John Coates, *Suppressing Insurgency: An Analysis of the Malayan Emergency, 1948–1954* (Boulder, CO: Westview Press, 1992); Noel Barber, *The War of the Running Dogs: The Malayan Emergency 1948–1960* (London: Fontana Books, 1973, 3rd impression); R.W. Komer, *The Malayan Emergency in Retrospect: Organisation of a Successful Counterinsurgency Effort* (Santa Monica: Rand Corporation, 1972); Edgar O'Ballance, *Malaya: The Communist War, 1948–1960* (London: Faber & Faber Ltd, 1996); Richard Stubbs, *Hearts and Minds in Guerilla Warfare: The Malayan Emergency 1948–60* (Singapore: Oxford University Press, 1989); Harry Miller, *Jungle War in Malaya: The Campaign against Communism 1948–1960* (London: Arthur Barker, 1972); Pennell J. Hickey, *Counterinsurgency Operations in Malaya, 1948–1960: The Role of Regular Forces* (Pennsylvania: U.S.

War College, 1971); and John Scurr, *The Malayan Campaign 1948–60* (Oxford: Osprey Publishing, 1982).

2. CO 1022/103. "Directive to General Sir Gerald Templer, 12 February 1952". See Appendix A.

3. John Cloake, *Templer, Tiger of Malaya: The Life of Field Marshal Sir Gerald Templer* (London: Harrap, 1985). After taking a history degree at Cambridge, Cloake joined the British Diplomatic Service in 1948, and worked for some time in the Foreign Office's Secret Information Research Department (IRD), which during the Cold War had close links with the CIA. He served in Baghdad, Morocco, New York, and in the Far East in Saigon, before becoming British Ambassador to Bulgaria from 1976 to 1980. Cloake, who was not well acquainted with Malaya, visited Malaya to interview people who had known or worked with Templer under arrangements made by Mubin Sheppard, a former senior Malayan Civil Service officer (MCS), who had stayed on in Malaya after independence. Cloake, rather jarringly, refers to Templer throughout his biography as "Gerald" which no doubt indicates his close connection with General Templer and his family, but the biography is well written.

4. C. Northcote Parkinson, *Templer in Malaya* (Singapore: Donald Moore Ltd, 1954). In 1950, Parkinson was Raffles Professor of History at the University of Malaya in Singapore, which subsequently became the National University of Singapore. He was a naval historian as well as a prolific writer of fiction and non-fiction, and wrote altogether sixty books. He became internationally known after leaving Singapore for his best-selling *Parkinson's Law. The Pursuit of Progress* (London: John Murray, 1958), which developed the theory that work expands to fill the time available for its completion.

5. Lieutenant General Sir Harold Briggs, KCIE, CB, CBE, DSO, was a retired regular British Indian Army officer. He was commissioned at Sandhurst in 1914 as an infantry officer, and had served throughout his career as a British officer in the Indian Army. He had thirty-four years' experience of soldiering and warfare in India, Southeast Asia, and the Middle East. His last army appointment was Commander-in-Chief Burma in 1948. He served in a civilian capacity in Malaya as Director of Operations (1950–51), and drafted the Briggs Plan in 1950 not long after his arrival. The official name of the Briggs Plan is the "Federation Plan for the Elimination of the Communist Organisation and Armed Forces in Malaya". See also Leon Comber, *Malaya's Secret Police 1945–60: The Role of the Special Branch in the Malayan Emergency* (Singapore: ISEAS/Monash University Press, 2008, reprint 2009), p. 76 fn. 26 and pp. 147–48.

6. ISEAS Library, Tun Sir Henry H.S. Lee Private Papers, HSL.031.057, 3 March 1952. Sir Donald MacGillivray joined the Colonial Administrative Service in 1928 and was Chief Secretary of Jamaica before taking up his Malayan

appointment. He was highly thought of as a colonial administrator. Like General Templer, he had not previously served in Malaya.

7. National Army Museum, Chelsea, ACC: 8011-132-3, Major General Lloyd Owen's letter dated 30 June 1976 to Major General J.M. Gow, Director, Army Training, Ministry of Defence, and *Federation of Malaya Annual Report 1952* (Kuala Lumpur: Government Printer, 1953), pp. 4–5.

8. CO 1022/100, Confidential, "General Templer's Address to the Legislative Council, 19 March 1952" and *Proceedings of the Legislative Council of the Federation of Malaya, 19 March 1952* (Kuala Lumpur: Government Printer, 1953).

9. Cloake, op. cit., p. 316. Beyond this, Cloake stated that Templer disliked politicians "as a tribe" [sic] (p. 381). See also PREM 11/113, "Personal and Confidential letter dated 12 March 1952, Templer to Secretary of State for the Colonies".

10. The term "hearts and minds" has often been attributed to Templer but it had a much longer genesis than this. It can be traced back to John Adams (second U.S. President) who argued that "The [American] Revolution was in the minds and hearts of the people ...The radical change in the principles, opinions, sentiments and affections of the people, was the real American Revolution." (quoted in a letter he wrote dated 13 February 1818). In more recent times it had been used too by Lieutenant Colonel C.E. Bruce, Indian Political Department, in his book about the North West Frontier of India, *Waziristan 1936–1937* (New Delhi: Gyan Publishers, 1996, reprint) in which he argued that military force should only be used with a policy of economic and political development that attacked the causes of the unrest.

    There is a strong revisionist school which now argues that the "hearts and minds" programme in Malaya was greatly exaggerated and used more as a political slogan rather than anything else. Lieutenant General Sir Geoffrey Bourne, who succeeded General Templer as Director of Operations in 1955, considered that the Chinese community had not developed any feeling of loyalty towards the British colonial government in spite of the "hearts and minds" programme, but it was the press who seized the slogan and ran with it (See Sergio Miller, "Malaya: The Myth of Hearts and Minds", *Small Wars Journal*, 16 April 2012).

11. ISEAS Library, Tan Cheng Lock Private Papers Collection, TCL 065, MCA President's Speech, 6th General Meeting, 27th December 1953. See, too, Victor Purcell, *Malaya: Communist or Free?* (published under the auspices of the Institute of Public Relations) (Stanford: Stanford University Press, 1955), p. 9, and Short, op. cit., p. 383.

12. See ISEAS Library, Tun Sir Henry H.S. Lee Private Papers, HSL 20.040c, Secret, "Home Guard in 1954".

13. In 1952, when Templer arrived in Kuala Lumpur, the Malay and Chinese

population figures were quite closely balanced. There were 2,716,899
Malaysians (Malays/Indonesians); 2,092,228 Chinese; 617,257 Indians/
Pakistanis; and 80,073 Others, making up a total population of 5,506,467
(*Federation of Malaya Annual Report 1952* (Kuala Lumpur: Government Printer,
1953)).

14. See Malayan Security Service (MSS), Secret. Fortnightly, *Political Intelligence
   Journal (PIJ)*, 1946–48, *passim.*
15. See also Cloake, op. cit., pp. 328–29.
16. Ibid., p. 224.
17. A.J. Stockwell, *Malaya.Part 1: The Malayan Union Experiment 1942–1948* (London:
   HMSO, 1995), p. xxxv.

1

THE BACKGROUND:
The Appointment of
General Sir Gerald Templer as
High Commissioner and Director
of Operations, Malaya (1952–54)

General Templer was appointed as High Commissioner and Director
of Operations in February 1952, following the murder in October 1951
by Communist insurgents of the previous High Commissioner, Sir
Henry Gurney, on his way up to Fraser's Hill from Kuala Lumpur.
His appointment marks a turning point in the long, long, war against
the Communist Party of Malaya's uprising (the Malayan Emergency)
against the Malayan Government during which the entire country was
turned upside down again so soon after the end of World War II and the
Japanese Occupation. When Templer left Malaya on 31 May 1954 after his
two-year proconsulship, as will be related, it was still very much a time
of living dangerously, and in spite of the tremendous efforts he put in to
defeat the Communist uprising, it still had another six years to run before
the Communists were defeated and the Emergency brought to an end.

Not long after Templer left Malaya, his successor as High Commissioner, Sir Donald MacGillivray, informed Lennox-Boyd, then Secretary of State for the Colonies, that the CPM's forces under arms "amounted to not less than 5,000 and they were still able to obtain as many recruits from the civilian population as they wish ... . The Emergency remains much more than an issue and it would be a grave mistake to think that its end is now in sight."[1]

The Malayan Emergency was the name given by the British colonial authorities to the uprising of the Communist Party of Malaya (CPM) which lasted from 1948 to 1960. The objective of the CPM was to overthrow the Government by force and establish a Communist People's Democratic Republic of Malaya. In all but name it was a war remarkable for the fiercely fought counterinsurgency operations in the Malayan jungle between the Government security forces and the CPM's guerrilla army, the Malayan National Liberation Army (MNLA). The CPM had no inhibitions, however, about the name used for the conflict and always referred to it in its own literature as a war, namely, "The Anti-British National Liberation War". The jungle war was waged concurrently with a political struggle for the hearts and minds of the Malayan people, that formed an important part of the two-pronged Directive that General Templer was given by the British Government when he assumed his appointment, which directed him not only to defeat the armed Communist insurrection but to guide Malaya on the path to self-government and independence and encourage its political advancement and economic development.

The focus of this chapter will be on the circumstances of his selection and appointment as a regular British Army officer as High Commissioner and Director of Operations in Malaya in 1952, and it will include comments on his appointment from British, Malayan, and Australian sources.

There was a noticeable hiatus before his appointment as High Commissioner and Director of Operations was announced by the British Government after Sir Henry Gurney's assassination. In the meantime, the CPM's MNLA continued its struggle against the Government and carried out a number of successful ambushes of security forces and spectacular derailments of the Malayan Railways' mail trains running from Singapore to Kuala Lumpur, which did nothing to restore public confidence that the British colonial Government was winning the war. On 7 November, only 17 miles (approximately 27.4 kilometres) from where Sir Henry Gurney had been murdered, 1,700 inhabitants of Tras, a small town in Pahang, were taken into detention under the Emergency Regulations as it was believed that they had given aid and supplies to the Communist terrorists who had taken part in Gurney's ambush. Service and civilian casualties in the jungle war against the MNLA continued undiminished. It was evident that the campaign against the Communist terrorists was not going as well as expected and questions about the deteriorating security situation in Malaya were asked in the House of Commons and the House of Lords.[2]

AUSTRALIAN COMMISSIONER IN SINGAPORE'S REPORT

In his annual report on British territories in Southeast Asia for the year 1951, T.K. Critchley, who was then acting Australian Commissioner in Singapore and a highly regarded independent commentator on the political scene in Malaya and Singapore, reported to the Department of External Affairs, Canberra, that the security situation in Malaya was serious and public confidence had been badly shaken by High Commissioner Gurney's murder.[3] Critchley commented that the Emergency measures introduced to combat the Communists had only met with limited success so far, and the *Min Yuen* or "People's Movement", the Communist organization on the jungle fringes that was aiding the Communists in the jungle with information, funds, food, clothing, medicine, and other necessities, was showing ingenuity in countering the Government's measures in restricting the movement of foodstuffs and other supplies which had been brought into force by Government decree on 17 June 1951 to prevent their being supplied to the Communists. Moreover, the Communists had intensified their efforts to intimidate and control the mainly Tamil labour force on rubber estates in an endeavour to regain control of the labour movement which they had lost when most of the trade union leaders went underground into the jungle at the outbreak of the Emergency in June 1948.[4]

The announcement of a replacement for Sir Henry Gurney was eagerly awaited, and when no appointment was made and the Government remained under M.V. del Tufo, the Chief Secretary, as Officer Administering the Government, there was a sense of let-down which gave rise to a flood of rumours and affected public confidence in the ability of the Government to contain the Communist terrorists.[5]

LIEUTENANT GENERAL SIR HAROLD BRIGGS

Before his death, Sir Henry Gurney had obtained, with the assistance of Field Marshal Sir William Slim who was then CIGS, the services of Lieutenant General Sir Harold Briggs, a distinguished retired British Indian Army officer then living in retirement in Cyprus, to assist him in planning, coordinating, and directing a new approach to fighting the Communist uprising. For the first time the services of the civil administration, Police, and the Armed Forces were coordinated and brought together in the fight against the Communist insurgents. Until then, Colonel Gray, the Commissioner of Police, had been responsible for coordinating counterinsurgency operations, but it was now felt that his Police duties had expanded to such a great extent that they warranted his full and undivided attention. On General Briggs' arrival at Kuala Lumpur on 3 April 1950, he took over as Director of Operations. He was appointed in a civilian capacity ranking equal with the Government's Chief Secretary, and was responsible for the performance of his duties to the High Commissioner. His civilian status was deliberate and undoubtedly helped to emphasize that Malaya remained under civil government, that martial law had not been declared, and that the role of the armed forces was in support of the civil power. He did not "command", as such the Police and military forces, but coordinated and directed operations that were carried out under their respective commanders.

Not long after his arrival in Malaya, Briggs carried out a rapid and extensive reconnaissance of the country at the request of Gurney, and prepared what has become known as the Briggs Plan, or to give it its official title, the "Federation Plan for the Elimination of the Communist Organisation and Armed Forces in Malaya", which became the overall long-term road map or strategy for defeating the Communist uprising. The Briggs Plan was essentially based on the integration of the security forces (Police and Armed Forces) and the civil administration in planning counterinsurgency operations, and the resettlement of mainly Chinese squatters and farmers into New Villages under police protection to make it difficult for the Communists to obtain intelligence, food and supplies from them. All these measures took some time to come into effect especially as they involved the resettlement of some half a million Chinese squatters and farmers into New Villages, which represented the largest mass movement of people in Malaya's history.[6] Chin Peng, the CPM's Secretary General, wrote subsequently in his autobiography that the Briggs' resettlement plan was the "Communists' Achilles heel". The Plan was approved by the then High Commissioner, Sir Henry Gurney and the British Defence Coordination Committee (Far East) for implementation with effect from 1 June 1950.[7] As stated in the Prologue, it was unfortunate that Briggs, who played an important and generally under-recognized role in the defeat of the CPM's insurrection, was not to live to see the success of his plan as he retired in ill health to Cyprus some two months before General Templer's arrival, where he died of cancer in the following year.

During Templer's two years' proconsulship in Malaya, it is often overlooked that he followed closely the Briggs Plan, which he implemented with his customary military determination and energy, and although Templer was punctilious in giving Briggs credit for it, Briggs' name is often forgotten. Perhaps more recognition should be given to him and the part he played in the eventual defeat of the Communist uprising.[8]

When Templer left Malaya in 1954 to return to the Army following his two-year proconsulship, the functions of High Commissioner and Director of Operations were separated as they had been previously. His deputy, Sir Donald MacGillivray, took over as High Commissioner and the baton of Director of Operations was taken over by Lieutenant General Sir Geoffrey Bourne, and three years later on Malaya's attaining independence, by Lieutenant General Sir James Cassell. The latter remained in post as Director of Operations until after the Communists were defeated in July 1960 and the Emergency declared at an end.[9]

After Briggs' retirement on medical grounds to Cyprus, his deputy Lieutenant General Sir Robert Lockhart took over temporarily as Director of Operations until General Templer, the new High Commissioner and Director of Operations, arrived on 7 February 1952, when he agreed to stay on as Deputy Director of Operations under Templer.[10]

Lockhart became, in effect, Templer's Chief of Staff, and in May 1952 Templer for the first time established a Research and Scientific Section as part of Lockhart's office to identify the strengths and weaknesses of the jungle campaign against the Communist terrorists and provide answers to such questions as what tactical mistakes were made by security force patrols that had suffered heavy casualties; what methods were adapted by Army patrols that avoided casualties; what was the most effective and efficient method of aggressive patrolling in the jungle; and what were the reasons behind the average number of casualties inflicted by the security forces on the Communist terrorists remaining so low.[11]

With all the changes that had occurred in the higher echelons of Government at this time, it was unfortunate that the Commissioner of Police (Colonel W.N. (Nicol) Gray) and the Director of Intelligence (Sir William Jenkin), two of the most senior and able officers concerned with the conduct of counterinsurgency operations against the Communist insurgents, both resigned and returned to the United Kingdom only three weeks before Templer's arrival at Kuala Lumpur. However, there had been serious differences of opinion between them for some time over the organization of police intelligence work and, indeed, between Gray and General Briggs, too, over the functions and role of the police in counterinsurgency operations. Both Gray and Jenkin returned separately to the United Kingdom in January 1952.[12]

OLIVER LYTTELTON, SECRETARY OF STATE FOR THE COLONIES

It was a time of political upheaval as well in the United Kingdom, and when the newly elected Conservative government came to power towards the end of October 1951, Prime Minister Winston Churchill lost no time in sending his newly appointed Secretary of State for the Colonies (Oliver Lyttelton, later Lord Chandos) on an urgent mission to Malaya in November to investigate the reasons for the deteriorating security situation and to make recommendations for dealing with it. It was clearly imperative for the British Government to appoint a successor for Gurney as High Commissioner as soon as possible, as well as a replacement for Colonel Gray. By 8 December 1951, after a rapid tour of Malaya, Lyttelton reported back to the Prime Minister that a "supreme commander" combining the functions of High Commissioner and Director of Operations should be appointed without delay, with General Lockhart as his Deputy Director of Operations. He recommended, too, for the first time in Malaya, that a Deputy High Commissioner should be appointed to relieve the High Commissioner of routine administrative duties so that he could concentrate on policy matters and the political side of the Directive he would be given as well as his military functions.[13] It was suggested at the time that the precedent of appointing a serving General to be High Commissioner and Director of Operations, combining both military and civil functions, may perhaps have been influenced by the appointment by the French Government of General de Lattre de Tassigny as Commander-in-Chief in French Indochina.[14]

LYTTELTON'S RECOMMENDATIONS FOR APPOINTMENT OF A MALAYAN SUPREMO

On his return to London, Lyttelton gave urgent attention to finding the right man to fill the appointment of supreme commander in Malaya combining the two functions he had in mind. He considered several senior service officers on a list that was prepared for him, which included General Sir Brian Robertson, Commander-in-Chief, Middle East; General Sir John Harding; Air Marshal Sir Arthur Harris; Field Marshal Sir William Slim; Air Marshal Lord Portal, Marshal of the Royal Air Force; Lieutenant General G.C. Bourne; and Lieutenant General Sir R. Scobie, former General Officer Commanding Greece[15] but after carrying out interviews, he found that he was still unable to come to a decision and he sought the help of the Secretary of State for War, Anthony Head, to recommend to him a further list of likely candidates from the senior ranks of the Armed Forces.[16] It was from this list that he recommended that General Templer should fill the appointment, subject to the Prime Minister's approval. Lyttelton said that he had spent three hours interviewing Templer to arrive at his decision. However, in his autobiography which he wrote several years afterwards, it is interesting to note that he said his first choice was General Sir Brian Robertson, but the latter declined the appointment as he had spent twenty-eight of the last thirty-one years outside Britain, and he wanted to enjoy some settled family life at home.[17]

With perhaps the exception of Slim, who came from a more modest background and had been for a short while a schoolteacher and a clerk before joining the Army at the outbreak of World War I, all these officers had similar social backgrounds. They had been through a process of education and training that had changed little over time. They had attended good British public schools, had been trained as officers at the Royal Military College (RMC) Sandhurst, the British army equivalent of West Point, and other similar military academies, had attended staff colleges, had risen through the regimental system, had exercised high command during World War II, and had been toughened on the anvil of war.[18]

There was something different, however, about Templer. He was then only fifty-three, and he had been the youngest Lieutenant General in the British Army in World War II. He had had wide experience in command. He had commanded the British 1st Division in North Africa, the 56th Division and the 6th Armoured Division in Italy, had been Director of Military Government in the British sector of occupied Germany, and after the war had been Vice-Chief of the Imperial General Staff, Director of Military Intelligence at the War Office, and was slated to be Chief of the Imperial General Staff in three or four years' time when the present incumbent was due to retire.[19] On 4 June 1950, some twenty months before he took up his appointment in Malaya, he was promoted to full General, and at the time of his appointment to Malaya, he was General Officer Commanding Eastern Command in the United Kingdom. He obviously had a bright future in front of him.

GENERAL TEMPLER'S MEETING WITH WINSTON CHURCHILL

After Lyttelton returned to London from Malaya, he lost very little time in recommending the various Malayan appointments to the Prime Minister but before they were announced, Churchill expressed a desire to see General Templer. He was instructed to fly to Ottawa to meet Churchill who was then visiting the United States to meet President Truman and address Congress. He was staying with Lord Alexander who was then Governor General of Canada.[20] Templer met Churchill at the Governor General's residence for two hours on 11 January 1952, at the end of which Churchill told him he would recommend to the Cabinet that his appointment should be confirmed.[21]

Templer's appointment as High Commissioner and Director of Operations was announced on 15 January 1952 together with those of Donald (later Sir Donald) Charles MacGillivray, former Chief Secretary in the West Indies, as Deputy High Commissioner, and Colonel A.E. (Arthur) Young, who was seconded from the City of London Police from February 1952 for a year, as Commissioner of Police.[22]

TEMPLER'S DIRECTIVE

While he was in Ottawa, Churchill asked General Templer to submit to him a short note on the job, and on the following day, Templer replied in a top secret note, as follows:

".... The problem is a fresh one to me, and I have had little time to study it but my mind is firm on five points." In his first point, which was probably the most important of all, he said

> "the general object is obvious — viz., to restore law and order, and to bring back peace to the Federation [of Malaya]. I am clear as to what must happen from the purely military point of view. I am not at all clear as to what H.M.G. is aiming at from the political point of view. Is it a 'united Malayan nation'? And if so, what exactly does this mean? Does it mean a merging of Malays and Chinese in one community — a long term project? I must have a clear policy to work on. I want to be given a directive from H.M.G. not so that I should shelter behind that directive — but rather that I can use it publicly to impress H.M.G's purposes ...."[23]

Templer did not have to wait long for the directive. The final version of an official Directive was approved by Lyttelton on 31 January, submitted to Churchill the next day, and handed over to Templer on 4 February to take with him to Kuala Lumpur before he left for Malaya on 5 February 1952 (see Appendix A).[24]

In amplification of Templer's duties, the Colonial Secretary said in a press interview:

> There will be no field of administration, civil, or military, beyond his [Templer's] control.... The Government remains convinced that making headway against the Communists is as much a political as a military task, and they are giving the new High Commissioner instructions which lay stress upon *the constitutional and political development* [emphasis by the author] of the Federation. He will direct the battle of ideas and concern himself with broad measures of social, economic, and political advance, especially in education. He will seek to reassure and enlist the Chinese community, without sacrificing in any way the interests of the Malays.... The Chinese terrorists can never be brought to book unless Chinese policemen, Chinese administrators, and Chinese citizens, take part in the struggle.... They are likely to remain merely onlookers so long as they feel that the best they can hope for in a self-government Malaya is to be treated as second-class citizens ... means will have to be found in giving the Chinese a more important sphere in local economic life.... Progress along these lines will be hard unless the cooperation of the Sultans can be won: they are suspicious of Chinese claims for fairer treatment and are loath to allow resettled Chinese squatters to enjoy permanent title to their new land.[25]

It is clear that Templer was being given supreme power and Lyttelton's words are important as they determined the measures Templer would have to take to carry out his task in Malaya and they more or less defined for him what his programme should be.

Nevertheless, in the meantime, the London *Daily Telegraph* reported shrewdly that General Templer's initial military plans for dealing with the Communist problem were unlikely to change materially the organizational and operational structure that had already been put in place under the Briggs Plan[26] and, indeed, Templer acknowledged his indebtedness to Briggs in correspondence with Major General J.M. Gow of the Ministry of Defence, sometime after he had left Malaya.[27]

MALAYAN AND AUSTRALIAN REACTIONS TO GENERAL TEMPLER'S APPOINTMENT

How was Templer's appointment received on the ground in Malaya? For the most part, and as expected, it was favourably received by European businessmen and planters in Malaya who were in favour of a military approach, although there was some criticism from local Malayan leaders and a note of caution was sounded, too, by Malcolm MacDonald, British Commissioner General for South East Asia, from his headquarters at Phoenix Park, Singapore, who expressed the view in a memorandum to the Colonial Office that he would have preferred a civilian rather than a serving Army officer to fill the appointment.[28]

It is worth noting, too, that Boris Hembry, who in 1951 was a member of the Federal War Council established by General Briggs and chaired by Sir Henry Gurney, commented à propos General Templer's appointment:

> To be fair to Sir Henry Gurney, who has never been given the recognition he deserves, many of these ideas [the strategies that were used to win the Emergency] had been accepted and put in hand before he was murdered. Templer was also lucky in that he had been granted almost unlimited powers, enjoyed direct access to Winston Churchill, the prime minister, and in Oliver Lyttelton had a very strong colonial secretary.'[29]

Northcote Parkinson said something similar in the Preface of his monograph, as follows:

> .... The main difficulty about describing the work in Malaya of Sir Gerald Templer is to avoid being grossly unfair to his predecessor and his colleagues. The temptation is to give him all the credit (as others may give him all the blame) for everything done in Malaya during his term of

office. But modern government does not work like that.... For half of his achievements he must share the credit with assistants of whose names the public will never hear. A man who loathes publicity, Templer is always conscious of this debt he must necessarily owe to the other members of his team. If now he must perforce accept a measure of the praise that is justly theirs, his consolation must be that he would likewise have had to accept the blame.... In a book of this size I can do little justice to Sir Henry Gurney and less to those who worked with him....[30]

Critchley, the acting Australian Commissioner in Singapore, who has been referred to earlier, reported that

".... Individually the appointments [of General Templer, MacGillivray, and Young] may be most satisfactory but some uneasiness has been caused among local leaders by the fact that none of these three have [sic] had any experience of Malaya. Sir Gerald himself is something of an unknown quantity and comment on his appointment has been tinged with some caution.... His experience for the position does not appear to have been exceptional although he served for a period as Military governor of a district in Germany and it is of interest to note that he had served as Director of Military Intelligence...."[31]

There were misgivings, too, by some senior Malayan Special Branch officers about his appointment on the grounds that they felt that an officer who was familiar with Malaya and its peoples should have been appointed, though they were not publicly expressed.[32]

A similar view was expressed by several Unofficial Members of the Malayan Legislative Council who felt that the High Commissioner should be an officer who was familiar with the country and its peoples. They probably had in mind del Tufo, who had been acting High Commissioner until Templer arrived. Del Tufo was a senior Malayan Civil Service (MCS) officer who had served throughout his thirty-year career in Malaya, spoke Malay and Tamil, and had a good knowledge of the country, but who had been passed over by Lyttelton and allowed to retire at the relatively young age of fifty-one.[33]

The Straits Times, for its part, disagreed with the appointment of MacGillivray as Deputy High Commissioner and considered that an Asian should have been appointed instead.[34] S. Rajaratnam, then a journalist but later to become Singapore's Foreign Minister in 1965, Second Deputy Prime Minister (Foreign Affairs), and founding Member of the Association of Southeast Asian Nations (ASEAN), writing in the *Singapore Standard* on 5 February 1952, went even further and described MacGillivray's appointment as "a slap in the face for Malaya".[35]

Tunku Abdul Rahman introduced an amendment in the Federal Legislative Council on 30 January to the acting Chief Secretary's resolution about MacGillivray's appointment in the Federal Legislative and proposed that the word "Asian" should be inserted before the words "Deputy High Commissioner".[36] Though after a prolonged debate, the Tunku's amendment was finally rejected by 36 votes to 27, it did emphasize the strong groundswell of opinion against the proposed appointment, and the Legislative Council recommended that the British Government should proceed with caution in doing so.

In his response to these comments, the Colonial Secretary, Oliver Lyttelton, explained that full consideration had in fact been given to the reservations "expressed by responsible leaders of opinion in Malaya that an officer with local experience should be appointed" and he expressed his confidence in MacGillivray as "a man who will bring a fresh line to bear on the many complexities of the present administrative machine".[37]

As the Australian Army General John Coates, who earlier in his career had served in Malaya during the Emergency, brought out in his study *Suppressing Insurgency: An Analysis of the Malayan Emergency 1948–1954*, there was undoubtedly "something of Templer's times in Malaya which resembles the tide in the affairs of men", and he commented that Templer's success was to some extent due to his being "the right man at the right time and the right place" and he was fortunate in being able to follow the ready-made Briggs Plan in the war against the Communist insurgents.[38]

A similar theme was taken up some time later by the Malayan *New Straits Times* in an editorial commenting that Templer did not originate the programme to resettle hundreds of thousands of Chinese squatters into New Villages which broke their contact with the Communist jungle army, and that he was fortunate to arrive in Malaya when the Communists were beginning to scale back their military activities to concentrate on more political activities, and although he arrived with a high reputation, the crucial test would be whether he left with one.

Meanwhile, it may not be inappropriate to include at this stage, especially as there are so very few first-hand descriptions of General Templer after his arrival at Kuala Lumpur in 1952 the first impression he made on John Davis, CBE, DSO, a former pre-war Malayan Special

Branch officer, an iconic figure in Malaya's colonial history who led the underground British Force 136 in the jungle in Japanese-occupied Malaya and had a most distinguished career after the war in several senior positions in the MCS during both Sir Henry Gurney's and General Templer's time. Davis wrote after his first meeting with Templer that he saw "a very strange fellow, a curious, nervy individual with pointed, sharp features, a thin moustache and the brightest of eyes. But behind his penetrating gaze there was a tough, even a harsh quality, an intimidating character, whose mordant tongue and vivid language would unquestionably make him some enemies in Malaya." Three months later, however, in May 1952, it seemed that Davis had somewhat changed his opinion as in a letter to his parents in England, he wrote: "I see Templer from time to time and like him ... he has made a great difference to morale already." Even so, Davis still harboured doubts:

> He [Templer] has not shown any signs of doing very much on the political side and I wonder if he will ever get a grasp of it... By and large, I would not say he is a great man, but he is the kind of man we need — he has jolly well got to be. We cannot go on waiting for ever ... . He is utterly tireless ... undoubtedly the most impressive — and frightening — man I have ever met. As a gentleman give me Gurney every time ... (author's emphasis).[39]

Meanwhile, in spite of the several criticisms of General Templer's and MacGillivray's appointments, the Colonial Secretary in London won the day and Templer and MacGillivray were appointed.

It was clear, however, that Templer's position was not going to be an easy one. Although he was an outstanding soldier, he was not well known outside the Army.[40] Aside from the above widespread reservations about his appointment, he had a most difficult task ahead of him in dealing at the same time not only with the military situation for which he was well qualified but also in implementing the political and socio-economic sides of his Directive, especially those relating to constitutional and political development which involved his dealings with local politicians. He was new to Malaya and there was a formidable array of political problems to be solved which would have taxed any colonial administrator, no matter how experienced, in a country in which there were three main races — Malays, Chinese and Indians — each with its own history, culture, religious beliefs and language, with political discussions being dominated by ethnocentrism and multiracialism. How Templer tried to deal with some of these problems will be examined in the chapters that follow.[41]

Notes

1. CO 1030/174, No. 11, 26 January 1955. Secret. "Security in Malaya: Despatch from Sir Donald MacGillivray to Mr Lennox-Boyd on Conduct of the Emergency".
2. *The Parliamentary Debates (Hansard)*, Fifth Series, Vol. CLXXV, House of Lords Official Report, "The Situation in Malaya", Second Volume of Series in 1951–52, 19 February – 4 April 1952 (London: 1952), p. 301.
3. Thomas Kingston Critchley was appointed Acting Australian Commissioner in Singapore in 1951. He was the first Australian Commissioner to be appointed to the Federation of Malaya in 1955 and subsequently Australian High Commissioner to an independent Malaya on 31 August 1957. His continuity of service in the Malayan territories was unique as Australian career officers were usually transferred after a tour of duty from two to four years, and his reports on the local political situation were acknowledged to be particularly well-informed and authoritative. See Peter Boyce, "Australian Diplomacy in Malaya", *Journal of Southeast Asian Studies* 4, no. 2 (September 1963), p. 72.

    The Australian Archives are of special interest as it is not generally realized that the Australian Commission in Singapore/Malaya during this period was tasked with a two-pronged function by the Australian Department of External Affairs, viz., (a) to cooperate and liaise with the British colonial power in Singapore/Malaya and relay back to Canberra any information obtained from it and, in addition, (b) to provide its own independent assessments and reports on political personalities and events of the time. The latter often provide a distinctly Australian perception of events as seen through Australian eyes and are not usually to be found in non-Australian archives such as the PRO Kew, the Singapore Archives, or the Arkib Negara, Kuala Lumpur.
4. National Archives of Australia, NAA: A1058, D/L 47/5/8a, Top Secret, "Far East Intelligence Reports from Singapore 1948–50", Australian Commission in Singapore to Department of External Affairs, Canberra, 29 April 1949. At the Regional Intelligence Conference held on 29 April 1949 at Phoenix Park, Singapore, the Political Secretary (Francis Stuart) of the Australian Commission in Singapore commented that the trade union movement in Singapore/Malaya was a "fertile ground for Communist propaganda and political agitation from the Left".
5. National Archives of Australia, NAA: A816, 19/321/18, Secret, "Annual Report for the British Territories in Southeast Asia for the year 1951", Australian Commissioner in Singapore to Department of External Affairs, Canberra.

6. *The Times* (London), 22 December 1952. It is interesting to note that Colonel H.S. Lee, a prominent MCA leader and a member of the Federal Legislative and Executive Councils, commented in a letter dated 29 November 1951 to J.T. Chappel, JP, President, Federated Malay States Chamber of Mines, that "the policy of the Briggs Plan is identical" to what he had advocated in July 1948 to the British authorities (see ISEAS Library Tun Sir Henry H.S. Lee, SMN, KBE, JP, Private Papers Collection, HSL.2.039, 29 November 1951, extract of letter to the Hon'ble J.T. Chappel).

   David Rooney claimed, too, in his biography of Brigadier Michael Calvert, *Mad Mike: A Life of Brigadier Michael Calvert* (London: Pen and Swords Books Ltd. 1997) that in the early part of the Malayan Emergency Calvert was asked by General Sir John Hardy (Commander-in-Chief, Far East) to make a threat assessment of the security situation and suggest means for defeating the Malayan Communist uprising. Calvert recommended that Chinese squatters and farmers should be moved into "fortified settlements" (rather similar to the "New Villages" under the Briggs Plan), and that a special commando unit (later known as the "Malayan Scouts") should be formed to operate for long periods inside the jungle to seek out and fight the Communists insurgents in the same way as the "Chindits", a British force under General Wingate that had operated behind the Japanese lines in Burma in World War II. Calvert had been a column commander of the Chindits. In 1951, Calvert, who was then a Lieutenant Colonel commanding the Malayan Scouts, came to see the author who was a Special Branch officer in the Johor State SB HQ to discuss the security situation but he did not refer to this matter, and it has not been possible to trace in the archives any report that Calvert may have prepared.

7. CAB 21/1681, MAL C (50) 23, Appendix, "Federation Plan for the elimination of the Communist Organisation and Armed forces in Malaya (the Briggs Plan) report by COS for Cabinet Malaya Committee." Briggs and Gurney discussed the Plan with the then Prime Minister Clement Attlee and J. Griffiths, Secretary of State for the Colonies, during their visit to London between 25 November and 1 December 1950 (see A.J. Stockwell, ed., *British Documents on the end of Empire. Malaya Part II: The Communist Insurrection 1948–1952* (London: HMSO, 1955), p. 272, and *The Times* (London), 14 December 1950.

8. See CO 1022/100, "General Templer's Speech from the Chair, 19 November 1952." In his speech, General Templer mentioned the part played by both Lieutenant General Sir Harold Briggs and Lieutenant General Sir Rob Lockhart.

9. *Singapore Ministry of Defence Journal*, "Personality File General Templer" 29, no. 4 (2003) and Ipoh World Archive Records <http://www.ipohworld.org/search8/result.asp?strid=2841> (assessed 27 October 2011).

10. Comber, op. cit., p. 129 fn. 55, and p. 183. Lieutenant General Sir Leslie Keith (Rob) Lockhart, KCB, CIE, MC (Indian Army retired) arrived in Malaya on 11 November 1951. He was the brother of Sir Robert Bruce Lockhart, the author, who had worked pre-war as a rubber planter in Malaya before joining the British Foreign Service. General Lockhart was recalled from retirement in England after having been Commander-in-Chief of the Indian Army 1945–47 and thereafter for a short while Governor of the Northwest Frontier Province. After taking over from 3 December 1951 to 6 February 1952 as Director of Operations in Malaya from General Briggs, he agreed to stay on as Deputy Director of Operations under General Templer when the latter arrived at Kuala Lumpur on 7 February 1952. It is interesting to note that General Lockhart, in a secret and personal letter dated 4 February 1952 to Field Marshal Sir William Slim, Chief of the Imperial General Staff, proposed that police headquarters should be reorganized along the lines of an Army Corps headquarters with separate divisions under senior police staff officers for police operations, training, intelligence, administration and supplies. Colonel Arthur Young, the newly appointed Commissioner of Police, who arrived in Malaya on 17 February 1952, subsequently reorganized federal police headquarters along similar lines though there is no record that he was aware of Lockhart's recommendations to the CIGS.

11. *The Times* (London), 19 July 1952.

12. Comber, op. cit., pp. 123–25.

13. PREM 11/639, f.51, Inward telegram from Lyttelton to Churchill, 8 December 1951 and CAB 129/48 C (51) 59, "Malaya: Cabinet memorandum by Lyttelton, Appendices 1-XV, 21 December 1951."

14. *The Times* (London), 14 January 1952.

15. PREM 11/639, Telegram no. T6/52 from Lyttelton to Churchill, 4 January 1952. The name of Lord Louis Mountbatten, too, had been suggested as "Supreme Commander" in a minute that E.J. Strachey, Secretary of State for War, submitted to Prime Minister Clement Attlee on 11 December 1950, following his earlier visit to Malaya in 1950 (see PREM 8/1406/23, "The Malayan Situation and the Far East, Minute by Mr. Strachey to Mr. Atlee urging the appointment of a regional Supremo"). It would appear from this the idea of appointing a "Regional Supremo" or "Supreme Commander" had occurred to Strachey earlier than it had to Lyttelton.

16. Oliver Lyttelton (Viscount Chandos), *The Memoirs of Lord Chandos* (London: The Bodley Head Ltd., 1962), pp. 381–82.

17. Lyttelton, op. cit., pp. 380–81. See also Short, op. cit., p. 326, and Lewis James Hawkins, "British Administration of Malaya during the Emergency, 1948–1957", MA History thesis, University of Delaware, June 1970, p. 43.

18. See David Benest, *British Leadership and Irregular Warfare* (London: British Army Review, Defence Academy of the United Kingdom. 2007), p. 2.

19. PREM 11/639, ibid; and <http://wikipedia.org/wiki/Gerald Templer> (accessed 26 March 2012).
20. *The Times* (London), 14 January 1952. For an account of Templer's meeting with Churchill, see Nigel Nicolson, *The Life of Field Marshal Alexander of Tunis* (London: Weidenfeld and Nicolson, 1973), pp. 301–2.
21. PREM 11/639, op. cit.
22. *Federation of Malaya Annual Report for 1952* (Kuala Lumpur: Government Printer, 1953), p. 3. Young's appointment was later extended to April 1953. Sir Donald MacGillivray's name is given incorrectly as "Sir David MacGillivray" in A.J. Stockwell, *British Documents on the End of Empire,* Series B, Vol. 4, *Malaya: The Communist Insurrection 1948–1953,* "Principal Members of Office 1948–1953", Pt. II, p. xvii.
23. CO 1022/103, Top Secret. Minute by Sir G. Templer to Mr. Churchill, 12 January 1952.
24. CO 1022/103, Directive to General Sir Gerald Walter Robert Templer, KCB, KBE, CMG, DSO, ADC, High Commissioner in and for the Federation of Malaya, by the Secretary of State for the Colonies on behalf of His Majesty's Government in the U.K., 1 February 1952.
25. *The Times* (London), 15 January 1952.
26. *Daily Telegraph* (London), 16 January 1952.
27. National Army Museum, Chelsea, ACC 8011-132-2, "Documents relating to General Templer's Period as High Commissioner, Malaya, 1952–54", General Templer's letter dated 5 January 1977 to Major General J.M. Gow, Ministry of Defence.
28. FO 371/1169, no. 14, "Inward telegram from Mr. M.J. MacDonald to Sir T. Lloyd", 5 November 1951.
29. Boris Hembry, *Malayan Spymaster, Memoirs of a Rubber Planter, Bandit Fighter and Spy* (Singapore: Monsoon Books Ltd., 2011), p. 356.
30. Parkinson, *Templer in Malaya,* p. i.
31. National Archives of Australia, NAA: A816, 19/321/18, Confidential, "Government Changes in the Federation of Malaya and Singapore — Appointment of Templer", Acting Australian Commissioner in Singapore to Department of External Affairs, Canberra, 4 February 1952.
32. See Lyttelton, op. cit., pp. 373–74; Short, op. cit., p. 337; and Comber, op. cit., p. 197, fn. 17.
33. Questions were asked in the House of Lords and the House of Commons about del Tufo's retirement, and the gist of Colonial Secretary Lyttelton's reply was that del Tufo had submitted a request to be allowed to retire on the grounds that the recent reorganization of higher posts in Malaya had radically changed his position, and he had acceded to his request. Awkwardly, it had fallen to Lyttelton, when he was staying with del Tufo during his mission to Malaya in December 1951, to inform him regretfully that he would not be confirmed in

his acting position as High Commissioner. In 1952 del Tufo was knighted by the British Government and he was later appointed the Federation of Malaya's delegate on the International Tin Council (*Straits Times*, 5 March 1956).

34. *Straits Times*, 30 and 31 January 1952. The same line was taken by the *Singapore Standard*, 30 January 1952.

35. ISEAS Library, Tun Sir Henry H.S. Lee Private Papers, HSL 031.023, *Singapore Standard*, 5 February 1952.

36. It is not generally known that on a visit to London in December 1948, Dato' Onn bin Ja'afar, then Mentri Besar, Johore, had recommended to the then Secretary of State for the Colonies A. Creech Jones that a Malay should be appointed Deputy High Commissioner of Malaya but nothing was done about it. (See CO 825/74/5, Secret. "Political Developments. The Appointment of a Malay as Deputy High Commissioner. Letter dated 23 December 1948 from Creech Jones to Sir Henry Gurney, High Commissioner, Federation of Malaya").

37. National Archives of Australia, NAA: A816, 19/321/18, Confidential, "Government Changes in the Federation of Malaya and Singapore — Appointment of Templer", ibid.

38. John Coates, *Suppressing Insurgency: An Analysis of the Malayan Emergency 1948–1954* (Boulder, CO: Westview Press, 1992).

39. Margaret Shennan, *Our Man in Malaya: John Davis (CBE, DSO), SOE Force 136 and Postwar Counter-Insurgency* (Singapore: Monsoon Books, 2014), p. 243.

40. See *Singapore Ministry of Defence Journal*, "Personality File General Templer", op. cit.

41. Perhaps the only bright (and light) note about the announcement of Templer's appointment was the comment by his wife, Lady Peggie Templer, who personifying the loyal Army wife, said at her home at Cobham, Surrey, on the eve of her departure for Malaya: "I go wherever my husband goes. That is the lot of a soldier's wife." As to be expected, General Templer said: "I am looking forward to having a go at what will be a tough job." (*Straits Times*, 17 January 1952).

2

THE EARLY DAYS:
General Templer in Kuala Lumpur —
Political Background

At the time of General Templer's arrival at Kuala Lumpur on 7 February 1952, the constitution in force was the Federation of Malaya Agreement 1948, which had replaced the Malayan Union. It came into being on 1 February 1948. It was called an "Agreement" but to all intents and purposes it was in fact a formal federal Constitution. The Federation of Malaya (in Malay *Persekutuan Tanah Melayu*) introduced in 1948, was the name given to the nine Malay States (Perak, Selangor, Negri Sembilan, Pahang, Johor, Kedah, Perlis, Kelantan, and Trengganu, and the two Settlements of Penang and Malacca). In this book, for simplicity, the Federation of Malaya is often referred to as "Malaya". Singapore was a separate colony. The Federation of Malaya became independent on 31 August 1957. In 1963 it was reconstituted as Malaysia with the inclusion of Singapore, Sabah, and Sarawak, although Singapore withdrew from Malaysia on 9 August 1965 and became a separate state.

The Preamble of the Federation of Malaya Agreement is important as it repeated the intention of the British Government to "move towards eventual self-government":

> His Majesty and Their Highnesses intend that progress should be made towards eventual self-government, and as a first step to that end, His Majesty and their Highnesses have agreed that, as soon as local circumstances and conditions will permit, legislation should be introduced for the election of members to the several legislatures to be pursuant to this Agreement.

The promise towards self-government within the British Commonwealth was, in fact, repeated by Clement Atlee, the British Prime Minister, in the House of Commons on 13 April 1949 and 28 March 1950.[1]

At the time of Templer's arrival in Kuala Lumpur, how did the British colonial Government function and what were its instruments of government?

Firstly, there was a Federal Executive Council, consisting of Templer as the High Commissioner as President [in Templer's time, the Deputy High Commissioner, Donald MacGillivray, was deputed by Templer to be *de facto* in charge of the Executive Council] aided by three *ex-officio* members (Chief Secretary, Attorney General, and Financial Secretary), with not less than twelve nor more than twenty-four members nominated by the High Commissioner. The function of the Federal Executive Council was to debate public policy matters and aid and advise the High Commissioner. As High Commissioner, Templer could only act against its decisions after reporting to the Secretary of State for the Colonies in London.

Secondly, there was the Federal Legislative Council consisting of the High Commissioner, three *ex-officio* members as per the Executive Council, a representative of each Settlement Council and the nine Malay States, and eleven Official and fifty nominated members.

The role of the Federal Legislative Council as defined in the Federation of Malaya agreement was to provide "advice and consent" to the High Commissioner and rulers in the making of law but in practice its functions extended beyond this as it exercised an influence in policy-making through the activities of its various committees, and more especially through the Standing Committee on Finance which was dominated by British commercial interests who were thus able to exercise a significant influence over public expenditure and the Government's budgets.[2]

In 1953, as part of a significant but gradual move towards self-government which General Templer introduced, he ceased to preside over the Legislative Council, and Dato Setia Wangsa Sir Mahmud bin Mat, CMG, OBE, former Mentri Besar, Pahang (1948–51) and Minister for Lands, Mines and Communications, was appointed in his place on 2 September as Speaker of the Legislative Council after six months' training at the House of Commons in London.

However, even before Templer's arrival in February 1952, his predecessor, the ill-fated Sir Henry Gurney who had been murdered by the Communists in October of the preceding year, introduced what was really the first significant move towards self-government, as mentioned in the Preamble to the Federation of Malaya Agreement, by appointing nine members of the Federal Legislative Council as "Members with Portfolios" with responsibility for groups of government departments. Most of them were community or political leaders, and it was in a sense, as Gurney correctly visualized, a forerunner of ministerial responsibility. Though the move was opposed by local die-hard British business interests, who for their own reasons were in favour of maintaining the status quo because of a fear that it would lead to a Malayanization of Malayan politics and perhaps even the imposition of restrictions on the remittance of profits to Britain which would lead eventually to the naturalization of British businesses in Malaya. However, Gurney was able to overcome their resistance and implement his plans.[3]

In 1952, Templer further developed the existing "member" system by expanding the Executive Council to include all Legislative Council Members with portfolios, and introduced, too, new legislation for citizenship (which had to be approved by the Malay Sultans) which he hoped would help to bring about a greater sense of Malayan identity and participation in Malayan affairs by the growing number of persons who were beginning to regard Malaya as their home. In 1952, the Malays and Chinese were quite closely balanced, in round figures 2.7 million Malays and 2 million Chinese, with 600,000 Indians and 80,000 Others, making up a total estimated population for the Federation of Malaya of just over 5.5 million.[4] All Malays were admitted to Federal citizenship, and it was estimated that an increasing number of non-Malays, but probably not more than one-third of the Chinese population, would be eligible for Federal citizenship under the new citizenship legislation.[5]

Nevertheless, in actual fact, these were still colonial times, with the British in the driving seat, and in effect political control was still exercised by an inner "Cabinet" of the Federal Executive Council made up of the High Commissioner (represented by MacGillivray), the Chief Secretary, the Attorney General, and the Financial Secretary.

Each of the Malay States had a Malay ruler, a State Council, and a State Executive Council, with a senior member of the MCS appointed to each State as a British Adviser to advise the Malay ruler on all matters except those pertaining to Malay customs and the Muslim religion. Each Settlement had a British Resident Commissioner, a Settlement Council, and a Nominated Council.

The Conference of Malay Rulers had power to consider: (a) legislation to be introduced into the Federal Legislative Council; (b) the salary schemes of Federal public officers; (c) every draft scheme for the creation of or major reorganization of any Federal department or service; and (d) the right of consultation upon Federal immigration and citizenship matters. As High Commissioner, Templer was responsible for dealing with the Malay rulers on behalf of the colonial Government.

The above involved political system was already largely in place when Templer arrived and there was no way he could overstep the Constitution and the law, and it therefore says much for his resolve that during his two years in Malaya he was able to work within this elaborate and complicated system, more especially so as the move towards self-government by local politicians, which had begun to make itself felt more noticeably after the Japanese surrender at the end of World War II, accelerated even further after his arrival and he had to devote much of his time to political matters.[6]

In 1955, the year following Templer's departure from Malaya, the Federal Legislative Council established under the Federation of Malaya Agreement was dissolved to make way for a general election, which marked the first time the people of Malaya went to the polls to elect their representatives to the federal legislature. It is noteworthy as it was actually well in advance of the timetable envisaged by Templer who, while he was High Commissioner, had resisted UMNO-MCA Alliance's demand for early self-government, and had taken a much more conservative view. In his view, Malaya would not be ready for federal elections before 1958 and self-government until 1960.[7]

GENERAL TEMPLER'S ARRIVAL AT KUALA LUMPUR

A few days after Templer's arrival at Kuala Lumpur on 7 February 1952 to take up his appointment, an official welcoming party called on him at King's House. It is worth recording the names of the persons who met him as they provide an idea of the top hierarchy of the British colonial administration in Kuala Lumpur at the time. The two senior-most members of the MCA were members of the welcoming party. It is not clear why UMNO was not represented in this group but it may well have been that the leadership of UMNO was in a state of flux at the time as Tunku Abdul Rahman had only recently taken over as the UMNO President after Dato' Onn bin Ja'afar's resignation.[8]

The delegation was led by M.V. del Tufo, the acting High Commissioner, accompanied by D.C. Watherston, Chief Secretary; Lieutenant General Sir Robert Lockhart, Director of Operations; Charles Mathew, Chief Justice; and Michael J.P. Hogan, Attorney General. The MCA delegates were Dato Tan Cheng Lock (later Tun Sir Cheng Lock Tan), a wealthy *baba* Chinese from Malacca, President of the MCA (1949–58), and Colonel H.S. Lee (later Tun Colonel Sir Henry Hau Sik Lee), a wealthy Chinese tin miner and banker, and member of the Federal Executive and Legislative Councils.[9]

Del Tufo had been on leave in Britain at the time of Sir Henry Gurney's murder in October 1951 and on hearing the news he had immediately returned by air to take over as Officer Administering the Government until a new High Commissioner was appointed. He was a senior MCS officer who had served throughout his career in Malaya.

Although Lyttelton did not say so, it seems likely that del Tufo was not confirmed in his acting appointment as Lyttelton had already decided during his mission to Malaya in November/December that Malaya needed a new leader at the helm who could provide a joint "military-political" approach which del Tufo, a quintessential MCS officer, would not be able to fill.

In order to provide the background to General Templer's arrival at Malaya, it may be opportune to summarize below the main points of del Tufo's last Budget Address that he gave to the Federal Legislative Council on 21 November 1951 only a short time before Templer's arrival. Some of the points are self-obvious but they do provide his view of the situation:

- The war against the Communist insurgents still gave rise for concern.
- The best practical way of dealing with the Communist insurgents was to obtain reliable information about their whereabouts, concentrate on cutting off their supplies, and intensify army and police patrols in areas where they were known to be active.
- The battle against the *Min Yuen* (literally "People's Movement"),

which acted as the eyes and ears of the Communist insurgents and sometimes likened to a "Communist Home Guard", was primarily a Police task.

- The Emergency was essentially a Chinese problem.
- The Emergency had to be fought simultaneously on three fronts: economic, political, and military.
- Facilities for education should be allowed to maintain their present rate of expansion regardless of the Emergency.
- The work of Rural and Industrial Development Authority (RIDA) (under Dato' Onn bin Ja'afar) in improving and developing the economy of mainly Malay rural areas should continue to receive government support so that it could be expanded.[10]
- The "member system" introduced by the late Sir Henry Gurney in April 1951 to appoint federal councillors to head "portfolios" to replace expatriate department heads had proved to be effective.[11]
- It was the announced policy of the U.K. Government to lead Malaya to self-government within the British Commonwealth as soon as it could "safely be achieved".[12]
- He expressed his deep sense of gratitude to General Briggs for his leadership during a critical period of the Emergency.[13]

However, in his capacity as "Officer Administering the Government" del Tufo provided a much more comprehensive and penetrating report on the Malayan situation in a top secret dispatch he had sent to the Colonial Secretary in London on 23 October 1951, which dealt with such matters as UMNO's protection of Malay rights; the MCA, which he described as active in acquiring equal rights for the Chinese in Malaya; and the MIC representing Indian interests, although he considered Indian opinion would be better voiced through the trade union movement than the Congress. In this respect, as it turned out, he was correct, as General Templer later made use of the services of P.P. Narayanan, a Federal Legislative Councillor and President of the Malayan Trade Union Council, to deal with the Indian labour movement which was mainly made up of Tamil rubber estate workers. Del Tufo also referred to Dato' Onn's decision to resign as UMNO's President which led to Tunku Abdul Rahman's taking over the party as President, as well as Onn's decision to form the Independence of Malaya Party (IMP), a non-communal party which Del Tufo thought seriously damaged the support Onn had hitherto received from Malay voters and marked the beginning of the end of the political power he wielded.[14]

In the meantime, upon General Templer's arrival in Malaya, he had decided that priority should be given to three matters:

(a) The reorganization and training of the Malayan Police, including the Special Constabulary;

(b) The reorganization of the intelligence organization;

(c) The reorganization of the Government's Information Services.[15]

Templer was successful, in due course, in achieving these objectives. The first with the assistance of Colonel Arthur Young, the newly appointed Commissioner of Police, who had been seconded from the City of London Police, and the second by appointing J.P. (Jack) Morton, a senior MI5 officer, the head of Security Intelligence Far East (SIFE) in Singapore, who was seconded from MI5 as Director of Intelligence (Templer himself always showed a personal interest in intelligence), and thirdly by the appointment, in July 1952, of A.D.C. Peterson as Director General of Information Services. These appointments did make an improvement in the situation though the Malayan public did not shed its scepticism of officially disseminated news.

DIRECTOR OF INTELLIGENCE

Towards the end of January 1952, before General Templer's departure from London to take up his appointment in Malaya, he visited the Colonial Office to discuss his proposals for appointing a senior intelligence officer to coordinate Malayan intelligence services and fill the vacancy left by Sir William Jenkin's resignation. He had in mind W.T. Williams, who was on Lord Montgomery's staff during the war, or failing that, one of the sons of the Archbishop of Canterbury whose name he was unable to recollect, who had held "an important intelligence post during the war".[16] Templer's proposal to appoint a senior officer to coordinate intelligence was, in fact, not new, and it echoed what Lyttelton had already recommended in his report on his mission to Malaya in November/December 1951.

The Colonial Office, however, felt that Templer should defer a final decision until he had taken up his appointment in Malaya partly because there were likely to be objections to his making a high-level appointment of this nature the emoluments of which would have to be voted by the

Malayan Legislature until he had consulted the views of local political leaders.

However, Templer did not waste any time in following up his discussions with the Colonial Office and on 13 February, a week after he arrived at Kuala Lumpur, he sent a telegram to Lyttelton repeating his proposal that "there is an urgent need for a Director [of Intelligence] to be responsible for the coordination and evaluation of intelligence from all sources". While he did not refer to the persons he had previously mentioned and there was no mention of his having to consult local political leaders, this time he requested the services of Dick White, a senior MI5 officer, whom he had known since the time Templer had been Director of Military Intelligence at the War Office.[17] White, however, declined the appointment, most likely because he was in the process of taking over as Director General of MI5. Templer then offered the post to J.P. (Jack) Morton, a senior MI5 officer, who was Head of the joint MI5/MI6 SIFE office in Singapore. As Templer wrote later to Major General Gow at the War Office:

> I know something about the organisation of intelligence…. [The man I had in mind] would have to head up the whole caboodle [sic]. This wasn't easy and it took time. The man who did the trick was Jack Morton, who had vast experience in the U.K., and quite a bit in the Far East itself.[18]

John Percival Morton, CMG, OBE, Indian Police Medal for Gallantry, had had a distinguished career in the Indian Police Special Branch before being transferred at India's independence in 1947 to London as "Principal, War Office", a cover name for MI5. He was subsequently seconded as Counsellor in the Commissioner General for South East Asia's office in Singapore as Head of SIFE (1949–52).[19] On accepting Templer's offer as Director of Intelligence, Malaya, he was seconded from MI5 for two years from April 1952. It was a fortunate choice because he worked well with Templer to coordinate Malaya's intelligence services during Templer's proconsulship although his remit was in an advisory capacity and it did not extend to his exercising executive control over the Malayan Police Special Branch or military intelligence in Malaya.[20]

GOVERNMENT INFORMATION SERVICES

In July 1952, General Templer appointed A.D.C. (Alec) Peterson to take over as Director General of Information Services. During World War II,

Peterson had established a reputation for himself as Deputy Director and Controller of "Black Propaganda" on the staff of Admiral Lord Louis Mountbatten, Supreme Allied Commander South East Asia Command, at his headquarters in Ceylon (Sri Lanka).[21]

General Templer showed personal interest in the work of the Government Information Services which he considered should keep the public aware of what the Government was doing. He was especially interested in psychological warfare.

An impressively wide range of activities were carried out by the Information Services' various divisions, which included the Malayan Film Unit, the Press Division, the broadcasting of news items in the four main languages of Malaya (English, Chinese, Malay and Tamil), and the running of Civics courses which were held in collaboration with the Department of Chinese Affairs and the Labour Department.[22]

The Information Services used "mobile units" for work in the field on a countrywide basis, which usually consisted of vehicles (vans or jeeps) equipped basically with a public address unit, portable recording machine, radio set, and, in those days, a gramophone.[23]

The Emergency Information Services, which had been established by General Briggs in 1950 before Templer arrived as part of the Information Services with responsibility for psychological warfare and countering Communist propaganda in the Emergency, now reported directly to Templer in his capacity as Director of Operations. Templer ordered the Public Works Department to give absolute priority to the construction of a new building for it, which was officially opened by him on 21 November 1952.[24] Until then, it had been temporarily housed in extremely cramped space on the third floor of the Oriental Building, Kuala Lumpur, on a site near the Selangor Residency.

Meanwhile, government approval had been given for "Surrendered Enemy Personnel" (SEPs), the name given to Communist insurgents who had defected to the Government, to accompany and assist State Emergency Information Officers (SEIOs) on their propaganda tours. However, this work did not always proceed as smoothly as intended. There was an occasion in early 1952, when the author who was then an officer at the Johor State Special Branch headquarters attended an open-air gathering of Chinese villagers in Johor where Hugh Howse, the Johor SEIO, a Cantonese-speaking British officer, accompanied by his special SEP assistant for Johor, Lee Choo, addressed them from the back of a mobile truck. After Howse spoke to them in Cantonese, the predominant southern Chinese dialect spoken in Johor, a Chinese villager who was squatting on the ground listening intently to what Howse was saying, commented to his friends in Chinese: "These 'foreign devils' are really very tricky! They must have arranged for a Russian to come and talk to us about the evils of Communism. I couldn't understand a word of what he said. He must have been speaking in Russian but it sounded very good." It was not until Lee Choo told them that Howse had been speaking to them in Cantonese that the audience applauded him.

Howse spoke fluent Cantonese but as he told the author afterwards, he often found that many Chinese villagers he spoke to did not seem to understand what he said because they did not expect him to be speaking to them in Chinese (there were, in fact, only a few Europeans capable of doing so in Malaya at the time) and it was somehow "difficult" at times for them to register that he was speaking in Chinese, even though he spoke good idiomatic Cantonese.[25]

While it is not possible to gauge accurately the effect on public attitudes and behaviour of all the measures that were taken by Templer to expand and improve the Government Information Services, the problem that remained even after the Information Services had been tightened up and improved, was that the public was still not completely won over to accepting on trust statements emanating from the Government.[26]

Dato' Onn bin Ja'afar, a member of the Federal Executive and Legislative Councils, who was interviewed on 5 October 1953 by Ian Hamilton, Public Relations Officer, Australian Mission in Singapore, praised the work of the Department of Information Services and particularly Radio Malaya for doing "a good job generally" (this is not surprising as he was the Member for Information Services and Broadcasting) , though he added that for administrative convenience he would prefer Radio Malaya to be located in Kuala Lumpur where it would be closer to the scene of action and not Singapore, "though he realised it was not practicable to do so at the present time".[27]

Meanwhile, in 1953, General Templer and Peterson were successful in obtaining permission from the Thai Government for a Malayan Information Services mobile broadcasting jeep to operate in south Thailand which had a porous border with the northern-most Malay States to broadcast anti-Communist propaganda in Chinese, Malay and Thai. The Malayan and Thai authorities had been aware for some time that elements of the Communist

Party of Malaya had moved across the international land frontier into the Betong Salient area of south Thailand for rest and retraining, where they would be immune from attack by Malayan security forces.

The Thai Communist Party (CPT), which was banned by the Thai Government in 1952, was also active in this area, and in November 1952 the Thai authorities declared a state of Emergency throughout the Thai-Malaya frontier area which came under the jurisdiction of the 9th Police Division of the Thai Police.[28]

The detailed arrangements for the operation were worked out by Peterson and G. Crossley, Assistant Regional Information Officer, Singapore, when they visited Songkhla between 2 to 5 March 1953 to discuss the operation of a Malayan mobile broadcasting vehicle in south Thailand with A.G. Evans, British Consul in Songkhla and the Thai Police Colonel Som Sun Thornrat, Chief Superintendent in Command of the 9th Police Division, Songkhla. As a result, it was agreed that a Malayan jeep mobile broadcasting unit should be made available to the Thais for six months, with the Malayan authorities assuming responsibility for its operating costs and providing training and salaries for the Thai personnel employed.[29]

It was indeed a breakthrough as it was only much later that a formal agreement was reached with the Thai authorities for Malayan security forces to operate across the international frontier "in pursuit of units of the Communist Party of Malaya", and even then they had to be accompanied by Thai security forces.[30]

LIEUTENANT GENERAL PHAO SRIYANONDH, DIRECTOR GENERAL OF THE THAI POLICE AND DIRECTOR OF THAI INTELLIGENCE

On 10 April 1953, not long after these arrangements were made, Lieutenant General Phao Sriyanondh, Director General of the Thai Police and Director of Thai Intelligence, met General Templer for discussions at King's House, Kuala Lumpur, about the general political situation in Siam (Thailand) and in Southeast Asia. Morton, the Malayan Director of Intelligence, and Major Thans, Phao's ADC, were in attendance.

Templer, who had been Director of Military Intelligence at the War Office and had helped reform the British Army's Intelligence Corps at the beginning of World War II, was very much in his element in the discussions with Phao as he was well aware as a soldier that the security situation in Malaya could easily be influenced by events in Indo-China and, still more so in Thailand where the Communists were reported to be gaining ground. The recent CPM forward movement from Malaya into the Malaya-Thai border area where the party leadership and its accompanying units straddled the Malaya-Thailand frontier gave cause for alarm should the security situation in Thailand deteriorate, and this must have been very much in his mind when he met Phao. The British Cabinet had, in fact, already appointed a committee under Anthony Eden (then Secretary of State for Foreign Affairs) to consider the defence of Malaya in the event of a French collapse in Indo-China leading to a Communist takeover in Thailand and its likely effect on the Communist insurrection in Malaya. Aside from political considerations, it was expected that such a situation would bring about a serious curtailment in the supply of rice from Thailand to Malaya on which Malaya greatly depended as it grew insufficient rice for its own requirements.[31]

General Phao said that Communism in Southeast Asia had its origins in the machinations of the Comintern, and that the principal Communist agent in Thailand was Nai Pridi, who was operating under the aegis of the Chinese Communist Party. It was due to Pridi's agents that the Thai Navy had recently staged an abortive coup d'état in Thailand.

General Templer asked him about the implications of the establishment by the Thai Communist Party of a Thai Autonomous Republic in Yunnan, and General Phao answered that the matter was not of great concern to the Thai Government as the situation was being closely watched and it would not be allowed to spin out of control. Templer enquired, too, about the activities of the large Soviet Diplomatic Mission in Bangkok and asked whether it was active in carrying out espionage activities in the area. Phao replied that its activities were being kept under close surveillance, and it was believed that it was mainly engaged with trade matters and not intelligence.

General Templer said that he appreciated that the security situation on Thailand's frontiers with French Indo-China (Vietnam) and Burma (Myanmar) would be of more concern to the Thai authorities than the situation resulting from the move of the CPM into the Malaya-Thai border region in the south, and he expressed his gratitude for the cooperation and assistance that the Thais had given to the Malayan security forces operating in the Malaya-Thai border region.[32]

Templer expressed his thanks, too, for the approval given by the Thai Government for the arrangements that had been made for the deployment of the Malayan mobile broadcasting unit in south Thailand, and Thailand's cooperation in signing the Malaya-Thai Border Agreement which allowed Malayan security units to operate in south Thailand in hot pursuit of MNLA insurgents. He noted, too, that several Communists had been arrested in Thailand under the recently promulgated Thai anti-Communist laws.

Although General Templer did not refer to it for obvious reasons, it is likely that he must have been aware at the time of the Malayan Special Branch's recent recruitment of a senior Thai police officer in Sadao as a secret agent on a monthly retainer of M$500 in return for providing copies of his monthly intelligence reports to Bangkok. This arrangement was, however, later discontinued as the intelligence obtained in this way was not found to add very much to what the Special Branch already knew from its own sources.[33]

The situation on the Malaya-Thai border that General Templer referred to was, in fact, later summed up in a memo that the British Colonial Secretary Lyttelton sent Major Niall Macpherson, MP, in reply to a question raised by the latter in the House of Commons about the security situation on the Malaya-Thai border. In his reply, Lyttelton informed him that there were an estimated 300 Malayan Communist insurgents operating in the border area, and they came under the operational command of the "CPM's Special Committee in Kedah and Perak" and the "CPM's Special Committee in Kelantan". He said that operations against them were being mounted jointly by Malayan and Thai army and police units.[34]

It is interesting to note that just before Peterson relinquished his appointment in 1954 as Director of Information Services to return to the United Kingdom, he mentioned in conversation with Lieutenant General Sir Geoffrey Bourne, who was then Director of Operations following Templer's departure from Malaya on 1 June 1954, that during his two-year stay in Malaya, which roughly coincided with Templer's, the attitude of the Chinese in the New Villages and on the rubber estates towards the Government had changed only slightly from "non-cooperation and apathy" to "reasonably friendly apathy". In his view this was not good enough and, in any case, "reasonable friendly apathy" did not accurately describe the situation in "the really bad New Villages where [Government] vocal and film propaganda had little effect" and in his view it was difficult to win over the hearts and minds of the Chinese villagers.

General Bourne duly passed on this information to the War Office with his comment that "appeal to patriotism or duty to Government, by vocal or film propaganda, has little effect on a population [Chinese] whose sense of nationhood has hardly started to develop. Fear is their dominant motive. In the bad areas they support the CT's [Communist terrorists] because they fear them. In areas where military success is achieved and security provided, fear subsides and they find it pays to cooperate."[35]

REORGANIZATION OF FEDERAL GOVERNMENT ADMINISTRATION

Not long after he arrived at Kuala Lumpur, General Templer informed Oliver Lyttelton, Secretary of State for the Colonies, by telegram on 28 February 1952 that he planned to reorganize from 1 March what he described as the "Government Administrative H.Q. machine". It was not a new proposal, however, as the idea had already been advanced in a memorandum to Lyttelton by Hugh Fraser, his Parliamentary Private Secretary, on 16 January 1952. Fraser had accompanied Lyttelton on his mission to Malaya and had stayed on for a while after Lyttelton left. Fraser had recommended it to avoid what he called a "split personality of government between civil-political and military".[36] It was an important step as it involved the merging of the functions of the "Federal War Council", which had been established earlier by Briggs as part of his "Briggs Plan", with those of the Federal Executive Council, and it affected both the civil administration and the security forces. The Federal Executive Council would then become the sole instrument of the Federal Government's policy.[37] There was much to be said for it as it helped to streamline bureaucracy at federal level, and it fitted in well with Templer's two-pronged Directive that he had been given by the British Government.

Templer informed Lyttelton, too, that he proposed to increase the number of Federal Executive Councillors to twenty by appointing five new members of whom at least two should be Malays. He proposed that one of them should be Tunku Abdul Rahman, who would be appointed in his personal capacity as a Member in charge of a Department and not as President of UMNO. However, Tunku nominated Dr Ismail, a senior member of UMNO, in his place as he was well aware that if he accepted the offer, he would be tied down to administering the Department he would be given, which would divert his attention from UMNO affairs, but he remained an unofficial member of the Council.[38]

The other four Federal Councillors appointed were General Sir Rob Lockhart (Deputy Director of Operations), J.D. Hodgkinson (Member for

Industrial and Social Relations), Leong Yew Koh (MCA), and Raja Uda bin Raja Muhammad (Mentri Besar, Selangor).[39]

On 29 September 1953, Dr Ismail and Colonel H.S. Lee joined the Federal Executive Council, the former as Member for Lands, Mines and Communications and the latter as Member for Railways and Ports.

The only members of the Federal War Council who did not find a place on the expanded Federal Executive Council were Dato Sir Cheng Lock Tan, MCA President; two European members who had represented rubber planters' interests on the Council; and the Keeper of the Rulers' Seal.[40]

The main function of the Federal Executive Council was to submit matters to the Deputy High Commissioner, MacGillivray, for action as necessary, so that he could either deal with them himself or refer them at his discretion to General Templer. In this way, a great deal of pressure was relieved from Templer's shoulders to enable him to deal with political and socio-economic matters.[41]

CLOSER LINKAGE WITH SINGAPORE

The British Government had been exploring for some time the possibility of a fusion between the Federation of Malaya and Singapore, and the Foreign Office and Colonial Office had in mind a wider association of all the British colonial territories in Southeast Asia, that is, Malaya, Singapore, Sarawak, and what was then British North Borneo (present-day Sabah), as well as Brunei, to form a "British Southeast Asian Dominion". From the strategic point of view, too, the concept found favour with the British Chiefs of Staff.[42]

Ivor Bulmer Thomas, a Labour MP who visited Malaya as early as October 1946 on his way back to London from attending the South Seas Conference in Canberra, reported that the separation of Singapore from Malaya (under the Malayan Union arrangement) was strongly denounced by many people to whom he had spoken, and he thought it inevitable that at some time Singapore should be incorporated in the Federation of Malaya.[43] Malcolm MacDonald, Commissioner General for South East Asia, too, had long advocated a closer association between Singapore and Malaya.

On 10 June 1952, MacDonald reported to Lyttelton, the Secretary of State for the Colonies, that he had attended the installation of John Nicoll (later Sir John) as Governor of Singapore, as well as the formal dinner party held afterwards which was attended by Nicoll, himself, and members of the Legislative Councils of the Federation of Malaya, the Borneo British territories, and Singapore. It was one of the rare occasions when members of the various Legislative Councils had come together in this way.

MacDonald related there was much favourable discussion at the dinner for a closer relationship between the British territories, and the idea of periodic meetings of this kind found favour too.[44] MacDonald commented further that "a number of prominent personalities in Singapore and the Federation of Malaya had publicly expressed their agreement" with a merger between the two territories, including C.C. Tan, a lawyer, who was a member of both the Singapore Legislative and Executive Councils and a prominent political figure in Singapore.[45] Dato' Onn, too, was known to be in favour of an ultimate closer association between Singapore, the Federation of Malaya and the British Borneo territories. Nevertheless, as MacDonald pointed out, it was noticeable that all the favourable comments in Singapore and the Federation for a merger came from the Chinese, Indian and other non-Malay communities and not from the Malays, which seemed to indicate that there was some reservation on their part. This was probably because of their concern that if a merger came about, they would be overwhelmed economically by the Chinese and it was possible too that their political strength would be affected.

When Templer left the United Kingdom to take up his appointment in Malaya in February 1952, he was tasked by the Colonial Office to continue to explore with the Governor of Singapore the possibilities of a closer linkage between Malaya and Singapore and after his arrival Templer was in contact with Gimson about this. There is no indication in the records, however, why he was not invited to attend the installation in June 1952 of Nicoll who was taking over as Governor of Singapore from Gimson as this would have undoubtedly provided him with a good opportunity to make Nicoll's acquaintance and pursue the matter further with him.

Thus it was at one of Templer's early visits back to London from Kuala Lumpur in December 1952, he rather surprised the mandarins in the Colonial Office by what they felt was his confused thinking about the lack of progress in bringing about a closer political development between Singapore and Malaya.[46] As J. J. Paskin, an Assistant Under-Secretary of State, minuted,

> To my astonishment Sir G. Templer asked me, at the meeting with C.O.S.[Chiefs of Staff] , whether there was any Colonial Office policy on the matter of a closer association between the two territories of Singapore and Malaya. I was quite taken aback by the question but I had to explain

that from 1945 onwards it *has* [emphasis in original] been Colonial Office
policy that there should be closer association between (a) the Federation
and Singapore and (b) the three Borneo territories, and that there was
also a "hope" that there would ultimately be a union of the Malayan *and*
the Borneo territories.[47]

Paskin went on to explain to Templer that the impetus for any closer
association between Singapore and Malaya would have to come from
Malaya itself and that if he felt the time was right, the proper course
was for him to get together with the Governor of Singapore and make a
joint representation to the Secretary of State. As Paskin put it, the retort
of General Templer was a "surprised" question whether policy on this
matter lay with the Secretary of State or with him and the Governor of
Singapore. Almost immediately afterwards, according to Paskin, Templer
commented that closer union between Singapore and the Federation would
mean "tearing up the Federation Agreement" although as "he himself
has repeatedly told us [this] could not be contemplated at present — or
indeed that nothing should be done to make the Malays feel that any such
move was in the wind." Paskin described the discussion as being "very
confused and in parts inconsistent but it served to show how disturbed
Sir G. Templer's mind is about the lack of progress in getting the two
territories together". On the evening of 10 December 1952, Paskin spoke
on the lines of his minute at a meeting with Lyttelton and Colonial Office
officials, which Templer attended.

According to MacDonald, who after the winding up of the Communities
Liaison Committee had been authorized by Lyttelton in May 1953 to form
a Joint Coordination Committee for Singapore and Malaya with the
approval of Malayan and Singapore Governments and the concurrence
of the Malay Sultans to continue discussing a closer association with
Singapore, "the main difficulty came from the Malays" who were wary of
a Chinese majority in the Malayan Councils and Chinese economic power
if a fusion with Singapore came about.[48] He also anticipated there would
be resistance from commercial interests in Singapore who were concerned
that their present monetary contribution towards the costs of the Malayan
Emergency would be increased.[49] His own inclination was to establish first
a federation of British North Borneo (Sabah), Sarawak, and Brunei which
could be joined later by Singapore and Malaya.[50]

It is possible that the reluctance of the Malays that MacDonald
referred to may have been influenced to some extent, but by how much

is not clear, by the "Pan Islamic Movement" emanating from the Middle East which was causing some concern to the British colonial authorities because Malay pilgrims for the haj on arrival at Mecca were increasingly subject to political propaganda when they were in a high state of religious emotion from the Supreme Islamic Council and the Ikhwan-el-Muslimin. From the official report submitted by the Malay Pilgrimage Officer, Haji Abdul Rahim, on his return to Singapore in 1947, for instance, there were protest movements against the partition of Palestine and Jewish encroachment, considerable unrest over the Anglo-Egyptian Treaty and the future of Sudan, and there were powerful xenophobic and Pan-Islamic trends at play favouring the inclusion of Malaya in the Indonesian Republic which would have been opposed to any fusion between Malaya and a non-Muslim (Chinese) Singapore.[51] For the policy-makers, the amount of evidence in the Malay Pilgrimage Officer's report seems to suggest they were worthy of serious concern as the ramifications for British policy were considerable.

At a further meeting at the Colonial Office on 18 May 1953 which was attended by Sir John Nicoll who had taken over from Gimson as Governor of Singapore and Templer who by then had been in Malaya for more than a year, both agreed that local feeling on both sides was opposed to any closer association of the two territories.[52]

Nevertheless, the question of a "fusion" between Malaya and Singapore and a possible closer association with the British Borneo territories continued to exercise the minds of the British authorities. MacDonald was quite sanguine that the prospects were good, and considered if the matter was handled boldly and prudently, it would be possible to overcome all difficulties.[53] The Secretary of State, however, did not concur with MacDonald's proposals straightaway and suggested that the matter should be given further consideration when MacDonald returned to London for consultations. At the same time, he expressed his appreciation and gratitude for all that had been achieved under MacDonald's guidance "to lay the foundations for the structure which will, I trust, in time to come, and in whatever shape is found appropriate, hold together the British territories in South East Asia in even closer association, for the benefit of their peoples and the well-being and prosperity of the region."[54]

There the matter seemed to rest, although there was much discussion behind the scenes. But it was not in fact until several years later that the Tunku reverted to what he described as a "Grand Malaysian Alliance" of Malaya, Singapore, Sabah (formerly British North Borneo), Sarawak and

Brunei in a speech he gave on 17 May 1961 at the Adelphi Hotel, Singapore, at a lunch arranged by the Foreign Correspondents Association of Southeast Asia. Exactly what role the British played behind the scenes in this proposal is not clear.[55] Of course, as mentioned previously, it was not the first time the idea had been proposed, and it had been mooted much earlier by MacDonald and advocated by several other organizations and persons, and over time, several different versions of the plan had emerged. One proposal was a union between Malaya and the three Borneo territories of British North Borneo (Sabah), Sarawak, and Brunei, excluding Singapore, but according to "unimpeachable Chinese and Malay sources", the British ruled this out and said, "you can't have Borneo without Singapore".[56]

During the period 1956–60, the idea of a union between Malaya and the Borneo territories had, in fact, attracted considerable UMNO support as it appealed to Malay nationalists who regarded the indigenous peoples of Borneo as *orang Melayu* (Malays), and saw in it a way to strengthen the position of the Malays vis-à-vis the growing Chinese population in Singapore and Malaya.[57]

By 1961, the Tunku was prepared to accept Singapore into Malaysia as he was persuaded by Singapore's Prime Minister Lee Kuan Yew that Singapore's ruling People's Action Party (PAP) was under threat by Communist elements from within and it would be more dangerous for Malaya to keep Singapore outside the Malaysian alliance than to allow it to come in. The Tunku himself said that for reasons of "national security and economy" the two countries should work together and it was hoped that by bringing in the Borneo territories the indigenous peoples of Borneo would help balance the influx of the large Chinese population of Singapore.[58]

Between May 1961 and September 1963, when Malaysia came into existence, there was a series of consultations and negotiations but when all was said and done, the real issue at stake was the relationship between the Chinese and Malays and whether they could get on well together.[59] It was apparent, however, that the Malays still felt apprehensive of their position. Tunku Abdul Rahman himself had touched on this matter when in his after-lunch speech referred to above, he said the tendency of the Chinese in Singapore was to make Singapore a "little China" while in Malaya "the Government is characteristically Malayan and bases its policy on a Malayan way of life and Malayan standards".[60]

The Sultan of Brunei was originally disposed to join Malaysia but he subsequently changed his mind most likely because of his concern over Brunei having to relinquish control of its lucrative oil revenue to the new

Federation of Malaysia and possibly, too, because he held the view that his status should be higher than that of the Malay Sultans of peninsular Malaya.

The Federation of Malaysia comprising Malaya, Singapore, Sabah, and Sarawak came into existence on 16 September 1963 but serious differences soon arose between Singapore and the Malaysian Government in Kuala Lumpur over the special rights of the Malays in the new Federation, and other matters, which led to the Tunku coming to the conclusion that the differences were so serious that they were irreconcilable. He thus informed the Singapore Prime Minister that it would be best for both parties if Singapore withdrew from Malaysia and went their separate ways to avoid the matter becoming out of hand and perhaps even leading to the spilling of blood on a large scale between the two territories, and on 9 August 1965 Singapore separated from Malaysia and became a fully independent Republic of Singapore.[61]

Notes

1. CO 1022/81, Dispatch No. 12 of 23/10, registered on 52849/100, "Political Background to the Situation in Malaya." On 13 April 1949, Atlee stated: "The purpose of our policy is simple. We are working, in cooperation with the citizens of the Federation of Malaya and Singapore, to guide them to responsible self-government within the Commonwealth", and 28 March 1950: "…. It is our firm intention to implement the policy which I then formed of steady democratic programs towards self-government within the [British] Commonwealth." "Self-government" has been described as a 'half-way house' to independence and the "British Commonwealth" replaced the former "British Empire". See also Ishak bin Tadin, "Dato Onn and Malay Nationalism, 1946–1951: The Birth of the UMNO," *Journal of Southeast Asian History* 1 (1960): 83.
2. See Martin Rudner, "The Structure of Government in the Colonial Federation of Malaya", *South East Asian Studies* 13, no. 4 (March 1976): 502, fn. 42 and 505.
3. Nicholas J. White, *Business, Government and the End of Empire. 1952–57* (London: Oxford University Press, 1996), p. 138 and. Rudner, op. cit., p. 502, fn. 42.
4. *Federation of Malaya Annual Report 1954* (London: HMSO, 1955), p. 9.
5. White, op. cit. However, it should be noted that L.F. McIntyre, Australia's Commissioner in Singapore, in a secret report to the Minister for External Affairs, Canberra, said that the focus in recent years had been to establish a common loyalty with which Chinese, Indian, and other non-indigenous groups could acquire the rights and privileges that are enjoyed by Malays but that registration as citizens of Malaya under the amended laws even though they

made full citizenship rights easier than before had fallen off considerably. His analysis was that "the Chinese are sitting on the fence waiting to see what happens in the rest of Southeast Asia, and the Indians cannot make up their minds. The three main groups of Malaya are still far apart by cultural, social, and temperamental differences, and mutual distrust." (See National Archives of Australia, NAA: A816, 19/321/18, Secret, "Movement towards Self-Government in Malaya", 23 September 1953, L.F. McIntyre, Australian Commissioner, Singapore, to Minister for External Affairs, Canberra).

6. For details of the above political background, see Russell F. Fifield, *The Diplomacy of Southeast Asia* (Archon Books, 1958), pp. 399–403; R.H. Hickling, *An Introduction to the Federal Constitution* (Kuala Lumpur: Federation of Malaya Information Services, 1960), pp. 10–12; *Report of The Federation of Malaya Constitutional Commission 1957* (Lord Reid, W.J. KcKell, B. Malik, Abdul Hamid, and Ivor Jennings) (Kuala Lumpur: Government Printer, 1957), passim; Martin Rudner, op. cit., passim; and *Malaya: The Making of a Nation* (London: Central Office of Information Reference Pamphlet No. 2, HMSO, 1957).

7. See CO 1022/86 (3), "Minutes of Political Talk with General Templer at Colonial Office, 3 December 1952" and CO 1022/86 "Minute by J.J. Paskin to Sir T. Lloyd re. Discussions with General Templer and the Chiefs of Staff, 10 December 1952."

8. YTM Tunku Abdul Rahman Putra al-Haj (1903–90), DMN, KOM, CH, MA (Cantab), Bar-at-Law (Inner Temple), President of UMNO (August 1951), was the seventh child of Sultan Abdul Hamid Halim Shah, Sultan of Kedah, by his Thai wife Nueng Nonthanakim. He became President of UMNO after Dato' Onn bin Ja'afar resigned to form the Independence of Malaya Party. The Tunku pledged that in spite of his royal background, he would work for the independence of Malaya by the people. The Tunku headed the UMNO/MCA Mission to London in January 1956 to negotiate Malayan independence which led to Malaya securing self-government leading to independence in August the following year. He was Malaya/sia's first Prime Minister and Foreign Minister after independence and is often referred to as "Bapa Malaysia" (Father of Malaysia) or "Bapa Merdeka" (Father of Independence), and more simply and popularly "The Tunku". After retiring from politics, he served as Secretary General of the Islamic Secretariat in Jeddah (1970–73).

9. The Malayan Chinese Association was formed in February 1949, with encouragement from Sir Henry Gurney, the former High Commissioner, to represent the interests of the Chinese in Malaya. While there was some ambiguity about whether the MCA was a political party, a colonial tool against the CPM, or the resuscitation of the Malayan Kuomintang (KMT) under another name, from its inception it had been formed to represent the political interests of the Chinese community in Malaya just as UMNO represented Malay interests and MIC represented Indian interests. Moreover, Tan Cheng

Lock unequivocally stated that the MCA was essentially a political and a social organization which has extended its activities to cover also social welfare and cultural work to benefit the masses (see ISEAS Library, Tan Cheng Lock Private Papers Collection, TCL 057, 5th Annual General Meeting of General Committee, MCA President's Address, Kuala Lumpur, 31 January 1953). In February 1952, it was clearly acting as a political party when it contested the Kuala Lumpur municipal elections in alliance with the Selangor branch of UMNO. Tan Cheng Lock (later Tun Dato' Sir Cheng Lock Tan, SMN, DPMJ (Johore), CBE, KBE, JP) was the MCA's first President. The MCA worked closely with UMNO and later (1954) with MIC to achieve independence on 31 August 1957. (See Margaret Roff, "The Malayan Chinese Association, 1949–65", *Journal of Southeast Asian History* 6, no. 2 (September 1965): 40–53, and Agnes Tan Kim Lwi, *A Son of Malacca: Tun Dato' Sir Cheng Lock Tan, SMN, DPMJ (Johore), CBE, KBE, JP* (Singapore: Lithographic Print House, 2006, 2nd edn).

10. RIDA was the responsibility of Dato' Onn bin Ja'afar, then Member for Home Affairs in the Legislative Council. Its main purpose was the development of rural areas so that the rural population (mainly Malays) could be encouraged to improve their social and economic life. (See *Federation of Malaya Annual Report 1953*, op. cit., p. 164). RIDA was established in 1951 by the late Sir Henry Gurney, who had a high opinion of Onn, as did several other senior British colonial officers including Malcolm MacDonald, the British Commissioner General for South East Asia, and General Templer, though the latter's view changed somewhat when it became apparent that Onn had lost the support of the Malays. In regard to RIDA, historian von Vorys comments that: "although on Templer's arrival, he said 'it was one of our main concerns to see that RIDA gets the full support of his government and it will have my own personal and full support', the actual effort behind RIDA was very modest indeed." The sum allocated was less than 1 per cent of the Federation's budget, and had no prospect of getting the Malays economically on par with the Chinese. See Karl von Vorys, *Democracy without Consensus: Communalism and Political Stability in Malaysia* (Princeton, New Jersey: Princeton University Press, 1975), p. 95.

11. See *Malaya: The Making of a Nation*, London: HMSO, 1957, p. 32; Rudner, op. cit., p. 503; and Victor Purcell, *Malaya: Communist or Free?* (Stanford, California: Stanford University Press, 1955), p. 67.

12. This was in fact almost identical to the opening sentences of the British Government's Directive given to General Templer by the Secretary of State for the Colonies, which read: "The policy of H.M. Government in the United Kingdom is that Malaya should in due course become a fully self-governing nation. H.M. Government confidently hopes that the nation will be within the British Commonwealth."

13. CO 1022/100, "Budget Address, 21 November 1951".

14. CO 1022/81. Top Secret. "Report on Recent Political Developments by the Officer Administering the Government, 23 October 1951."
15. Short, *Communist Insurrection in Malaya*, pp. 356–57.
16. CO 1022/51, Secret, "Meeting with General Templer re. Appt of Director of Intelligence, 29 January 1952."
17. CO 1022/51, "Meeting with General Templer", Extract from JIC (52) 15 itrg Directors dated 31 January 1951 and CO 1022/51, Confidential, Templer to Secretary of State for the Colonies, "Director of Intelligence, 13 February 1952." Dick White (afterwards Sir Dick White, KCMG, KBE), a senior MI5 officer, became Director General of MI5 (1953–56) and Head of MI6 (SIS) (1956–68). He was transferred from MI5 to MI6, which was unusual, in the wake of the "Crabb Affair", which had damaged Soviet-British relations and embarrassed MI6. Commander Lionel Crabb, RNVR, GM, OBE, was employed on a top secret MI6/CIA mission to inspect the underwater hull of the Russian cruiser *"Ordkhonikidze"* moored in Portsmouth Harbour, which had brought the Russian President Nikhita Kruschchev and Bulganin Nikdai to Britain on a goodwill mission in 1956. He disappeared on this mission and was never seen again, although a headless body was later recovered from the harbour, and he is presumed to have lost his life on the mission.
18. National Army Museum, Chelsea, ACC: 8011-132-2, "General Templer's letter to Major General J.M. Gower, 5 January 1977." Templer had been Director of Military Intelligence at the War Office (1946-48).
19. The author met Morton in the 1950s at SIFE, Phoenix Park, Singapore, to discuss the possibilities of using the KMT in Malaya as a "Third Force" to fight the Communists.
20. CO 1022/51, See "Extract from Memorandum on Cabinet Paper C (51) 59, 21 December 1951" (Original on SEA/1/03) and CO 1022/51, Confidential Telegram No. 206, "Director of Intelligence, Gen Sir G. Templer to Secretary of State for the Colonies, 13 February 1952."
21. Alexander Duncan Campbell Peterson, OBE, was Director General, Malayan Information Services, during the two years that Templer was in Malaya (1952–54). During WWII, he had been Director, Psychological Warfare, South East Asia Command, and Deputy Chief of the Far Eastern Publicity Division of South East Asia Command, on Admiral Lord Louis Mountbatten's staff in Ceylon (Sri Lanka). He was educated at Radley and Balliol. At the time of his appointment to Malaya, he was the headmaster of Newport Grammar School, Shropshire. On returning to Britain, he became headmaster of Dover College, and later Director of Educational Studies, Oxford University (1958–73). He became a recognized authority in the field of Comparative Education and a leading exponent of Internationale Baccalaureate studies in the United Kingdom. See "Federation of Malaya Information Services. An Authoritative Survey", *Journal of Association of British Malaya* (February 1953), pp. 87–90.

22. *The Times* (London), 3 September 1952.
23. *Federation of Malaya Annual Report 1953,* op. cit., pp. 312–14.
24. See "Federation of Malaya Information Services. An Authoritative Survey. Mr. A.D.C. Peterson, Director-General of the new integrated Information Services of the Federation", *Journal of Association of British Malaya* (February 1953), pp. 87–90.
25. After leaving Malaya, Hugh Howse, OBE, became Head of the "English by Radio and TV" Division of the BBC in London, which included Southeast Asia and the PRC within its remit, and he was able to put to good use his knowledge of Chinese. (Author's personal notes).
26. *Federation of Malaya Annual Report 1953,* op. cit., p. 315.
27. National Archives of Australia, NAA: A5954/1, 2292/5, Confidential, "Interview with Dato' Sir Onn on 5 October 1953", Ian Hamilton, Public Relations Officer, Australian Commission in Singapore, to Department of External Affairs, Canberra, 15 October 1953.

 Dato' Sir Onn bin Ja'afar, DK, DPMJ, KBE, a member of the Executive Council and Member for Home Affairs in the Federal Legislative Council (1948–55), had responsibility for an extremely wide-range of portfolios, including Information Services, Broadcasting, RIDA, Immigration, Aborigines, Registration of Citizens, Co-operative Development (except Wholesale and Consumer Co-operatives), and Pilgrim Affairs (see *Federation of Malaya Report 1953,* op. cit., pp. 377 and 379), and was a member, too, of the CLC (Communities Liaison Committee). During the Japanese Occupation, he had been appointed by the Japanese as Head of the Food Control Bureau for Johor State. His grandfather, father, and two elder brothers had been Mentris Besar (Chief Ministers) of Johor, and his son Tun Hussein Onn, who had not been in Malaya during the Japanese Occupation, and had served in WWII as a Captain in the Hyderabad Regiment of the British Indian Army, became Malaysia's third Prime Minister. After WWII, Onn headed the first united Malay political movement against the Malayan Union and was successful in getting it superseded by the Federation of Malaya Agreement. His mother was Circassian (Turkish) and he had spent some years at school in England as a boy and had an excellent command of English which gave him a unique background. General Templer found Onn "more balanced and easier to understand" (see Mubin Sheppard, *Tunku: His Life and Times. The Authorized Biography of Tunku Abdul Rahman Putra al-Haj* (Petaling Jaya: Pelanduk Publications (M) Sdn Bhd, 1995), p. 83. However, he may not have had such a favourable view of him had he known Onn had tipped off William Kuok Hock Ling (alias Peng Cheng) of the well-known Kuok family in Johor Bahru, who was a close friend of James Puthucheary and other University of Malaya leftists at the time, that he was about to be arrested by the Malayan Special Branch for having Communist connections, which resulted in Kuok joining the

Communist terrorists in the jungle. Kuok later came to an untimely end as he was killed by the security forces in an attack on a Communist jungle camp in Pahang in September 1953 (see Ooi Kee Beng, *The Reluctant Politician: Tun Dr Ismail and His Time* (Singapore: Institute of Southeast Asian Studies, 2006), p. 9.

Onn was the founder President of UMNO and probably the most prominent Malay politician in the immediate post-war period, and was referred to as "Britain's Great Malay Hope" (see Nicholas White, *Business, Government, and the End of Empire: Malaya 1942–1957* (Kuala Lumpur: OUP, 1996), p. 136. After leaving UMNO when he failed to convert it into a "United *Malayan* National Organisation" with non-communal membership [author's emphasis], he founded Independence of Malaya Party (IMP) but once again he failed to obtain Malay support to convert it into a multi-racial party. Thereafter he launched in February 1954 Parti Negara (National Party) which appeared in some ways to be an extension of IMP as most of its members were former IMP members but, once again, it too failed to receive widespread support. He resigned as Member for Home Affairs in January 1955. Finally, in the 1959 General Elections, he became MP for Trengganu Selatan (South Trengganu). (See CO 537/733, No. 10, "Dato Onn and the Independence of Malaya Party: letter from Sir H. Gurney to J.D. Higham", 13 June 1952; Zainah Anwar, *Three Who Built Malaysia, Legacy of Honour* (Kuala Lumpur: Yayasan Mohamad Noah, 2011), pp. 154, 158–59, 161, 163; Cheah Boon Kheng, *Malaysia: The Making of a Nation* (Singapore: Institute of Southeast Asian Studies, 2002), p. 30; and Leon Comber, *13 May 1969. A Historical Survey of Sino-Malay Relations* (Singapore: Heinemann Asia, 1983), p. 44.

28. CO 1022/205 CIS (52) (2), Final. Top Secret, "The Situation on the Thai-Malayan Frontier as at 15 April 1953"; *Federation of Malaya Annual Report 1954*, Kuala Lumpur: Government Printer, 1955; and Comber, *Malaya's Secret Police 1945–60*, op. cit., p. 257.

29. CO 1022/87, Confidential, "Review of Field Operations of a Mobile Information Unit in South Thailand, Dispatch No. 49, 16 March 1953."

30. *Federation of Malaya Annual Report 1954*, op. cit., "The Malayan-Thai Border Agreement", pp. 411 and 455.

31. CAB 134/898, FE (0) (53) 6, "Political effects that a deterioration of the situation in Indo-China would have in British colonial and protected territories, 13 June 1953." Malaya depended on imports for about half of its total rice requirements. (See *The Economic Development of Malaya*, International Bank for Reconstruction and Development, Washington, D.C., September 1955, p. 10). See also National Archives of Australia, NAA: A5799, 9/1957. Top Secret. Report of the Australian, New Zealand, and Malaya Intelligence Meeting, Singapore, November 1956, attaching a copy of the JIC Report No. 6/1957 "Threat to Malaya from Communist dominated Thailand."

32. CO 1022/37. Secret. "Note on Discussions with Gen. Templer and Lt. Gen Phao Sriyanond, Director-General of Police, Thailand, at King's House, Kuala Lumpur, on 10 April 1953." In September 1957, General Phao was ousted in a coup led by Field Marshal Sarit Thananarat and he escaped to Switzerland where he remained until he died a few years later (see Comber, op. cit., p. 266, fn.35). See also National Archives of Australia, NAA, A5799, 9/1957, Top Secret, "Report of the Australian, N.Z., and Malaya Intelligence Meeting", Singapore, November 1956, attaching a copy of Joint Intelligence Committee Report No. 6/1957, "Threat to Malaya from Communist-dominated Thailand".

33. Comber, op. cit., p. 256.

34. CO 1022/37. "Situation on Malayan-Siamese Border, Memo from Lyttelton to Major Niall Macpherson, MP, 11 June 1953."

35. WO 216/874, 174831, Secret. "Report by Lt. Gen. Bourne", Appendix "A" to DEF/DO/1, 17 July 1954.

36. CO 1022/22 No. 1, "Reorganisation of government: memorandum by Mr Fraser to Mr Lyttelton, 16 January 1952."

37. CO 1022/60, Secret. "Merging of Federal War Council and Executive Council of Malaya" (closed until 1983), 29 February 1952. See also "The Federal Changes", *Straits Times*, 3 March 1952.

   Lyttelton congratulated General Templer on abolishing the Federal War Council and said that when he was in Malaya in December 1951 he had reluctantly accepted the view of del Tufo at that time that it would take "several months" to bring it about. The Federal War Council had originally been established under the Chairmanship of General Briggs as Director of Operations, and it was responsible to the High Commissioner, Sir Henry Gurney, for policy matters, and the provision of resources to State War Executive Councils to enable them to implement the Briggs Plan. (See CAB 21/1681, MAL C (50) 23, Appendix, "The Briggs Plan", 24 May 1950). Nevertheless, a "Director of Operations Committee" continued to exist with Templer as Chair, which operated within the policy laid down by the Federal Executive Council and controlled the conduct of the Emergency through the State (SWECs) and District War Executive Committees (DWECs).

38. Ooi Kee Beng, *The Reluctant Politician: Tun Dr Ismail and His Time* (Singapore: Institute of Southeast Asian Studies, 2007, 2nd reprint), pp. 60–61.

39. ISEAS Library, Tun Sir Henry H.S. Lee, Private Papers Collection, HSL.031.057, "Templer scraps Federal War Council", *Malay Mail*, 3 March 1952.

40. The Keeper of the Rulers' Seal is charged with the custody and use of the Rulers' Seal on behalf of the Conference of Rulers and is Secretary of the Conference of Rulers.

41. *Straits Times*, 3 March 1952.

42. See CO 1022/61, no. 19, "Closer Association of British territories. Minute by J.P. Higham to J.J. Paskins"; CO 537/3669, no. 3, "Closer Association with Federation of Malaya and Singapore. Colonial Office meeting with Mr M.J. MacDonald on 16 April 1948"; and CO 1022/86, "Closer association of British territories. Minute by J.J. Paskin to Sir T. Lloyd on discussions with Sir G. Templer and Chiefs of Staff, 10 December 1952."

43. CO 537/2141, no. 28 [Constitutional proposals] "report by Mr Thomas on his visit to Malaya 9–16 February 1947" dated 22 February 1947.

44. CO 1022/61, no. 15, Inward telegram no. 73. "Closer Association of British territories", from M.J. MacDonald to the CO. Minutes by J.D. Higham and Sir T. Lloyd, 10 June 1952.

45. Ibid.

46. CO 1022/61, No. 19, "Closer Association of British territories. Minute by J.P. Higham to J.J. Paskins"; CO 537/3669, No. 3, "Closer Association with Federation of Malaya and Singapore. Colonial Office meeting with Mr M.J. MacDonald on 16 April 1948"; and CO 1022/86, "Closer association of British territories. Minute by J.J. Paskin to Sir T. Lloyd on discussions with Sir G. Templer and Chiefs of Staff, 10 December 1952."

47. Ibid. See also CO 1022/61, Secret, 29 January 1952. (Closed until 1984). "Closer Association between Federation of Malaya and Singapore." According to an unsigned minute on the file, it was agreed to take gradual steps towards a closer association between *all* British territories in Southeast Asia [emphasis by author]. See, too, CO 1022/61, 5 March 1952, Minute by J.J. Paskin, Asst. Under-Secretary of State, Colonial Office, suggesting that Malcolm McDonald, General Templer, and Sir John Nicoll, the Governor of Singapore, should undertake a review of the policy to bring about a fusion of Federation of Malaya and Singapore. See also CO 1022/61, Secret, 10 March 1952, in which Sir Franklin Gimson, the former Governor of Singapore, stated that he was not in favour of a closer association between Singapore and Malaya and considered if it came about it would result in Templer pressing for stronger counterinsurgency measures being taken in Singapore. According to Gimson, Templer was well known to have little regard for the Government of Singapore, especially the Singapore Special Branch.

48. The Malay Sultans were assured that their positions as rulers of the Malay States would not be affected if there was closer coordination between the two territories.

49. NAA:A816, 19/321/18, Confidential, Memo no. 475, "Singapore. Joint Co-ordination Committee", 2 May 1953.

50. Clyde Sanger, *Malcolm MacDonald. Bringing an End to Empire* (McGill-Queen's University Press, Montreal, 1995), pp. 338–40.

51. See Malayan Security Service (MSS), Secret, *Political Intelligence Journal*

1/1948, Supplement no. 1, "The 1947 Muslim Pilgrimage Season and the Pan-Islamic Movement", 15 January 1948.

52. CO 1022/61, No. 40, "Closer association between Federation of Malaya and Singapore. Colonial Office note of meeting with Sir G. Templer and Sir J. Nicoll, 18 May 1953".

53. CO 1030/163, no. 1, "Closer association of British territories: Despatch no. 3 from Mr M.J. MacDonald to Mr Lennox-Boyd., 2 April 1955".

54. CO 1030/163, no. 2, "Closer association of British territories: Despatch (reply) no. 150 from Mr Lennox-Boyd to Mr M.J. MacDonald, 2 June 1955".

55. See Cheah Boon Kheng, op. cit., p. 97. Cheah's book provides a comprehensive account of the formation of Malaysia. The author attended the Foreign Correspondents Association of Southeast Asia's lunch at the Adelphi Hotel at which the Tunku gave his speech.

56. Mohamed Noordin Sopiee, *From Malayan Union to Singapore Separation: Political Unification in the Malaysia Region, 1945–65* (Kuala Lumpur: Universiti Malaya, 1974), pp. 125–27.

57. Ibid.

58. See Lee Kuan Yew, Prime Minister of Singapore, *The Battle for Merger* (Singapore: Government Printing Office, 1961), in which the Prime Minister expounded on the threat posed to Singapore by the Communist Party of Malaya.

59. R.S. Milne and Diane K. Mauzy, *Politics and Government in Malaysia* (Singapore: Federal Publications, 1978), p. 69.

60. Leon Comber, *Singapore Correspondent: Political Dispatches from Singapore (1958–1962)* (Singapore: Marshall Cavendish International (Asia), 2012), p. 184.

61. *Social and Economic History of Modern Singapore* (Singapore: Curriculum Development Institute of Singapore/Longman Singapore Publishers, 1985), pp. 222–30.

3

THE TEMPLER PLAN:
The Implementation of
General Templer's Political Directive

On 19 March 1952, some six weeks after his arrival in Malaya, General Templer, as President of the Federal Legislative Council, addressed the opening session of the Council to outline the manner in which he intended to implement the political Directive he had been given by the British Government. It dealt with an impressively wide range of social, economic, and political matters which brought out clearly his views on the immense number of complex problems with which he had to grapple.

Templer sent a draft of his speech to Lyttelton in London, which he said was "entirely in accord with Her Majesty's Government's policy", and in his telegram of 12 March to Lyttelton, which he copied to Malcolm MacDonald, British Commissioner General for South East Asia in Singapore, he said that it had been "gone through yesterday by the Executive Council".[1]

In his telegram to Lyttelton, Templer said that during the past few weeks he had held a number of discussions with Dato' Onn, Dato E.E.C. Thuraisingham, a Ceylonese Tamil, who was the Member for Education, and other local politicians about responsible local government at grass roots level, which Templer referred to as the "parish pump level". On 7 March, the *Singapore Standard* in a critical article written by S. Rajaratnam [then a newspaper journalist who later joined the People's Action Party (PAP) and became Singapore's first Minister for Culture and subsequently Singapore's longest serving Foreign Minister and Deputy Prime Minister], said it was Templer's intention to limit Malaya's advance to self-government, to use Templer's own phrase, to "parish pump" level.[2] This mention of the term "parish pump" which was to incur Templer's wrath, attracted a lot of attention, and Templer informed Lyttelton that he intended to issue a statement about it in his forthcoming address to be delivered on 19 March to the Legislative Council along the following lines:

> I now turn to the question of political progress. Ten days or so I was criticised in a newspaper for saying that I would confine political progress to the Parish pump level. Who gave that information to the newspaper in question, I have no idea, since I have been careful not to make any statement whatsoever on this subject until I could make a considered one at the opening of this new session of the Federal Legislative Council. I am, of course, aware of the responsibilities placed on all of us in regard to the election of members to the several legislatures, by the penultimate sentence in the preamble to the Federation Agreement. But, I am a firm believer in first things first. Or, to put it another way, that it is politically unsound and structurally impossible to put the roof on the building until the foundations of it are well and truly laid, and until the uprights or, anyway the corner posts, are in position and firmly fixed. I believe it right to ensure that truly responsible local government at Rural community and Municipal Council levels is firmly established, and as quickly as possible. Not for one moment would I suggest that this should be postponed in any way at all because the so-called "Emergency" is upon us. On the contrary, it is all the more necessary — because of the Emergency — to press on with this measure. I firmly believe, from the bottom of my heart, in the principle of responsible local government by local people. I will do all in my power to foster this and the quicker we can start on it the better. This is the firm foundation on which political progress must be based....[3]

Templer commented that this passage was singled out by members of the Executive Council with whom he had discussed his speech on the previous day, and there was criticism principally from Colonel H.S. Lee and Dato' Onn, though they were not political allies, that his reference to confining "political progress to the Parish pump level" disposed too abruptly of the question of elections to the State and Federal Legislatures, and gave the impression that the matter would be shelved indefinitely. Other members were anxious, too, that a sentence should be included indicating his intention to bring about "a more territorially representative distribution of membership of the State and Legislative Councils and the Federal Legislative Council until such time as the franchise can be extended throughout the Federation for the election of Members of these several legislatures."

To meet these points, Templer said that he was contemplating the inclusion of the following words, subject to agreement, at the end of the second sentence of the original draft about confining political progress to the Parish pump level:[4]

> .... and we shall not put out of mind the arrangements it will be necessary to make to give effect to this purpose as soon as circumstances and local conditions will permit; and there may be a case meantime for a more territorially representative distribution of membership of these Legislatures.[5]

It was clear that the main problem which brought about criticism from Lee and Onn was Templer's omission to say anything about elections beyond "parish pump" level to State and Federal Legislatures. They considered that Templer's remarks disposed "too abruptly" of the question of elections to the legislatures and gave the impression that the matter would be postponed indefinitely. The matter of the issue of the timing of elections to the State and Federal levels was to remain at the heart of a continuing serious disagreement in the months to come between Templer and the UMNO-MCA Alliance — UMNO and MCA were the two leading political parties in Malaya — and there was some disagreement about the matter, too, among the mandarins in the Colonial Office.[6]

A.S. Gann, a Colonial Office Principal Secretary, argued for advance as soon as possible to State, Settlement and Federal Council elections, and T.C. Jerrom, another Principal Secretary, disagreed with Templer's intention to work upwards from "parish pump" level. J.D. Higham, Assistant Secretary, Head of the Colonial Office's South East Asia Department, agreed with both of his colleagues and wrote "I do not myself entirely accept the theory that one must work upwards gradually from the 'parish level'." However, he added: "But I think Gen. Templer's line of policy on this has been discussed here and generally agreed." However, the minutes indicate there was still considerable ambivalence on the part of the Colonial Office mandarins themselves in arriving at a final decision about the question, and it was finally agreed that the matter should be included on the agenda for Templer's next visit to London with a note that "it may well fall to Mr MacGillivray rather than to General Templer to handle these problems in future."

To revert to Templer's speech to the Legislative Council, no one seems to have thought to mention, especially perhaps Dato' Onn who was a Malay, a matter that was later brought to Templer's attention on a visit to Kelantan by Bill Bangs, Kelantan State Development Officer who had lived there for many years and was well conversant with Kelantan Malay culture, that it was the custom of Malays to build the roof of a house first before attaching it to the uprights or corner posts.[7] However, this practice may well have been confined to Kelantan, and it has not been possible to find reference to it elsewhere in the literature.[8]

In regard to Templer's assertion that he had been careful to make no statement before the Legislative Council meeting of the term "parish pump" level, Michael Davidson, the foreign correspondent of *The Observer* (London), in a cabled report to London on 19 March stated that Templer had actually referred to the term in a conversation with him in the presence of three other persons at King's House, Kuala Lumpur, on 16 February, a month before the Legislative Council meeting. According to Davidson's account, he had asked Templer what his election policy would be, and the conversation had gone like this: "'No', he [Templer] replied firmly; then, after a pause, he added: 'There will be no election above parish pump level. Those I want to see carried out as widely and quickly as possible. But nothing above the parish pump."

"I suggested that State elections might ease his dealings with the Malay States by giving the people, as well as the rulers, a say in affairs. 'State elections?' the General had exclaimed. 'That's very high level. In England we didn't have county council elections immediately after Magna Carta.'"[9]

In his cabled report, Davidson followed this up by saying:

.... enigmas now present themselves: will the elections to the Johore State Council, already planned to follow hard on the heels of this year's town board elections in that State, be cancelled? And what does "as soon as circumstances and local conditions permit" mean? That is a phrase open to definite interpretation. There is good reason to believe that in this matter the High Commissioner is acting against the counsel of some of his best qualified advisers with whom repeated discussions on the subject have been held recently.

There is yet another question unanswered. With all its qualities of imagination and its will to constructive action, today's speech could not help sounding like an election speech by a candidate who seeks the rural votes and the votes of the middle class and "the Right" generally, but who is not interested in the wage earners' vote. It offered great gifts in the field of health, education, and tenure, industrialization and agricultural technique — all vital, of course, to Malaya's future. But one omission was noteworthy; there was no mention of trade unions or indeed of "labour" at all. The encouragement of sound trade unions has been a prime plank in Government policy since 1948 or earlier. The absence of any reference to them today is bound to lend support to the recent belief that the workers' organisations are going out of official favour.... The High Commissioner's speech has set the Administration and the peoples of Malaya some splendid heights to climb along the road towards a united self-governing nation — the goal, he insisted throughout of all his energies. But he was careful to say that he was formulating principles and that their translation into action could often be fraught with difficulty.[10]

However, Davidson's comments do not appear to have been taken up further by Templer and the matter was allowed to rest there.

THE TEMPLER PLAN

To revert to General Templer's speech to the Legislative Council which lasted fifty minutes, it was the first important policy speech he had made after his arrival at Kuala Lumpur from London.[11] In fact, aside from some other politically less important matters, it constituted his blueprint and road map for the political and economic development of Malaya for the remainder of his two-year proconsulship in Malaya.

He made eighteen points as follows:

- The easing of citizenship rights.
- The retraining of the Malayan Police.
- The creation of a Malayan Army.
- The improvement of medical and health services.
- The development of a national education policy.
- The importance of land tenure for agriculturists.
- The encouragement of youth movements.
- The improvement of the Government's information services.
- The importance of progressive political progress.

- The strengthening of the economic position of the Malays.
- The overhauling of income tax.
- The encouragement of industrial development.
- The improvement of road communications.
- The training of the civil service, both overseas and locally to equip Malayans for higher posts in the Government service.
- The importance of economy in financial matters in view of the possibility of a sharp fall in the prices of rubber and tin.
- The expansion of electric power resources.
- The building up of the economy of the Malays.
- The increase of local food production and agricultural output to render the country less dependent upon imports.

They were all very ambitious and noteworthy plans and the *Malay Mail*, which referred to them as "The Templer Plan", came out in favour of them,[12] although it noted that many of the points were in fact already covered in Malaya's 1950 Development Plan, the implementation of which had been hampered by the continuance of Communist terrorism.[13] The *Malay Mail* continued: "they must command the attention of all who profess to be working for the good of Malaya" and "the pace of progress in this direction is governed largely by the degree of willingness on the part of the Malays and Chinese to recognize that both communities have much to give to the future [of] Malaya, and to what extent they are willing to submerge communalism in the greater cause."[14] Some of these topics, too, had been considered by the Communities Liaison Committee (CLC), which had been formed by Malcolm MacDonald before Templer's arrival.

But there were voices of dissent, too, about Templer's speech, particularly from the *Singapore Standard*, where the columnist S. Rajaratnam said that "it was no radical departure from policy that has always guided speeches of our rulers", and that

> the same principles have been common property of speech makers for a great many years and in fact some of them were enunciated as far back as the reign of Queen Victoria. Since liberation, every leader and administrator worth his salt has bowed his head to a united Malaya, common citizenship, promotion of racial harmony, self-government, RIDA and the expansion of medical, educational and other social services, and ending the Emergency. But what General Templer has done is to restate in effective language the accepted principles of the Administration.... Although Templer thought he showed great enthusiasm for elections at parish pump elections, he was less so about Federal and State elections.[15]

Meanwhile, Templer opened his address at the Federal Legislative
Council by saying:

> It is my privilege on this my first attendance at a meeting of the Federal
> Legislative Council to address you at the opening of its 5th session. We
> have just witnessed the ceremony of the presentation of the Mace. This
> in itself is symbolic of the solemnity of the occasion.[16]
>
> When I arrived to take up my duties as High Commissioner,
> I made it plain that it is a tenet of my faith that the Emergency cannot be
> overcome by military measures alone. The campaign must be fought on
> social, economic and political fronts as well. In framing the measures to
> be taken on all these fronts this Chamber has a great part to play.
>
> Shortly after my arrival you will have seen that I circulated an
> instruction to Government officers to the effect that the Emergency
> element of Government could not be kept in a water-tight compartment,
> separated from what may be described as the normal peace-time processes
> of Government. That applies not only to Government itself, but also to
> all the activities of the country today. There is no one who is not affected
> in his daily life by the Emergency.... The Emergency is a thread which
> runs through the pattern of all our lives, whether we are employed in
> the Government, in commerce, in industry, in our own business or in
> winning a livelihood from the soil ....[17]

Templer had got off to a good start by emphasizing that the Emergency
would not be won by the "rifle and bayonet" approach, which many of his
detractors had been concerned about when his appointment had been first
announced, and making it clear that he realized the importance of social,
economic, and political matters and he intended to enlist the support of
all sectors of society in his plans.[18]

He continued:

> .... I am glad to see that it [the Directive] was the subject of a formal
> statement made by the Secretary of State Dean Acheson on behalf of the
> United States Government on the 5th March, in which he stated that the
> United States Government welcomed the statement that the defeat of
> communist terrorism in Malaya was not to be achieved by military action
> alone, but also by an imaginative and progressive policy of assisting the
> diverse peoples of Malaya towards the longer-term objectives: the forging
> in due course of a united and self-governing Malayan nation....[19]

Meanwhile, the following summary of some of the more relevant and
important points of Templer's speech, with background comments added
to place them in a historical context, will be of interest as they provide an
indication of the complexity of Templer's task and the problems he faced:

1. *The Easing of Citizenship Rights* — The bringing about of a common form of citizenship for all those who regard the Federation or any part of it as their real home and the object of their loyalty.

Comments

The question of citizenship had in fact long been a complex issue in Malaya and since at least 1949, Malcolm MacDonald, Commissioner General for South East Asia, had been working hard on citizenship issues through the CLC (1949–51), a semi-official body made up of Malay, Chinese and other community leaders which he had helped to form, although he kept in the background,[20] to discuss major political problems, develop closer Sino-Malay relations, and tease out an agreed approach to Malayan citizenship.[21]

The opening of the citizenship door had, in fact, been discussed a few years earlier at a meeting in Penang on 28 December 1949 of the CLC attended by Malcolm MacDonald, where Dato' Onn and another member, Zainal Abidin,[22] had voiced their view that Federal citizenship should be given to every person born in the Federation. However, in a despatch to the Colonial Office, Sir Henry Gurney, then High Commissioner, described this view as "miles ahead of Malay opinion", and commented that "we are thinking on the lines of two generations of birth and of converting citizenship into nationality". Onn had resigned as Mentri Besar, Johor after falling out with the Sultan of Johor in October 1949, and the Mentri Besar of the other Malay States had taken him to task for the views he had expressed on citizenship and had told him that he had no authority to speak for the Malays on any issue unless he had first obtained permission from them and the Malay Sultans.[23]

Nevertheless, Onn continued to advocate at the UMNO General Assembly in August 1951 the granting of "Malayan nationality for all races to replace the existing citizenship regulations" which would include the opening of UMNO membership to non-Malays, but both proposals had met with little favour as UMNO traditionally stood for the preservation of the "special position and rights" of the Malays under the Federal Agreement. It was, in fact, on this issue that led to Onn resigning as President of UMNO and the Presidency being taken over by Tunku Abdul Rahman.[24]

In this connection, it is interesting to note that as early as 11 April 1949, the late Sir Henry Gurney had taken a bleak view of the prospects of bringing about a common federal citizenship, although it was an ideal to be greatly desired by the British Government, and had reported to Creech Jones, then the Colonial Secretary, that very few Chinese, who made up nearly half the total population, "had a Malayan outlook or feel they own allegiance to this country and are reluctant to commit themselves to pro-Government policies."[25]

This was the background to the Bill which Templer laid on the table at the Federal Legislative Council meeting on 19 March 1952. The Bill owed its existence to a study of the subject by a Select Committee which had been deliberating the matter since the previous June long before his arrival. It was an improvement on the current legislation, and Templer hoped that it would open the way for more Chinese and Indians to become Federal citizens. In numbers, he thought that the Chinese would gain the most from it, with the Indians to a lesser degree. However, when all is said and done, it was clear that the new legislation would not grant the Chinese nor the Indians the same citizenship rights as the Malays who automatically became Federal citizens as *bumiputeras* or "sons of the soil".

In his speech introducing the new legislation, Templer said that in the first place the law of citizenship must play a great part in the strengthening of loyalty [to the nation] and that he was glad that the Select Committee "had reached agreement on the way to remove present restrictions on the acquiring of citizenship".[26] The new citizenship law basically provided two avenues for acquiring citizenship: (i) by being a citizen of the United Kingdom and the Colonies, and (ii) by satisfying the provisions required for qualifying as a subject of a Malay ruler.[27]

Perhaps Templer was too sanguine to expect that the new laws would answer all the questions which were so deeply rooted and complex. The problems had in fact, already been brought out into the open in a debate on Malayan citizenship in the British House of Lords on 27 February 1952, a month before the Malayan Legislative Council meeting, where the Marquess of Salisbury outlined some of the inherent problems involved and, in particular, those relating to the Chinese who then represented more than 40 per cent of Malaya's population.

In his speech, the Marquess said:

> The Chinese or, at any rate, a great many of them, are not yet true members of the Malayan community. This, of course, brings up the whole question of citizenship .... The Chinese can hardly be expected to play a full part in the political life of the Federation [of Malaya] until more have been

admitted to federal citizenship. The importance of this form of common citizenship is underlined, as I have already said, in the directive to General Templer .... I do not pretend .... this is likely to be an easy task....

Nearly one third of the Chinese in Malaya are in fact already federal citizens; and the new Bill which I mentioned just now, will, when it becomes law, add 250,000 non-Malays to this number ....[28]

The estimated population in the Federation of Malaya at the time totalled 5,698,200 made up of 2,808,400 Malaysians; 2,155,700 Chinese; 651,100 Indians and Pakistanis; and 83,000 Others.[29]

By September 1953, Templer had been in Malaya for more than one-and-a-half years and registration for Malayan citizenship under the amended citizenship laws had been in force for a year. However, while it made full citizenship rights easier than before, registration had fallen off considerably. L.F. McIntyre, the Australian Commissioner in Singapore, who was a witness and reporter of the Malayan political scene whose views did not always echo those of the British colonial power, observed in a secret report to the Minister for External Affairs, Canberra, that "the Chinese are sitting on the fence waiting to see what happens to the rest of Southeast Asia, and the Indians can't make up their minds". He opined that the three main groups [Malays, Chinese, and Indians] "are still far apart by cultural, social and temperamental differences and mutual distrust". The local preoccupation with racial harmony in Malaya had begun to give way to a strong desire for self-government and "within the last few months there had been a lively interest in the possibilities of holding elections for a central legislature" with "a tendency to regard elections and self-government as more or less the same".[30]

Further confirmation of the unsatisfactory state of the new legislation was provided some two years after McIntyre's report when Lennox-Boyd, then Secretary of State for the Colonies, commented that the "present [Malayan] citizenship laws are unsatisfactory in that they deny citizens' rights to large sections of the Chinese community", and they also "tend to admit as citizens of the UK and Colonies persons whose loyalty to the Crown is doubtful".[31]

Many more years have passed and much water has passed under the bridge since then, but citizenship issues have a long history in Malaya and they still remain a thorny problem to this day in an independent heterogeneous Malaysia, where ethnicity and race still play an important part in the political equation and there are still so many loyalties at play.

2. *The Retraining of the Malayan Police* — **The retraining and reorganization of the Malayan Police and the recruitment of Chinese into the Uniformed Branch of the Police.**

Comments

Templer correctly referred to the retraining and reorganization of the Malayan Police as an important matter to be dealt with and by saying this he was merely echoing the remarks of Oliver Lyttelton, the Colonial Secretary, in his report on his mission to Malaya in November/December 1951.[32] It was already generally accepted that the most important element of the security forces fighting the Communist terrorists was the Police, which had a knowledge of the country, its peoples and languages, and more especially the Police Special Branch, which was well placed to obtain both political and operational intelligence about the Communist terrorists (who were predominantly Chinese), rather than the other Armed Forces which did not have this local knowledge.[33] The civil Government thus remained supreme throughout the Emergency, martial law was not declared, and the army operated in aid of the civil power. Templer, although a regular soldier, was well aware of the situation and accepted it.

Although Templer did not refer to it in his speech, Colonel Arthur Young, the newly appointed Commissioner of Police, had already selected Assistant Commissioner J.N.D. Harrison, former Chief Police Officer (CPO), Negri Sembilan, and until recently CPO Perak, to be in charge of the Police training programme, and he had decided that there would be three phases of retraining, that is: (a) gazetted police officers, (b) regular police constables, and (c) Special Constables.

In his speech, Templer said that arrangements had been made for providing training courses for all gazetted police officers (that is, officers above the rank of Inspector) who had been appointed after the start of the Emergency in June 1948 and had not yet passed the required gazetted police officers' examinations in law, colonial regulations, Malayan Government regulations, and Malay, before being confirmed in their appointments. At the same time, it was estimated that 37,000 Special Constables, who were mainly employed in guarding rubber estates and tin mines and 22,000 regular police constables, would have to be retrained at Contingent (State) level, that is, a total of 59,000 rank-and-file police, which in itself would be a formidable undertaking.

He said that the Police Training Depot in Kuala Lumpur would continue to train and turn out up to 200 recruits each month, as well as a small number of wireless operators and other specialists required by the regular police.[34]

The urgent need to reorganize the police referred to by Templer had, in fact, been brought up even long before Lyttelton's report by Field Marshal Sir William Slim, then Chief of the Imperial General Staff, when he visited Malaya in October 1949. While acknowledging the improvements to the general organization of the police that Colonel Gray, then Commissioner of Police, had introduced since July 1948, he put his finger on the crux of the problem when he pointed out that both the police and the administration did not have enough Chinese-speaking officers "capable of dealing with the Chinese population" and the Police Special Branch should have "a proper central Headquarters".[35] To remedy the situation, he recommended the transfer of some Chinese or Cantonese-speaking British Special Branch officers and uniformed branch Chinese of other ranks from the Hong Kong Police to the Malayan Police. Hong Kong was then a British colony. Though this recommendation was not followed up, a few Cantonese-speaking British police officers were transferred from Hong Kong to Malaya to serve in the Special Branch.

It is also relevant to note that Slim's visit was followed by a Police Mission from November 1949 to February 1950 appointed by the Colonial Office and chaired by Sir Alexander Maxwell, a former Permanent Under-Secretary at the Home Office, to examine the organization and training of the police. As a result, in July–August 1951, the Government attempted to overcome the shortage of Chinese-speaking officers in the police and administration by providing short Chinese language courses in colloquial Cantonese and Hokkien at a Chinese language school that was established in the Cameron Highlands under Robert Bruce, a British Council officer and a former missionary in China.[36] Thus there was a long history behind Templer's referring to the problem in his Federal Legislative Council speech.[37]

In furtherance of his plans, a few days after the Legislative Council meeting, General Templer issued an appeal to Chinese youths to join the police. He said that at present there were only 800 Chinese in the uniformed branch of the Malayan Police as opposed to about 3,200 in the Criminal Investigation Department (CID).[38]

However, *The Times* (London) Singapore correspondent, Louis Heren, wrote rather disparagingly about Templer's plans and said:

It was ridiculous that the Chinese community of more than two millions should be policed by Malays unable to speak their language and furthermore largely antipathetic to the race they considered to be alien; and reports of reprehensive behaviour by some Malay policemen in resettlement areas [which were largely Chinese] have been too numerous to be ignored. As a consequence many Chinese have no confidence in the police and find it no more expensive to "buy" protection from the terrorists.

He pointed out, too, that the revised rates of pay offered to Chinese recruits were still too low to attract the right kind of Chinese to apply.[39]

Templer was clearly rankled by Heren's criticisms in this article and other articles he had written for *The London Times,* and when Templer visited the Colonial Office on one of his regular visits to London in 1953, he complained specifically about an article Heren had written on 1 December 1952 in which he said that the improvement in the security situation was not due to Templer's arrival in 1952 but to the introduction by the CPM of its "October 1951 Resolutions" or "Directives" which called for less terrorist activities and increased United Front work.[40]

The CPM's October 1951 Resolutions were later modified in 1953, when Chin Peng realized that the instructions that had been given in the October 1951 Directives which had resulted in less aggressive action being taken against the security forces and a general curtailment of terrorist activities were beginning to affect Communist morale and reduce party influence over the masses. In practical terms, too, at ground level, the CPM found that the growing of their own food in isolated parts of the jungle was more difficult than had been anticipated. To counter this, a new set of directives were issued in 1953 that attacks on selected as opposed to random targets should be resumed, and it was clarified that food cultivation was not to be considered a fundamental party policy but as a temporary measure to deal with the situation with which they were faced as a result of action being taken by the security forces under the Briggs Plan to cut off the leakage of food from the New Villages to the Communist jungle army.[41]

During his London visit, Templer pressed hard for Heren's dismissal or removal from Singapore but the Editor of *The Times,* Sir William Haley, refused to do so and Heren remained where he was.[42]

At the same meeting, Templer complained to the Colonial Office about the perceived anti-British bias of the doctor/novelist Han Suyin's Malayan novel … *And the Rain My Drink* which he wanted banned or withdrawn as it allegedly presented a misleading picture of the hardships suffered by Chinese squatters in Johor during the Emergency. However, he was not successful in this either as the publishers pointed out that it had already been widely distributed throughout the world, though a senior Colonial Office mandarin promised to see what could be done by sending out Vernon Bartlett, a MP who was a journalist of the London *News Chronicle*, to provide a more favourable account of the situation.[43]

To revert to Templer's plans to encourage Chinese young men to join the Malayan Police, in April 1952 a Government recruiting campaign was launched in Perak where there was a large Chinese population, but it was not very successful.

The shortage of Chinese policemen in the regular Malayan Police, Home Guard, and other auxiliary police units as at March 1952, as well as the great imbalance in numbers between Malays and Chinese in the Police, is brought out in Table 1.

Nevertheless, while it was well known that Malayan Chinese were traditionally disinclined to serve in the Army or the uniformed branch of the Police, it did not seem they were averse to serving as detectives in the CID or the Police Special Branch, where they were not required to wear uniform or be subject to such strict discipline as they would in the regular uniformed branch.[44]

There were cultural and historical reasons for this disinclination as the profession of arms, which in the public eye included both military and police, was not regarded with great favour according to the traditional Chinese social hierarchy. In China, during the warlord period of the early

TABLE 1
Ethnic Breakdown of Regular Police and Home Guards, March 1952[a]

	Malays	Chinese	Indians	Others	Total
Regular Police	16,239	1,223	1,279	301	19,042
Special Constables	33,629	1,425	1,623	155	36,832
Auxiliary Police	17,051	2,546	1,029	–	20,626
Extra Police Constables	3,175	304	256	21	3,756
Home Guards	110,295	73,610[b]	9,429	4,876	198,210
Total	180,389	79,108	13,616	5,353	278,466

Notes: a. CO 1022/165, extracted from letter reference INF.No. 360/49/110, 3 March 1952, from J.N. McHugh, Director Information Services, Federation of Malaya, to the Colonial Office.
         b. Chinese Home Guards were mainly employed to guard Chinese New Villages.

twentieth century, many of them were considered in the eyes of the civilian population to be little better than ruffians and criminals themselves, while in Malaya the Chinese often quoted for their own purpose the well-known Chinese adage: "You don't use good steel to make nails and you don't use good men to make soldiers" to explain their reluctance to serve in the Army or Police. However, when it was pointed out there were Chinese serving in the rank-and-file of the colonial Police Forces in Singapore and Hong Kong, they replied that the situation was quite dissimilar as Chinese policemen in Singapore and Hong Kong were working among predominantly Chinese populations that had similar historical, cultural, and linguistic backgrounds to themselves, whereas the situation in peninsular Malaya was not the same.

While there is no evidence to suggest that Tan Cheng Lock, the leader of the MCA, was privy to several official reports that were in existence at that time dealing with the problem of helping the Government obtain greater Chinese support to fight the Communists, it did emerge, however, that he and his colleagues in the MCA had been thinking along similar lines.[45] In May 1950, for instance, Tan had submitted a confidential memorandum to the Colonial Secretary (Creech Jones) and the Secretary of State for War (John Strachey), who were both then visiting Malaya, advocating the greater use, as Tan put it, of "Chinese to fight Chinese". He urged the setting up of what he called a "Malayan Chinese secret service" and a "Malayan or Chinese Brigade" under the command of British Special Branch officers to fight Communist terrorists.[46] Tan's proposals, however, were not taken up by the colonial Government at the time probably because the Special Branch expressed concern that if they were accepted, an opportunity would be provided for former Kuomintang (KMT) Army officers then living in Malaya to participate in and form what would virtually be a "Third Force" to fight the CPM. The KMT had been proscribed in Malaya in May 1949 and the British Government had recognized the Chinese Communist Government in China after the KMT forces under Generalissimo Chiang Kai-shek had been driven into exile in Taiwan.[47]

The three main constituent parts of Tan's plan were as follows:

- To create, train and equip a Malayan Chinese Brigade under British officers to be deployed as a counterinsurgency force.
- To form a Malayan Chinese Constabulary and a force of *kampung* guards under British control to police squatter settlements and New Villages to assist the regular police and win over the confidence and cooperation of the Chinese villagers.

- To create, train, and maintain a large "Malayan Chinese secret service" under the Special Branch to penetrate the Communist network that existed in the population outside the jungle. As Tan put it, "the best man to catch the Chinese bandit [sic], Communist agent, or rebel is the Chinese policeman, Chinese spy, or Chinese soldier."

It was evident, therefore, if Templer's plans to increase the number of Chinese in the police were to succeed, which was a laudable measure in itself, new ways and means would have to be found to overcome their objections to serving in a colonial police force in Malaya.

At a meeting between representatives of the MCA and General Templer at King's House, Kuala Lumpur, on 21 April 1952, Tan submitted a proposal to increase the number of Chinese police recruits and said that the MCA would be able to help by providing about 2,000 Chinese police recruits, at a rate of approximately 175 per month.[48]

Tan's proposal called for the MCA to work closely with the police recruiting teams that would visit each State and Settlement in Malaya, and in return, the MCA requested the Government not to enforce the National Service Ordinance to call up young Chinese men for national service except in case of dire emergency, and to grant citizenship papers to Chinese recruits after three years' satisfactory service in the police.[49]

At the meeting, Templer read out a report submitted by the Commissioner of Police on the Government's recruiting campaign in Perak, which he described as "encouraging", and the Secretary for Chinese Affairs reported that the MCA in Negri Sembilan, Malacca and Johor had already held preliminary meetings to discuss preparations for police recruiting campaigns in their respective States.

The MCA delegation suggested that under their proposed scheme the recruits rate of pay should be supplemented by monthly stipends provided by the MCA, which would be classified in the MCA's accounts as "Welfare Work" and paid out of the proceeds of the MCA's sweepstakes. The MCA announced that it would be prepared to set aside M$500,000 for distribution to the families of recruits to make up the difference between the salaries Chinese workers could expect to earn in private employment and the lower salaries they would be paid as police constables.

The MCA's proposals, however, did not find favour with Templer, who wrote to Tan on 24 April, three days after the meeting, that it would not be possible for the Government to accept the MCA scheme as the payment of a "bounty" or "stipend" would be a virtual admission that the police rates of pay were low and "would cause dissatisfaction and complaints from members of other racial communities already in the force" and, moreover, the subsidizing of Chinese recruits would strike at the "essential impartiality and independence of the police and should be rejected on those grounds alone".[50]

In spite of this setback, however, the Government seemed to have it both ways as in spite of Templer's letter, it did not seem to prevent the MCA paying a bounty to Chinese recruits once the recruiting campaign was launched. The Government decided to organize a recruiting drive in April before invoking the powers of call-up provided for in the National Service Ordinance as a way around the impasse, and though the Federal Legislative Council had already accepted the 1950 National Service Bill in principle to conscript Chinese young men for service in the Armed Forces, it was not implemented for the time being.[51] It was a *quid pro quo* situation in which the Government tacitly accepted the MCA's assistance in recruiting Chinese recruits for the Police Force in return for making certain concessions to accommodate the MCA's requests not to enforce the National Service Ordinance.

Meanwhile, the MCA established special sub-committees at every MCA centre to deal with the recruitment of Chinese recruits. To allay the reservations expressed by Chinese recruits, they were reassured they would not have to eat Malay (*halal*) food (which they did not find to their taste) while they were undergoing training at the Police Training Depot, Kuala Lumpur; they would not be required to wear the pill-box style hat then worn by Malay policemen which they disliked; there were both Chinese and Malay instructors at the Police Training Depot; and they would be eligible for Federal citizenship after three years' service. As a result, 2,059 Chinese recruits were enlisted.

According to the MCA's Central Working Committee at the time, the MCA had already spent "hundreds of thousands of dollars (sic) to recruit a mere fraction of the Police Force" and a proposal to spend a further M$200,000 to recruit a further 1,000 Chinese recruits was not approved.[52]

It was well realized by the MCA, however, that the Chinese prejudice against serving in the Armed Forces was deeply rooted and Tan Cheng Lock suggested in a memorandum to the Federal War Council that perhaps a better way of dealing with the situation would be to encourage Chinese to join the Home Guard, making use of long-established and accepted Chinese principles of self-defence through loyalty to the family and society.[53] It was almost a Confucian solution. The Government's reply to his suggestion is not on record. However, the all-Chinese Kinta Valley Home Guard which was afterwards enrolled and trained jointly by the MCA with Government support, see Chapter 5 *infra*, was a good example of how an important Chinese Home Guard unit was formed along these lines to guard the numerous Chinese tin mines in the Kinta Valley area.

3. *The Creation of a Malayan Army* — The formation of a "Malayan Army" to consist of the existing Malay Regiment and a new multi-ethnic Federation Regiment.

Comments

In 1933 the War Office agreed to the formation of the Malay Regiment as a locally formed infantry unit of the British Army. The rank-and-file was made up entirely of Malays while most of its senior officers were British. The Malay Regiment that was formed pre-war earned for itself an outstanding record for bravery in World War II especially during the closing days of the Japanese onslaught in Singapore at Bukit Chandu in the Pasir Panjang area where they fought to the last man against overwhelming odds.

After the war, and before Templer's arrival in 1952, the Malay Regiment was reformed and four operational battalions came into being.[54] This increase formed part of the British plan to establish a local Malayan army which would form the nucleus of the regular defence forces after independence. As Malcolm MacDonald, Commissioner General for South East Asia, commented in August 1950 to James Griffiths, then Secretary of State for the Colonies, "nothing is more likely to assist a new state to stand squarely on its own feet in the cockpit of South East Asia than ... well-trained forces".[55] And the Malay Regiment was one of them.

In August 1951, Griffiths hoped it would be possible to expand the Malay Regiment to include non-Malays (read mainly "Malayan Chinese") in its ranks thus making it a multi-racial force.[56] However, it seemed the Chinese were sitting on the fence and they did not show any interest in enlisting in the army for more or less the same reasons that had prevented them from joining the uniformed ranks of the Malayan Police.[57] If they were interested at all, it was only as serving as officers or perhaps in specialized technical units of the armed forces.

After General Templer arrived in 1952, however, he did not give up the idea of creating a Malayan army and as a way round the impasse he thought of forming an all-Chinese Regiment which would have the advantage, too, of involving the Chinese community more directly in the war against the Communists but the Malay rulers whose assent would be required for such a move did not look favourably on the idea perhaps because the traditional numerical supremacy of the Malays in the country's Armed Forces would be affected. Nevertheless, he was able to obtain the Malay rulers consent to a compromise which would involve establishing up to three battalions of a multi-racial Federation Regiment, open to enrolment by Chinese, Indians and Eurasians, on the understanding that with the formation of each battalion of the Federation Regiment a battalion of the Malay Regiment would be formed.[58]

On 3 July 1952, the Federation Regiment Bill was passed by the Federal Legislative Council, and it seemed, therefore, that the way was paved for the development of Malaya's first multi-ethnic army. Recruitment for the Federation Army started almost immediately. The first task, as Templer put it, was to find twelve "super men" who would be sent for officer training. But this was easier said than done as Templer insisted that the health requirements for entry into Sandhurst should be adopted and only nine young men could be found who met these high standards and none of them was Malay. Templer admitted "I could not possibly announce the result", and the medical standards had to be lowered so that three Malays, who were hurriedly sought, could be selected. Eventually the "twelve super men" quota was made up of six Chinese, three Malays, two Indians, and one Eurasian.[59]

Recruitment of rank-and-file for the Federation Regiment began in Penang on 18 August as well as other recruiting centres throughout the country. However, Templer's hope that Chinese would be encouraged to enlist in the Regiment ran into the same cultural problems that had been encountered over Chinese recruitment for the police.[60] Moreover, another reason put forward was that they could not live on the low pay offered to recruits although it was identical to the pay and conditions of service offered to Malay recruits for the Malay Regiment. It is possible, too, though it was not clearly expressed at the time that there was a more fundamental reason behind their disinclination to serve in the army which was that they were still inclined to consider themselves as "sojourners" in Malaya owing allegiance to their ancestral home (China) and not to Malaya, and they could not see what benefits national service would offer to them in the political system in Malaya at the time.[61]

Nevertheless, once again the MCA stepped into the breach by offering special monetary incentives to recruits, and by the end of June 1953 it had managed to recruit 855 Chinese youths to serve in an Engineer Squadron of the Federation Regiment and the Boys' Companies that were being formed as feeders into the Federation Regiment.[62] General Templer's plans, however, ran into further problems. It was not easy to find the right kind of British officers he had in mind to be seconded from the British Army to serve in the Malayan Army. It became clear, too, that insufficient consideration had been given to budgeting for the extra costs involved in face of the ever increasing costs of running the Emergency which in turn was exacerbated by the downturn in the economy brought about by a sharp fall in the price of tin and rubber which were Malaya's main exports.

General Templer originally planned to expand the regular military forces in Malaya by raising three additional battalions of the Malay Regiment and three battalions of the new Federation Regiment "in the shortest possible time" to form the Malayan Army.[63] However, in May 1953, when it became apparent that the Government had not factored in the additional expenditure required to cover this expansion, the plans had to be revised downwards to cover the raising of only one additional battalion of the Malay Regiment in 1954, with a second and third battalion to follow "several years later", and one battalion of the Federation Regiment, to be followed later by two more battalions, with the proviso "if and when funds became available".[64] This presented a serious setback to Templer's more ambitious plans to establish a Malayan Army and the best that could be said was that while some progress had been made, it did not measure up to the plans that he had envisaged.

4. *The Development of a National Education Policy* — A national education system to be brought about through the medium of a common language.

Comments

In his speech to the Legislative Council, General Templer said that Malaya required an education system by which, in due course, every man, woman, and child would be able to have at least some contact with members of other communities through the medium of a common language in addition to their own. He envisaged that agreement would soon be reached on the recommendations of the Special Committee on educational policy which had been set up before his arrival in September 1951 by the Legislative Council. The Report was submitted for approval by the Legislative Council in October 1952 by the Attorney General, M.J. Hogan, and it became law as the Education Ordinance, No. 63 of 1952.[65]

The education system has always been a contentious issue in Malaya, especially as the Chinese educational world approached any innovation with caution. Historically, Chinese schools in Malaya had a different origin from Malay, Indian or English schools. The Chinese in Malaya established their own schools because there was no provision for their schooling and they were funded by clan associations and donations from wealthy Chinese benefactors and they were not dependent on financial support from the Government. They used textbooks imported from China which promoted a Chinese and not a Malayan point of view and most of the teachers were recruited from China. As a result the trends in education and politics in China had a spin-off effect on Malayan Chinese schools, and the burgeoning nationalist influence on education in China led to the spreading of both KMT and CCP political propaganda among Malayan Chinese schools and to the Malayan Chinese population as a whole.

After World War I, however, for the first time, the colonial Government in Malaya became interested in Chinese schools and aware of the political influence they exercised among the Chinese community, and some of the schools were given a limited amount of government aid in return for which they then came under the Chinese Protectorate and an officer of the Chinese Protectorate was attached to the Education Department as Assistant Director of Education (Chinese). It was, in fact, only after World War II that they came completely under the Education Department, and then for political and not educational reasons.[66]

The rationale of the Government in providing education was that while education in the vernacular schools should be free for all Malay children "Malay is the *lingua franca* of the country, it was not thought necessary to provide education for the children of an alien temporary population in their own language".[67]

Meanwhile, the 1931 Census revealed for the first time that Malays were outnumbered in their own country by non-Malays, that is, the combined Chinese and Indian elements of the population. Local-born Chinese now made up 38 per cent of the population in the pre-war Straits Settlements and 31 per cent in Malaya, and they began to make it clear that they were no longer content to be treated as "aliens" and discriminated against by the colonial Government. In 1947, Tan Cheng Lock was disturbed by the idea that a powerful Malay State Council dominated by Malays and a pro-Malay British Resident and senior colonial officials would soon be in a position to determine Government policies over education, land rights, and other matters. He expressed his disquiet over a Government policy which he perceived as "discrimination against non-Malays". With regard to the Government's education policy, he pointed out that free education was only provided in the Malay language while the Government contributed hardly anything towards the maintenance of Chinese vernacular schools.[68]

It was clear that racial harmony and cooperation at ground level were still a long way off. Government policy was perceived to be directed as having separate vernacular schools for Malays, Chinese, and Indians, which only tended to foster a centrifugal tendency, even though it was recognized that one of the ways to bring about integration in a multi-ethnic society is through education.

Much had happened before General Templer arrived in 1952. In 1951, the Government appointed a commission headed by Leonard Barnes to look into the system of Malay vernacular education, and the resulting Barnes Report recommended that children of all races should attend National Schools where only Malay and English would be taught as part of an integrated system. The most important feature of the primary National Schools was that they would be bilingual and all pupils would be taught English and Malay. The best students would then proceed to English-medium secondary schools.[69] But the Chinese were dissatisfied with the conclusions of the Report and felt that their problems had been side-stepped. Another committee was appointed in 1951 headed by Dr W.P. Fenn and Dr Wu Teh-yao to investigate and report this time on Chinese education in Malaya, and inevitably the recommendations of this committee were radically different from those of the Barnes Report. While it acknowledged that education should have a local Malayan orientation, it proposed that a system of belonging could be inculcated by maintaining the different cultures and separate school systems of the main ethnic groups in Malaya.[70]

The conflicting views of the above two committees were studied by yet a third committee which concluded this time that National Schools should be formed using Malay and English as the media of instruction, while accepting that Chinese and Tamil could be taught as subjects as a third language, but that Chinese and Indian medium schools would remain outside the National Schools system.

It was this policy that was enshrined in Education Ordinance No. 63 which Templer presented at the Legislative Council meeting on 19 March 1952. It was in a sense a compromise. Though insisting that National Schools should be the pattern to be followed, it was still permissible for Chinese or Tamil to be taught as a third language. Chinese and Indian medium schools would be allowed to exist outside the system but to do so they still had to comply with the regulations laid down by the Government regarding the provision of acceptable school premises and equipment, the recruitment of students and staff, the use of approved textbooks, and so on, until such time as there were sufficient National Schools into which they could be incorporated, when it was proposed to withdraw Government grants-in-aid from them.[71] In the meantime, existing Government-aided Chinese and Tamil schools, which were largely missionary-funded or self-funded, would be encouraged to convert to National Schools and abide by the conditions laid down by the Government for National Schools, such as the provision of acceptable school premises and equipment, the enrolment of students, the use of approved textbooks, and the teaching of English or Malay. Chinese as a separate subject could only be taught in National Schools if requested by parents or guardians provided there were at least fifteen students at the same level or standard in the school.

Under this system, English-medium schools in the National Schools system would teach Malay as a subject from the third year onwards whereas Malay-medium schools would teach English from the first year onwards.

The new Ordinance tabled by General Templer aroused strong opposition from both the Chinese and Tamil communities at what they perceived to be the unfair way Chinese and Tamil education was being treated, and hundreds of educational bodies sent petitions and letters to the Government. The MCA took up the cause of Chinese schools and Tan Cheng Lock established the MCA Chinese Education Central Committee in April 1953 to lead the opposition to the new Ordinance. He wrote to Templer to ask him to revise the Ordinance as it was perceived to be "harmful to Chinese education". Among the eight points he raised in his letter was the long-standing and re-occurring fear and suspicion among the Chinese community that the Government was pursuing a policy that would eventually lead to the elimination of the teaching of the Chinese language and literature and the eradication of Chinese culture.[72] He had, in fact, already written on this topic many years earlier in 1943 during his enforced exile in Bombay during the Japanese occupation of Malaya when he had addressed a lengthy memorandum to Colonel Oliver Stanley, then Colonial Secretary, on the future of Malaya. Among other matters, he wrote about the problem of Chinese education and recommended that "the teaching of Chinese as a language subject should be made available to all Chinese students in English secondary schools".[73]

The objections by Chinese teachers to the Government's policy led to the formation of UCSTA (United Chinese School Teachers Association) on 25 August 1951, which was notable as it was the first pan-Malayan Chinese school teachers' organization in Malaya, and the opposition to the Ordinance was led by the MCA's Chinese Education Central Committee which coordinated the efforts of the UCSTA and the UCSCA (United Chinese School Committees Association).[74]

Tan Cheng Lock's appeal was, however, rejected by Templer. The irony of the situation, which seems to have escaped the authorities, was that it was not possible in any event to introduce the new National School system as the Government did not have the necessary funds to do so. Moreover, even if the Chinese and Tamil schools agreed to convert to National Schools, there were insufficient qualified teachers with the necessary language skills to teach in them.[75]

In May 1953, the MCA and MIC jointly presented another appeal to Templer about the new Education Ordinance but this, too, was rejected.[76] Tan then addressed a memorandum to Madame Vijavalakshmi Pandit, the President of the UN General Assembly, on the subject though the records are silent as to what happened about it.[77] Nevertheless, the ongoing *contre temps* between the MCA and Templer only added to the strained relations that were beginning to grow between them from the time that the MCA's proposals for providing Chinese recruits for the Police, had been rejected.

The widespread opposition to the new Ordinance by the Chinese community brought about a demand for the Chinese language to be recognized as one of the official languages of Malaya in addition to Malay and English, and in November 1952, after the promulgation of the new Ordinance, the Deputy High Commissioner, MacGillivray, tried to defuse the situation by inviting a delegation of UCSCA to meet him to discuss the matter, explaining that under the Federation of Malaya Agreement only English and Malay were designated as official languages and no other languages could be used. However, his reply did not satisfy the UCSCA and on 18 August 1954 at a UCSCA meeting in Kuala Lumpur, the UCSCA President called for the Chinese community to continue to struggle for the recognition of Chinese as one of Malaya's official languages.[78] Most of the Chinese educators regarded it as a splintered education system with different communities pulling in different directions and they were opposed to any scheme which they considered could lead to the death of Chinese education.

This was the situation up to the time Templer left Malaya in 1954, but even in more recent times, the status of Chinese education in the national educational system has still not been completely settled, and it remains a controversial and sensitive issue for the present Barisan Nasional government in power.[79]

5. *The Importance of Land Tenure for Agriculturists* — The question of land and the resettlement of squatters.

Comment
As Templer said in his Legislative Council speech:

> The process [of resettlement] has been a hurried one, and without the opportunity for careful sociological and economic survey and planning which would normally preclude so abrupt a disturbance of a long established pattern of rural life.... None of these problems is, I believe, of greater importance than that of land holding .... It must surely be our endeavour to ensure that these new communities are founded on a stable economy and that, to this end, land reasonably close to it and capable of the production of food supplies is made available to the peasant farmers of these new communities. The tenure of land is, as always has been, the fundamental stabilising influence in the life of any country.[80]

General Templer was mainly concerned with problems which arose from the resettling under the Briggs Plan in 1950–52 of half a million or more Chinese, as well as some Malays and Indians, into 550 New Villages in order to dislocate their contact with Communist terrorists and to prevent their becoming an important source of supplies, information, and recruitment for the terrorists. This vast programme that involved about 10 per cent of Malaya's population was in itself an unprecedented undertaking which inevitably brought in its train hardships as it separated many of the New Villagers from their usual places of employment as agriculturists and market gardeners, rubber tappers, workers on tin mines, and so on.[81] It is true that in some cases their hardships were ameliorated at that time by the coincidental increase in the price of rubber and tin (see Chapter 5) which enabled them to find employment as rubber tappers and tin mine workers but this was not always the case and there is no doubt, especially in those New Villages which were badly sited and lacked social services due to the speed at which the resettlement programme was carried out, that the lives of many of the New Villagers were adversely affected. Unfortunately little information is available about the facilities that were made available to them or to what extent they were offered titles to agricultural or other land, or found other employment.

Templer did not go into this matter in any great detail in his speech to the Legislative Assembly but the constitutional structure of Malaya, and the religious, historical, and economic differences between the Malays and Chinese who were mostly affected, as well as the Islamic law of inheritance, combined to make the problems of land tenure and the allocation of land extremely complex.

In this connection, it may be of interest to look at the promulgation of the first Malay Reservations Enactment in the Federated Malay States in 1913 and similar legislation in the Unfederated Malay States between 1930 and 1941, which in a sense resulted from the large-scale Chinese immigration into Malaya in the latter half of the nineteenth century which changed the whole demographic picture of Malaya.[82] The towns and urban centres became predominantly Chinese settlements, and Chinese farmers and agriculturalists spread out to fill vacant spaces in rural areas. Aliens had always been entitled to hold land but the Malays soon came to be concerned they would be driven off the land if this movement continued and they would be reduced to becoming tenants of Western, Chinese, and Indian (Chettiar) landlords. Representations were therefore made to the colonial Government that Malays should be afforded special protection to safeguard the land held by them under customary tenure and prevent it being acquired by non-Malays, and the colonial Government created Malay reservations in which land could only be alienated to Malays and not transferred into non-Malay hands. Thus Malay reservations came into being. However, non-Malays were allowed to retain land acquired before the various enactments were promulgated.

The principle followed was based on the formula that in no State in the Federated Malay States should the ratio between cultivable area in Malay reservations and the whole cultivable area of a State fall below

60 per cent, although as far as can be traced no public announcements were made to this effect. While it was true that the legislation made it impossible for Malays to transfer reservation land to non-Malays, it did not prevent their pledging the land as security for a loan or an advance. This loophole permitted Chinese and Indian money-lenders and speculators to obtain effective control of the land, with the Malays remaining owners in name only.

In 1933, the Malay Reservations Enactment of the Federated Malay States was therefore amended to forbid charge or lease of land to non-Malays, and similar laws were introduced in other States.

The legal position was that the owner of land in a Malay State either derived his title from a grant by the Crown or by the Sultan of the State or from rights created by the clearing and cultivation of land which was recognized when rights in land were investigated and recorded on the introduction of land registration. All unalienated land in the Malay States was invested in the Malay Sultans and land titles in each State were granted only on the authority of the Ruler-in-Council.[83]

It was this lack of a unified land code for the whole country and the political and legal problems involved that made the matter so complicated and difficult for General Templer to deal with.[84] While the Malays regarded the reservations as necessary to protect their special rights as cultivators, the Chinese took an opposite view and looked upon the reservations as another example of the "protection" afforded to Malays by the colonial Government.[85]

It was a politically sensitive issue, too, and Templer had to explore with the Malay Sultans the possibilities of their agreeing to make available land to New Villagers, which was not always an easy task. While he made some progress, it was not always possible to overcome the residual reluctance on the part of some Malays to let Chinese have a stake in the land.

6. *The Encouragement of Youth Movements* — Particularly non-communal youth movements and a cultural renaissance under British patronage.

Comment
Templer emphasized in his Legislative Council speech that the Government would encourage the formation of multi-racial youth movements which he regarded as a way of bringing together the young people of Malaya to realize their future responsibility towards their country, and that such a

movement would receive his utmost support. It clearly fitted in well with the British Government's intention to create a united Malayan nation, which was one of the central objectives of the Directive that Templer had been given, although it led to what has been described by some critics as a surfeit of various organizations to which youths of all races could belong, such as Boy Scouts, Cubs, Girls Guides, Boys and Girls Clubs, and so on.[86] In doing this, Templer built on and improved the arrangements that had already been put in place by General Briggs between April 1950 and November 1951 when he issued a comprehensive series of Directives in support of the implementation of his Briggs Plan, which had laid down elaborate plans for the organization of a wide range of social welfare services similar to what Templer now had in mind. These included the provision of medical clinics, the establishment of schools in New Villages, visits by small cinema vans, the opening of cooperative shops, the setting up of Boy Scouts' troops, and so on, which must have been of great value to Templer and his staff in the preparation of their own plans.[87]

In 1953, Boy Scouts and Girl Guides Ordinances were promulgated to extend and protect the activities of the two movements throughout Malaya. Templer, who had been appointed Chief Scout of Malaya, took great interest in these movements, and he wore the Scouts badge in the lapel of his coat whenever he was wearing civilian clothes.[88]

Together with his encouragement of the youth movement, Templer envisaged a "cultural" renaissance under British patronage to foster what he thought of as a "civilized nation" according to the British pattern, and where they already existed, he encouraged support of museums, zoos, libraries, and local arts and crafts.

There were two museums in Malaya before World War II, the Perak Museum in Taiping which had been built in 1886 and the Selangor Museum in Kuala Lumpur, which had been built in 1904. In March 1945, towards the end of World War II, the Selangor Museum was destroyed by bombs dropped by American B29 aircraft attacking the Malayan Railway marshalling yards at Brickfields, Kuala Lumpur, not far away and on the opposite side of the road from the Museum, and the present-day National Museum of Malaya that replaced the old Selangor Museum owes its existence to the support Templer gave to the inspiration of a retired former senior Malayan Civil Service officer, Tan Sri Dato' Dr Mubin Sheppard, to establish a national museum.[89]

On 12 September 1952, Templer wrote to Tan Cheng Lock to inform him of his wish and to ask for his support to "engender an interest in Malayan history by the youth of the country" and told him that "the Museum is doing this in a small way in Kuala Lumpur, and early the next year the [Museum] Department will be organizing a travelling exhibition."[90]

The study of the history and geography of Malaya at the University of Malaya was encouraged, and Templer agreed to become the patron of the *Malayan Historical Journal*. A far-sighted British book publisher in Singapore, Donald Moore, with a branch in Kuala Lumpur, began to publish a number of booklets and monographs dealing with local Malayan subjects, and Moore's wife, Joanna, edited *The New Malaya* magazine which brought together contributions from various authors about Malayan arts and culture.[91]

In July 1951, before General Templer's arrival, a Malayan-wide Adult Education Association had already been formed with the political support of Dato' Onn and Independence of Malaya Party (IMP), and by the end of October 1952, the colonial Government had provided M$250,000 to support its 587 Basic English classes.

The MCA had its own New Village Adult Education programme, too, which was extensive and widely publicized with the object of helping to eradicate adult illiteracy. It included, for instance, the preparation of a textbook on Malayan civics to meet the demands of labourers and factory workers in New Villages. Civics was a popular subject as there were few books explaining how the Malayan Government worked and the procedures it followed, and MCA-run evening classes in bookkeeping, mathematics, Chinese and Malay became popular in New Villages.[92] The MCA used funds derived from its popular lotteries for running its Adult Education classes and other welfare projects.

The MCA Adult Education programme was helped, too, by the United States Information Services (USIS) in Singapore providing "desirable literature", which meant, in other words, textbooks or reading material with an anti-Communist bias for use in its adult classes.[93]

In May 1953, however, the Malayan Federal Treasury informed the MCA that its application for remission of tax on the proceeds of the lotteries had been rejected and that approval would not be granted for the running of further lotteries after August 1953 on the grounds that the MCA had become a "political party".[94] In the Government's view it had sufficient reserves to continue to pay the annually recurrent charges on its New Villages' welfare activities for at least another two years without running lotteries. The matter was discussed at some length at a meeting of the MCA Working Committee in Malacca on 8 May 1953 and it was decided that Tan Cheng Lock would head a small MCA delegation to see General Templer to discuss the matter.

At the meeting, Tan pointed out to Templer that the Government's intention to impose tax on the lottery would mean that out of a net profit of M\$750,000 from the M\$2,500,000 lottery, the MCA would now have to pay the Federal Treasury M\$500,000 per sweepstake which was held every six weeks. This would result in a serious curtailment of the MCA's welfare work and in particular it was pointed out that a reduction in the availability of funds of this nature would have serious repercussions in the following areas that were heavily dependent on support from the MCA:

(a) The widespread welfare work that had been carried out in New Villages for several years including the provision of capital expenditure to be used for amenities and facilities such as schools, community halls and centres, sports requisites, Boy Scout and Girl Guide uniforms and equipment;

(b) The relief of distressed and destitute persons.

(c) Grants to Government-approved charitable organizations and other institutes of public character such as Adult Education in New Villages.

(d) The relief of detainees and ex-detainees and their families under the Emergency Regulations.

Tan pointed out, too, that applications for funds had been received on 3 October 1952, for instance, M\$16,000 from St John's Ambulance Brigade and M\$10,000 from the Red Cross Society.[95] Moreover, when these two organizations arrived in Malaya in 1952, the MCA had granted them a total of nearly M\$500,000 to purchase the necessary transport for the work they intended to carry out in the New Villages.[96]

As Tan pointed out, the assistance provided by the MCA was clearly extensive as it had provided funds over a wide area of charitable endeavours undertaken by many religions including St Michael's Catholic Action, the Convent of the Holy Infant Jesus (Malacca), the Home for the Aged (Penang), and the Ramakrishna Mission (Penang). It had provided funds, too, towards the costs of building the Lady Templer Tuberculosis Hospital at Cheras, Kuala Lumpur, named after General Templer's wife, the foundation stone of which had been laid by the Duchess of Kent during her visit to Malaya in October 1952.[97] Tan explained that the MCA had received several appeals for charitable causes from Lady Peggie Templer herself and that the MCA had assisted the Government in providing low-cost housing at Petaling Jaya, Kuala Lumpur, and funds for the Grow More Food Campaign and settling Chinese rice planters in Cangkat Jong (Perak). It had responded, too, to an appeal for funds from General Templer's wife for the Federation School for the Deaf which was established in Penang.[98] Further, in July 1953, the MCA had established a Malay Welfare Fund with M\$500,000 from its lottery proceeds which could be used by UMNO for the Malay community.

However, Tan was not successful in persuading Templer to remove the ban on MCA lotteries and it remained in force.[99]

In June 1953 General Templer banned all welfare lotteries run by political parties which he considered were being siphoned off for purely political purposes, and said that he intended to replace them with Government-sponsored lotteries. In his view, the MCA "had behaved very badly in amassing funds for its own political purposes". His biographer Cloake reported that Tan Cheng Lock considered that the MCA's efforts were being unfairly denigrated and he became "vehemently anti-Templer".[100]

Meanwhile, the Government licence to run UMNO's third lottery in 1953 was cancelled, which Tunku Abdul Rahman and Dr Ismail described as being unduly harsh.[101] As Cloake states, Templer had a "distrust of the Tunku's policies".[102]

In regard to the provision of amenities in New Villages, the important part played by Christian missionaries should not be forgotten. In February 1954, for instance, the position before Templer left Malaya, was that the Malayan Christian Council had 125 resident workers stationed in 43 New Villages, and the Catholic Church 56 workers in 176 New Villages. Crèches for the children of rubber tappers had been established, some practical training had been provided in crafts and trades, and mini-libraries established in New Villages (though they often had Christian tracts in them).

Templer had a hand in the employment of missionaries as he had approached the College of Propaganda in Rome for assistance in providing missionaries, who had had experience in China and spoke Chinese, to help in Malaya although this was considered rather a sensitive area as there were difficulties over a possible conflict in what was seen as the propagation of Christianity in a country where the predominant religion was Islam.

Dato' Onn guarded carefully, too, the domain of RIDA and especially the work missionaries were doing in agrarian reform, and as a result the Government had to reassure Mentris Besar in the Malay States that the work of Christian missionaries in New Villages was geared solely to "fighting Communism" and they would not be permitted to evangelize or propagate Christianity.[103]

The Malayan Film Unit (MFU) deserves special mention. Although it was already in existence by the time Templer arrived in 1952, he attached great importance to the use of propaganda to win over the hearts and minds of the public in the struggle against the CPM, and he asked the Foreign Office for the services of Tom Hodge to head its Film Unit. While it was not publicly announced at the time, Templer took a personal interest in what Hodge was doing and instructed him that the underlying presence of the British colonial Government was always to be portrayed in the most favourable light. As the British Film Institute commented in its recently published book, *End of the Empire: Cultural Histories of Cinema* (2011): "What was kept discreetly in the background was Britain's hand in the choice of the political leaders to head the new Nation — those who would were amenable to the British colonial government and safeguard its economic interests." The MFU's films helped enhance Templer's image as a hero in every film in which he appeared, and supported wherever possible his viewpoint and his social and economic activities, and "although he was noted for his dictatorial manner, ensured that he was always portrayed smiling and mingling with the ordinary people and shaking their hands wherever he went".[104]

7. *The Importance of Progressive Political Progress* — General Templer's election policy.

Comment

As referred to earlier in this account, Templer said in his speech to the Legislative Council that he had been criticized in a newspaper for saying that he would confine political progress to the "parish pump level". He now wished to elaborate further on this, and stated that he regarded

Municipal and Town Council elections as the next step towards democratic government and they would be followed in due course by a much slower and deliberate move to State and Federal elections, which he thought of as being some years away.

But, in fact, the first steps towards democratic government had already been taken before his arrival at Kuala Lumpur in January 1952 when UMNO and MCA had formed an alliance at municipal level to defeat Dato' Onn bin Ja'afar's IMP, which Onn had formed after he relinquished the leadership of UMNO.[105] The idea of forming a political alliance of this kind came from Colonel H.S. Lee, the Chairman of the MCA Selangor Branch, a banker and a millionaire Chinese tin miner, his deputy Ong Yoke Lin, a local Chinese businessman who then had an electrical goods shop in Kuala Lumpur, and Dato' Yahya, the Chairman of the UMNO Kuala Lumpur branch.

Colonel H.S. Lee received a letter of congratulations from Tunku Abdul Rahman, the UMNO President, for the cooperation between the two political parties he had brought about. The Tunku hoped that as UMNO-MCA were the largest ethnic political parties in Malaya, the successful cooperation which had been started in the Kuala Lumpur Municipal elections should be repeated throughout the country, and he suggested that he and Tan Cheng Lock should meet to discuss the extension of the cooperation between the two parties to other States and Settlements. The Tunku said that it was clear the public had no confidence in IMP, which was only successful in winning two seats in the Kuala Lumpur Municipal elections by a very small majority of 500 odd votes, whereas MCA candidates had won all their seats by hundreds of votes.[106]

Lee informed Tan that he had had several meetings with the Tunku and found him a "very sincere and reasonable" person and that the Tunku was writing to the Chairmen of the various UMNO State and Settlements' branches to suggest that they should meet and cooperate with their MCA counterparts. The Tunku considered this to be the first step to bring about "elected State and Settlement Councils to be followed by an elected Federal Legislative Council".[107]

Some years afterwards, the Tunku provided his own version of the course of events which resulted in the political alliance of UMNO and MCA and he gave credit to the part played by Colonel H.S. Lee, Ong Yoke Lin, S.M. Yong, Datuk Yahya, Encik Ramli and Encik Ali Taib. He said that the idea of holding a Round-Table Conference between UMNO

and the MCA came about because of Dr Victor Purcell's visit to Malaya
(see Chapter 4).

> Sir Cheng-lock Tan asked me to meet Dr Purcell, who had some proposals
> to make to me on behalf of the MCA. The UMNO General Assembly which
> was then in session at Butterworth, objected strongly to Dr Purcell, whom
> the Malays always considered to be anti-Malay. Much as I disagreed with
> the UMNO General Assembly, I had to give in to prevent the proposed
> liaison between UMNO and MCA from breaking down. I sent a telegram
> to Sir Cheng-lock Tan suggesting that members of the UMNO and the
> MCA should meet in a Round-Table, without the services of Dr Purcell or
> any middle-man for that matter .... The MCA agreed with this proposal,
> and so the first Round Table Conference between members of UMNO
> and the MCA took place on February 3, 1953 .... The meeting turned out
> to be a complete success.[108]

The political alliance between the two parties in the Kuala Lumpur elections
was thus repeated in other municipal and town elections, and the Alliance
partnership emerged as the dominant political organization in Malaya. The
success of the Alliance in the municipal and State elections undoubtedly
helped to solve many of the problems that had hitherto hindered Sino-
Malay political cooperation.[109]

The UMNO-MCA Alliance's success, however, was something of a
setback for Templer who had up to then viewed Dato' Onn's IMP favourably
as it was an inter-communal party fitting in closely with his own views
of forging a united Malayan nation and he had hoped that it would
replace the UMNO-MCA alliance and emerge as the dominant political
party in Malaya. Onn, no doubt, too, had harboured his own ambitions of
becoming the dominant Malay figure in Malayan politics and for his part
was prepared to support General Templer's view that self-government
should be a gradual process as this would fit in with his own ideas and
provide him with time to further his own political ambitions.

On the other hand, General Templer did not have a high opinion of
Tunku Abdul Rahman when the latter took over from Onn as President
of UMNO, as he had urged that Malaya should be given independence
immediately and was critical of Templer's "parish pump" policy and
what he perceived to be the colonial Government's unnecessarily slow
and gradual move towards self-government and independence.[110]

In summing up at this stage, it is nevertheless indeed remarkable
that Templer, as a professional soldier, was able to focus as he did in his

first address to the Legislative Council so soon after his arrival in Malaya on so many diverse political, social, and economic problems that needed attention, while at the same time directing the war against the Communist terrorists in the Malayan jungle, although it is worthwhile noting as Professor Northcote Parkinson shrewdly commented in his book, *Templer in Malaya*, "For half of his achievements he must share the credit with assistants of whose names the public will never hear."[111]

Templer's task, however, was not made any easier by his having to deal at the same time with the economic insecurity resulting from the serious downturn in rubber and tin prices on which the Malayan economy depended, which had the effect of restricting public expenditure on critical infrastructure projects such as health, education, and social and political developments. These will be further referred to in due course.[112]

Meanwhile, many historians have remarked at the pace at which Templer was working, and have commented that he was already beginning to show signs of the pressure and strain of high office, and perhaps his abrasiveness and brusqueness which have often been remarked on may to some extent be attributed to this.[113] His lack of tact is, in fact, often mentioned by Cloake, his biographer, who refers to Lady Templer helping her husband out on occasions by intervening to soften ruffled feelings caused by his rudeness. Cloake, for instance, relates an occasion when Templer's wife had to intervene to avert an awkward situation when her husband (then VCIGS at the War Office) was discourteous to Emmanuel Shinwell, Secretary of State for War, and comments that she often had to soften the ruffled feelings of persons her husband offended.[114]

As the *Straits Times* reported on 17 April 1952, quoting the remarks made by Albert Hogg, Singapore's Chief Delegate to the District Rotary International Conference in Kuala Lumpur, at which Templer gave the keynote speech: "General Templer looked a tired man, working under great strain and who was suffering physically. The High Commissioner gave his speech seated."[115]

Yet further confirmation of the strain under which he was working was provided by his Military Assistant, Major David Lloyd Owen, who referred to Templer looking "fatigued and tired out" in a secret and personal letter he wrote to Lieutenant General Sir Nevil Brownjohn on 9 June 1952.[116]

R.V. Jones, a member of the London Joint Intelligence Committee (JIC), provided the following impressions of Templer when Templer visited

London in 1953 to brief the Committee on the situation in Malaya: "The problems of the Malayan Emergency were clearly telling on him [Templer] for I have never before or since seen a man under such manifest strain. He chain-smoked cigarettes incessantly with trembling hands the whole time he was speaking to us, and I wondered how long he could last."[117]

Notes

1. CO 1022/298, Confidential. Inward Telegram no. 348, "Gen. Sir G. Templer to Secretary of State, 12 March 1952", indicating the lines Templer proposed to take on elections in his forthcoming speech to the Legislative Council.
2. Ibid. S. Rajaratnam joined the Singapore People's Action Party (PAP) in 1954, and became Minister for Culture (1959–65), Minister for Foreign Affairs (1965–80), and Deputy Prime Minister (1980–85). Before that he had worked as a journalist with *The Tribune* (1947) before joining the *Singapore Standard* as leader writer and features editor when it was launched in 1950. He became well-known for his trenchant style and he often took an anti-colonial stand. He expounded his views of the local political scene in his *I Write as I Please Column*. (See Irene Ng, *The Singapore Lion: A Biography of S. Rajaratnam* (Singapore: Institute of Southeast Asian Studies, 2010), pp. 119–59).
3. CO 1022/298, Confidential. Inward Telegram no. 348, "Gen. Sir G. Templer to Secretary of State, 12 March 1952", op. cit.
4. With all the talk about elections at "parish pump" level, one wonders what the phrase meant to the ordinary person in the street in Malaya who would be the voter, as the phrase has a distinctly "ye olde English" touch to it which could not have been very familiar to Malayans.
5. Ibid.
6. CO 1022/298, no. 30, 18 October 1952. "[Elections]: letter from D.C. MacGillivray to J.D. Higham on current plans. Minutes by A.S. Gann, T.C. Jerrom and J.D. Higham."
7. Cloake, op. cit., p. 306.
8. Author's notes. The author who was Commissioner of Police, Kelantan, during the British Military Administration September 1945 – April 1946 (the post was afterwards redesignated Chief Police Officer after the civil government took over) had observed the same practice while he was in Kota Baru.
9. CO 1022/100, No. 5977, Observer Foreign News Service, London, "From Michael Davidson by cable from Kuala Lumpur, 19 March 1952".
10. Ibid.
11. CO 1022/100, Confidential, "General Templer's Address to the Legislative Council, 19 March 1952". Templer and MacGillivray had spent much of their time after their arrival at Kuala Lumpur at the beginning of February in drafting Templer's speech.

12. ISEAS Library, Tun Sir Henry H.S. Lee, Private Papers Collection, HSL.031.085, "The Templer Plan", *Malay Mail*, 21 March 1952.

13. CO 1022/485, "World Bank Mission to Malaya: Revision of Development Plan for Federation of Malaya: Malayan Section of Colombo Plan for end 1944 – mid 1950, 9 May 1952". Dato' Onn bin Ja'afar represented the Malayan Government at the Colombo Plan Consultative Committee meeting in Karachi that discussed *inter alia* various proposed fields of economic and social development plans for Malaya, which were circulated to the Federal Executive Council. They were referred to as the "Yellow Book". The Colombo Plan was the chief instrument of U.K. economic aid to independent Commonwealth and foreign countries. See also *The Economic Development of Malaya. Report of a Mission organized by the International Bank for Reconstruction and Development at the request of the Government of the Federation of Malaya, the Crown Colony of Singapore and the United Kingdom* (Singapore: Government Printer, 1955). The eighteen subjects of the Templer Plan and several others too, were, in fact, referred to in the World Bank Mission report, and though the Mission Report was not mentioned by Templer in his speech, it is likely that O.A. Spencer, his Economic Secretary, would have been aware of it as he had written to J.D. Higham in 1952 to suggest that a World Bank Mission should visit Malaya (See CO 1022/485, no. 2, 9 May 1952, "Letter from O.A. Spencer to J.D. Higham suggesting a World Bank Mission to Malaya.").

14. *Malay Mail* (Editorial), 21 March 1952. Some of the same points had been adverted to by del Tufo before Templer's arrival. In his column for the *Singapore Standard* on 29 February 1952, S. Rajaratnam had said that the bulk of Malayan Chinese were not "calculating politician fence sitters", and they were simply caught in the cross-fire of two forces contesting for mastery over them, and that the government was inclined to treat them as "second-class citizens" (See ISEAS Library, Tan Sir Henry H.S. Lee Private Papers Collection, HSL.7.058, "Fortnightly Press Digest, Department of Information Services, Federation of Malaya, No. 4/52 for period 16 February – 29 February 1952, English Language Press").

15. *Singapore Standard*, "The Land of Promises", 21 March 1952.

16. The Mace referred to was presented to the Federal Legislative Council by the Malay Rulers in 1952 and it represented symbolically the supreme authority and prestige of the Council (see *Official Portal of the Parliament of Malaya*, "Parliamentary Democracy in Malaysia", Kuala Lumpur, 1963).

17. CO 1022/100, op. cit.

18. Counterinsurgency is often described in the literature as "75 per cent political and 25 per cent military". See Cloake, op. cit., p. 262; Paul Dixon, "Hearts and Minds? British Counterinsurgency from Malaya to Iraq", *Journal of Strategic Studies* 32(3), p. 359; and Lieutenant Colonel David Galula, *Counterinsurgency Warfare: Theory and Practice* (Westport, CT: Praeger, 1994), reprint 2006, p. 63.

19. ISEAS Library, Tun Sir Henry H.S. Lee, Private Papers Collection, HSL.031.069, "US Backs Policy in Malaya, 7 March 1952". The statement was made by the U.S. Secretary of State, Dean Acheson, at a news conference on his return to the United States from a meeting of the North Atlantic Council in Lisbon.

20. The CLC was an organization which attracted little public notice. It initially consisted of six representatives each from the Chinese and Malay communities, and one each from the Indian, Eurasian, Ceylonese and European communities. It had its genesis at a dinner party at Dato' Onn bin Ja'afar's house in Johor Bahru towards the end of 1948 when Malcolm MacDonald suggested to Tan Cheng Lock and others that ten Chinese and ten Malays should meet informally to discuss Sino-Malay cooperation. Onn was then Mentri Besar, Johor. At a further meeting in Penang on 9 January 1949, Tan and Onn agreed to form what they referred to as the "Sino-Malay Liaison Committee", which was later renamed the CLC, with MacDonald as its adviser. The agenda of the meeting centred on the resolution of ethnic issues, Sino-Malay cooperation, citizenship for non-Malays, and *bumiputera* (Malay) special rights. However, although the CLC was a brilliant idea, it had a short lifespan which only extended from early 1949 to late 1951. (See ISEAS Library Tun Sir Henry H.S. Lee Private Papers Collection, HSL.029/1, "Statement on Communal Relations in Malaya, 8 November 1952" and Heng Pek Koon, *Chinese Politics in Malaysia: A History of the Malaysian Chinese Association* (Oxford: Oxford University Press, 1988), pp. 147–56.

21. CO 967/84, no. 70, "Brief for Mr. Rees Williams Tour of Hong Kong, Singapore and Malaya, Oct/Nov 1949" and CO 537/4741, no. 78, 28 December 1949. At this time (October 1949), the CLC was in favour of all persons born in the Federation of Malaya qualifying for federal citizenship.

22. Zainal Abidin was the Vice-President of RIDA of which Onn was the President.

23. CO 537/4741, no. 78. "Letter from Sir Henry Gurney to J.J. Paskin, Colonial Office", 2 December 1949.

24. CO 537/4741, No. 78, 2 April 1949. Though it was unsuccessful, the idea of a non-communal party found favour with the British at the time and Templer and MacDonald initially supported the formation of the non-communal IMP which Onn inaugurated after he stepped down as UMNO President, and they initially gave Onn their political patronage. In the early 1950s, Onn was the most prominent Malay figure in the wholly nominated Federal Executive Council. (See Heng, op. cit., p. 180).

25. CO 537/4751, no. 80, 11 April 1949, "Gurney to Creech Jones, enclosing joint paper by Lt Col Gray and Major General Boucher". Gurney must have overlooked, however, the presence of the local-born Peranakan Chinese community who had made Malaya their home, with roots going back centuries in Malaya's history, who were loyal to the British Establishment, and he was

presumably referring to the more recent immigrants from China who still thought of themselves as "Chinese", regarded China as their home, and did not have a Malayan outlook.

26. CO 1022/100, Confidential, "General Templer's Address to the Legislative Council, 19 March 1952", and Denis Warner, Correspondent, *The Scotsman* and *The Daily Telegraph*, "Gen. Templer's Programme for Malaya", 20 March 1952.

27. Victor Purcell, *Malaya: Communist or Free?* (Stanford: Stanford University Press, 1954), p. 218.

28. The Parliamentary Debates (Hansard), Fifth Series, Vol. CLXXV. House of Lords, Second Volume of Series, 19 February 1952–58 April 1952, "The Situation in Malaya", p. 323. See also ISEAS Library, Tun Sir Henry H.S. Lee Private Papers Collection, HSL.2.045, Secret, "Memo on the Chinese Community in Malaya in July 1952". There is an unsigned memo on this file stating that the principle of *jus soli* for citizenship had not been accepted and that Chinese applicants for citizenship were discriminated against by being required to take a Malay or English language test.

29. *Federation of Malaya Report of the Committee Appointed to Examine the Question of Elections to the Legislative Council* (Kuala Lumpur: Government Printer, 1954), p. 40.

30. National Archives of Australia, NAA: A816, 19/321/18, Secret, "Movement towards Self-Government in Malaya", 23 September 1953, "L.R. McIntyre, Australian Commissioner in Singapore to Minister for External Affairs, Canberra".

31. CAB 129/76 CP (55) 81, "Federation of Malaya: Constitutional Developments. Cabinet Memorandum by Mr. Lennox-Boyd, 20 July 1955".

32. CAB 129/48, C (51) 59, "Malaya. Cabinet Memo by Mr. Lyttelton, Appendixes I – XV, 21 December 1951".

33. Harry Miller, *Jungle War in Malaya: The Campaign against Communism, 1946–60* (London: Arthur Barker, 1972), p. 25.

34. CO 1022/165, extract from *The Straits Budget*, 17 April 1952.

35. CO 537/4374, no. 3, "Notes on Tour of South-East Asia, October 1949. Report by Field Marshal Sir William Slim on the Importance of Civil Action in Counterinsurgency". Also CO 537/3741, no. 76, letter dated 5 December 1949, from Secretary of State for the Colonies to Sir Henry Gurney, High Commissioner, Federation of Malaya, deals with the points raised in Slim's report. See also Leon Comber, *Malaya's Secret Police 1945–60: The Role of the Special Branch in the Malayan Emergency* (Singapore: Institute of Southeast Asian Studies, 2008), reprint 2009, pp. 112–16.

36. Comber, op. cit., pp. 115–16.

37. See *Report on the Police Mission to Malaya* (Kuala Lumpur: Government Printer, 1950).

38. CO 1022/165, *The Times* (London), "Police Recruits in Malaya, 1 April 1952."
39. CO 1022/165, "Police Recruits in Malaya. Sir G. Templer's Call to Chinese, 31 March 1952".
40. See also Heren's article "Stalemate in Malaya" which appeared in *The Times* (London), 1 and 2 October 1953.
41. National Archives of Australia, NAA: A8816, 19/321/18, Malaya File 3, Top Secret, "Malaya: The Emergency", Australian Commissioner's Office, Singapore, to Department of External Affairs, Canberra, 4 December 1954.
42. CO 1022/85, no. 36, 18 November 1953, "Protection of Malayan Students from Undesirable Influences"; Hack, op. cit., p. 144; Adrian Threlfall, "The Malayan Emergency. A Historiographic Analysis", BA honours thesis, School of Social Science, Victoria University, 2003, p. 35; Susan L. Carruthers, *Winning Hearts and Minds. British Government, the Media and Colonial Counter-Insurgency, 1944–1960* (Leicester University Press, 1998), pp. 86–87, 120 n.74; Louis Heren, *Growing Up on the Times* (London: Hamish Hamilton, 1978); and *The Independent*, "Louis Heren's Obituary", 28 January 1995.

    Louis Heren was a good friend of S. Rajaratnam and had shared with him a translation of the 1 October 1951 CPM Directives which had come into his hands which formed the basis of his article in *The Times* that Templer had complained about. (See Irene Ng, op. cit., p. 522, fn. 24). Irene Ng writes that Rajaratnam had "approvingly" reproduced Heren's article in *The Standard*.
43. In 2013, Monsoon Books Pte Ltd, Singapore, reprinted a commemorative edition of Han Suyin's Malayan novel … *And the Rain My Drink*, after her death in Lausanne, Switzerland, in November 2012. It has two Forewords, one written by the author who was Han Suyin's husband at the time she wrote it, describing the genesis of the book and the sources of information she used for it, and the second by Professor Kirpal Singh discussing its literary merits. Further details concerning the genesis of the book and its aftermath are given in Cheong Suk-Wai's article in the *Straits Times* dated 3 January 2009.
44. CO 1022/165, *The Scotsman*, 16 February 1952, in which Michael Davidson, the newspaper's Special Correspondent in Singapore, referred to the Chinese aversion to serving in the Police as a constable as "degrading and underpaid".
45. Alexander Maxwell, J.F. Ferguson and R.L. Jackson, *Report of the Police Mission to Malaya* (Kuala Lumpur: Government Printer, 1950), pp. 10–12.
46. CO 1022/148, "The Organisation of Chinese Resistance to Communism in Malaya, Proposed by Tan Cheng Lock for Formation of a Secret Chinese Organisation to Combat Terrorism in Malaya (closed until 1983) and CO 1045/484, "Papers including Communist Influence in Chinese Schools in Malaya 1959". See also CAB 129/40, CP (50) 125, dated 13 June 1950,

"Preliminary Report on a visit to Malaya and Singapore: Cabinet Memorandum by Mr. Griffiths"; CAB 21/1681, MAL C (1950) 1, dated 17 June 1950, "The Military Situation in Malaya: Memorandum by Mr. Strachey for Cabinet Malaya Committee"; CAB 128/17, CM37 (50) 1, dated 19 June 1950, "Malayan Cabinet Conclusions on Reports by Mr. Griffiths and Mr. Strachey following their Visits to Malaya"; and CAB 21/1681, MAL C6 (50) 1, dated 19 June 1950, "The Civil Situation in Malaya: Cabinet Malayan Committee Minutes".

47. Lee Su Yin, *British Policy and the Chinese in Singapore, 1939 to 1955. The Public Service Career of Tan Chin Tuan* (Singapore, Talisman Publishing, 2011), p. 77.

48. Arkib Negara, Kuala Lumpur, SP/13/A/41, "Malayan Chinese Association. Scheme on Recruiting of Chinese into the Police Force for Submission to H.E. the High Commissioner; Malacca. Chinese Police Recruiting Campaign. Questions and Answers; and Recruitment of Chinese into the Police Force. Memorandum for the consideration of the Delegation to the Conference at King's House on Monday, 21 April 1952" and National Archives of Australia, NAA: A816, Cablegram, "MCA Plans for the recruitment of Chinese into the Malayan Police", 5 July 1952.

49. ISEAS Library, Tan Cheng Lock Private Papers Collection, TCL 3.274, 21 April 1952, "Meeting of MCA Reps. at Federal Executive Council Meeting Room". There was a large attendance at this important meeting including on the Government side: General Templer, General Lockhart (Deputy Director Operations), Colonel A.E. Young (Commissioner of Police), the Acting Secretary for Chinese Affairs (David Gray), and representing the MCA, Dato Sir Cheng Lock Tan, Colonel H.S. Lee, Tan Siew Sin, and Leong Yew Koh.

50. Ibid., "Letter from General Templer to Sir Cheng Lock Tan, 24 April 1952".

51. Heng Pek Khoon, *Chinese Politics in Malaysia: A History of the Malaysian Chinese Association* (Singapore: Oxford University Press, 1988), p. 125. ISEAS Library, Tun Sir Henry H.S. Lee Private Papers, HSL. 24.018a, "MCA Plan to recruit 2.000 Police Recruits".

In November 1950, before Templer's arrival, a National Service Bill was laid on the table covering conscription for military or para-military service for Malayan youths between the ages of eighteen and twenty-four which caused an outcry from the Chinese community. The Chinese press was most outspoken against the proposals. Tan Cheng Lock argued that Chinese traditionally own loyalty first and foremost to their family rather than to the nation (which would not have gone down very well with General Templer) and asked that the eldest and only sons of Chinese families should be exempt from national service. See Leon Comber, *13 May 1969: A Historical Survey of Sino-Malay Relations* (Kuala Lumpur: Heinemann Asia, 1983), p. 39.

52. Heng, op. cit., pp. 125–27.

53. Ibid., p. 122.
54. Karl Hack, *Defence and Decolonisation in Southeast Asia: Britain, Malaya and Singapore 1941–68* (Richmond, Surrey: Curzon Press, 2001), p. 145.
55. DEF 7/421, Commissioner General to Colonial Secretary, J. Griffiths, 9 August 1950.
56. Hack, op. cit.
57. Hack, op. cit. and Heng, op. cit., p. 12.
58. National Archives of Australia, NAA: A816, 19/321/18, Secret, "Singapore: The Federation Regiment", 12 August 1952, Australian Commissioner, Singapore, to Minister for External Affairs, Canberra.
59. Hack, op. cit.
60. National Archives of Australia, NAA: A816, 19/321/18, Secret, op. cit.
61. See Kwok Kian-Woon, Kwa Chong Kuan, Lily Kong, Brenda Yeoh, eds., *Our Place in Time* (Singapore: Singapore Heritage Society, 1999), p. 54.
62. Heng, op. cit., pp. 126–27.
63. See CO 229, T 220/282, ff. 211-212, "Aid to Malaya. Minute by A.H. Clough (Treasury) of a meeting between Mr Gaitskell and Mr Griffiths about UK financial assistance", 28 November 1950. The Federal Government of Malaya had already authorised the raising of four battalions of the Malay Regiment, and the Chiefs of Staff had recommended the raising of two more battalions. The first of these two extra battalions (5th Battalion) would be completed by about the end of 1951 and the other (6th Battalion) in 1952.
64. *Federation of Malaya Annual Report 1953*, op. cit., p. 325. See also CO 1022/100, "Gen. Templer's Programme for Malaya. Federation Regiment Planned"; and Denis Warner, *The Scotsman*, 20 March 1952. The financial cost of fighting the Communist insurgents soared from US$83,000 to over US$234,000 a day in 1953 and amounted to one-third of that year's Malayan annual federal expenditure. (See Cheah Boon Kheng, "The Communist Insurgency in Malaya, 1948–90: Contesting the National State and Social Change", *New Zealand Journal of Asian Studies* (1 June 2009), pp. 132–52.
65. "Report on the Special Committee appointed on the 20th September 1951 to Recommend Legislation to cover all aspects of Educational Policy for the Federation of Malaya", Kuala Lumpur: Government Printer, 1952, and *Education Ordinance*, No. 63 of 1952, Kuala Lumpur: Government Printer, 1952.
66. See *The Economic Development of Malaya: Report of a Mission organised by the International Bank for Reconstruction and Development at the request of the Governments of the Federation of Malaya, the Crown Colony of Singapore and the United Kingdom* (Singapore: Government Printer, September 1955), pp. 325–28; Norton Ginsburg & Chester F. Roberts, Jr, *Malaya* (Seattle: University of Washington Press, 1958), p. 157, 304–10; and Leon Comber, *Singapore Correspondent: Political Dispatches from Singapore (1958–1962)* ("Chinese Education in Malaya 1962"), op. cit., pp. 166–77.

67. Rupert Emerson, *Malaysia: A Study in Direct and Indirect Rule* (Kuala Lumpur: University of Malaya Press, 1966, reprint), p. 511.

68. Tan Cheng Lock, *Malayan Problems: From a Chinese Point of View* (Singapore: Tannsco, 1947), p. 76.

69. Heng, op. cit., pp. 191–200. See also Francis Wong Hoi Kee and Ee Tiang Hong, *Education in Malaya* (Hong Kong: Heinemann Educational Books (Asia) Ltd, 1971), pp. 52–53, and Comber, op. cit., p. 41.

70. *Chinese Schools and the Education of Chinese Malayans: The Report of a Mission Invited by the Federation Government to Study the Problem of the Education of Chinese in Malaya* (Kuala Lumpur: Government Press, 1951); Wong and Ee, op. cit., pp. 54–55; and W.R. Roff, *The Origins of Malay Nationalism* (Kuala Lumpur: University of Malaya Press, 1967), p. 49.

71. *Education Ordinance*, No. 63 of 1952 (Kuala Lumpur: Government Printer, 1952); Lee Ting Hui, *Chinese Schools in Peninsular Malaysia: The Struggle for Survival* (Singapore: Institute of Southeast Asian Studies, 2011), pp. 66–69; Leon Comber, *13 May 1969: A Historical Survey of Sino-Malay Relations* (Kuala Lumpur: Heinemann Asia, 1983), pp. 40–41; and Purcell, op. cit., p. 29. The best accounts of Chinese education issues at this point of time are Tan Liok Ee, *The Politics of Chinese Education* (Oxford: Oxford University Press, 1997) and Lee Ting Hui, op. cit.

72. ISEAS Library, Tan Cheng Lock Private Papers Collection, TCL.058. This file contains the speech "Chinese should have a worthy place in Malayan National Schools", that Tan gave (in English) at the Conference of Chinese School Committees and Teachers, Chinese Assembly Hall, Birch Road, Kuala Lumpur, on 20 April 1953.

73. Tan, *Malayan Problems*, op. cit., pp. 27–30.

74. Heng, op. cit., p. 198.

75. Lee Ting Hui, op. cit., p. 68. See also *Federation of Malaya Annual Report 1953*, op. cit., pp. 175–76.

76. Lee Ting Hui, op. cit.

77. ISEAS Library, Tan Cheng Lock Private Papers Collection, TCL.010, 14 August 1954, "Memo on Education Ordinance 1953, Federation of Malaya", addressed to Madame Vijavalakshmi Pandit, President, UN General Assembly.

78. ISEAS Library, Tan Cheng Lock Private Papers Collection, TCL. 70, 21 August 1954, Speech on "The Future of Chinese Education" by Tan at MCA Chinese Education Central Committee Meeting.

79. See *Straits Times*, "Malaysian Politics. Chinese schools press too far with demands", 27 April 2012, p. A 38.

80. CO 1022/100, Confidential, "General Templer's Address to the Legislative Council, 19 March 1952".

81. Kernial Singh Sandu, "The Saga of the New Villages", *Journal of Southeast Asian History* 5, no. 1 (March 1964), pp. 143–77.

82. See *Malay Reservation Enactment*, 1 January 1914, covering Perak, Selangor, Negri Sembilan. Similar enactments were later introduced in the other states of Kelantan, Terengganu, Kedah, Perlis and Johor. (See *Official Portal of Director General of Lands & Mines, Ministry of Natural Resources and Environment*). See also Sharon Md. Ariffin, "Malay Reservation Land — Unleashing a Century of Trust", *International Surveying Research Journal* 3, no. 2 (2013), pp. 1–28.

83. *The Economic Development of Malaya, Report of a Mission Organised by the International Bank for Reconstruction and Development* (Singapore: Government Printer, 1955), p. 226. See also Vernon Bartlett, *Report from Malaya* (London: Derek Verschoyle, 1954), pp. 104–105, and Mohamed Amin and Malcolm Caldwell (eds.), *Malaya. The Making of a Neo-Colony* (London: Spokesman Books Ltd, 1965), p. 251.

84. *The Economic Development of Malaya*, op. cit., pp. 223, 226.

85. Rupert Emerson, *Malaysia, A Study in Direct and Indirect Rule* (Kuala Lumpur: University of Malaya Press, 1966 reprint), pp. 478–79; *The Economic Development of Malaya*, op. cit., pp. 57–61, 227; R.D. Hill, *Rice in Malaya: A Study in Historical Geography* (Kuala Lumpur: Oxford University Press, 1977), pp. 45–46, 80–81, 112, 119, 122–25, 136–37, 196.

86. Bartlett, op. cit., p. 109.

87. Briggs Plan, Directive No. 13 (February 1951), see also T.N. Harper, *The End of Empire and the Making of Malaya* (London: Cambridge University Press, 1999), p. 185.

88. Purcell, op. cit., p. 245.

89. Mubin Sheppard (subsequently Tan Sri Dato Dr Mubin Sheppard) (1905–94), read history at Cambridge, and was appointed a Cadet Administrative Officer in the MCS in 1928. He filled many senior administrative posts in British colonial Malaya before and after World War II. During the campaign against the Japanese in World War II, he served as an officer in the Federated Malay States Volunteer Force and became a prisoner of war in Singapore for three-and-a-half years. He was a Malay scholar and on retiring from the British colonial service, he converted to Islam, adopted the name Mubin Sheppard, and decided to remain in Malaya. He wrote many books about Malayan culture and history including the authorized biography of Tunku Abdul Rahman, the first Prime Minister of Malaysia.

90. ISEAS Library, Tan Cheng Lock Private Papers Collection, TCL.5.3007, 12 September 1952.

91. See Harper, op. cit., pp. 275–79. The Arts House, Singapore (the former Singapore Parliament building) organized many years after he had left Singapore an exhibition about Donald Moore and his legacy ("Rediscovering Donald Moore: Singapore's Arts Pioneer") from 6 to 29 August 2014, at which the author was one of the speakers.

92. ISEAS Library, Tun Henry H.S. Lee Private Papers Collection, HSL.4.024/1, quoting *The Malay Mail*, 25 October 1952.
93. Heng, op. cit., p. 112–13.
94. ISEAS Library, Tan Cheng Lock Private Papers Collection, TCL.14.460/1-5, "Confidential letter dated 15 May 1953 from Tan Cheng Lock to General Templer".
95. ISEAS Library, Tun Sir Henry H.S. Lee, Private Papers Collection, HSL. 15.24. "Minutes MCA HQ 5th Cabinet Meeting. 5 October 1952".
96. Heng, op. cit., p. 128.
97. The Lady Templer Tuberculosis Hospital had rather a sad and chequered history. It was closed as a hospital in 1985 and then became the Poliklinic Cheras, a government medical clinic. In later years, the polyclinic was closed and the building was eventually abandoned and allowed to become run-down and derelict. It was reputed to be haunted.
98. ISEAS Library, Tan Cheng Lock Private Papers Collection, TCL. 8/37/1, "Letter dated (?) May 1954 from Lady Templer to Tan Cheng Lock appealing for funds for the Federation School for the Deaf".
99. Heng, ibid.
100. Cloake, op. cit., pp. 309–10 and Heng, op.cit., p. 146.
101. Tunku Abdul Rahman, *As a Matter of Interest* (Kuala Lumpur: Heinemann Asia, 1981), p. 65.
102. Cloake, op. cit., p. 316.
103. Harper, op. cit., pp. 97, 182, 185. There are several excellent studies of resettlement and New Villages in Malaya. A good, first-hand account, written by a missionary, of what it was like to live in a New Village in close proximity with the New Villagers (which is seldom referred to) is Amy McIntosh's, *Journey into Malaya* (London: China Inland Mission, 1956).
104. Lee Grieveson & Colin McCabe, eds., *End of Empire: Cultural Histories of Cinema* (London: British Film Institute, 2011). See also CO 537/657A, "Malayan Film Unit Proposed Reorganisation 1949–50".
105. At the time Onn inaugurated IMP in September 1951, he was a Government official and the Member for Home Affairs. (Purcell, op. cit., p. 99.)
106. ISEAS Library, Tan Cheng Lock Private Papers Collection, TCL. 9.33.1, "Letter 18 February 1952 from Colonel H.S. Lee re. MCA/UMNO co-operation in Kuala Lumpur Municipal Elections".
107. Ibid., "Letter 22 February 1952 from Colonel H.S. Lee to Tan Cheng Lock".
108. Tunku Abdul Rahman, *Viewpoints* (Kuala Lumpur: Heinemann Asia, 1978), p. 90.
109. Richard W. Stubbs, "UMNO, MCA and Early Years of the Malayan Emergency, 1948–55", paper presented at the Annual Conference of Canadian Society for Asian Studies, Laval University, Quebec, 28/29 May 1976, pp. 4 and 9.
110. ISEAS Library, Tan Sir Henry H.S. Lee Private Papers Collection, HSL.7.058,

The Fortnightly Press Digest, Department of Information Services, Federation of Malaya No. 4/52 for the period 16 February – 29 February 1952, reported a statement made by Tunku Abdul Rahman on 20 February 1952 that Malaya should be given "independence now" and have a date fixed for independence. See also Joseph M. Fernando, *The Alliance Road to Independence* (Kuala Lumpur: University of Malaya Press, 2009), p. 38.

For another view of the Tunku, this is what Tan Siew Sin, Tan Cheng Lock's son, said when the Tunku in due course became Malaya's first prime minister after General Templer's departure from Malaya, "in the last analysis what converted not me but many other Chinese, was your [the Tunku's] magnificent leadership. It is no exaggeration to say that had anyone but you been at the helm of the Alliance in the early years of independence, the history of Malaya, and later Malaysia, could well have been different." (See Tunku Abdul Rahman Putra al-Haj, *Looking Back* [Kuala Lumpur: Pustaka Antara, 1977], pp. 175–81).

111. See Parkinson, "Preface", op. cit.
112. In 1955, the year after General Templer left Malaya, the Emergency was costing M$150 million per anum, that is a quarter of Malaya's national income, which drew on funds that could otherwise have been used for the building of hospitals, schools and roads.
113. See the official journal of the Singapore Armed Forces (POINTER, "Personality Profile, General Templer," 29, no. 4 (2003)) in which he is described as having "a sharp tongue and ruthless efficiency". Field Marshal Lord Carver described him as "A martinet in appearance and manner — his displeasure — even his presence was intimidating". See "Templer, Sir Gerald Walter Robert", *Oxford Dictionary of National Biography* (Oxford: Oxford University Press, 2004); "Criticism of Templer" in Anthony Short, *The Communist Insurrection in Malaya 1948–60* (London: Frederick Muller Ltd, 1975), pp. 379–87 (reprinted by Cultured Lotus Press as *In Pursuit of Mountain Rats*); and V. Osipov, "Templer Loses His Temper", *Soviet Press Translations* 8, no. 3 (1953).
114. Cloake, op. cit., pp. 175 and 450.
115. *Straits Times*, "Templer was a tired man", 17 April 1952.
116. National Army Museum, Chelsea, ACC: 8301-6, "Correspondence of Major D.L. Lloyd Owen as Military Assistant to High Commissioner, Malaya, March 1952–September 1953, Secret and Personal letter to Lieutenant General Nevil Brownjohn, KBE, CB, CMG, CBE, dated 9 June 1952".
117. R.V. Jones, *Reflections on Intelligence* (London: Mandarin Publishers, 1990), p. 23.

4

VICTOR PURCELL AND FRANCIS CARNELL, HONORARY MCA POLITICAL ADVISERS, AUGUST–SEPTEMBER 1952

On 12 June 1952, Mrs B.H. Oon, a prominent member of the Penang MCA Branch, unofficial member of the Federal Legislative Council, and a partner of the well-known Penang law firm, Lim, Lim and Oon, wrote to Colonel H.S. Lee to enclose a copy of a letter she had received from Dr Victor Purcell in the United Kingdom to say he and a colleague would welcome an invitation from the MCA to visit Malaya "in order to correct certain misleading reports and ill-informed criticisms that had appeared in the press in Britain" and to ascertain the facts about the present position of the Malayan Chinese. Mrs Oon said that she read out Dr Purcell's letter at a meeting of the Penang MCA Branch on 17 May and had sent a copy of it to the MCA President, Tan Cheng Lock, and she hoped it would be possible for the MCA to extend an official invitation to him and his colleague, Francis G. Carnell, a lecturer in Colonial Government at Oxford University, to come to Malaya.

Dr Purcell was an old friend of the Malayan Chinese who had specialized in Chinese Affairs during his long service with the Malayan Civil Service (MCS) (1922–46). He spoke Cantonese and Mandarin and had held a number of senior appointments in the Chinese Affairs Department, and was internationally recognized as a scholar and sinologue.[1] On retiring from Malaya, he was employed by the United Nations as Secretary of the Working Group of 12 Nations on Asia and the Far East, and had last visited Malaya in 1947 and 1950.

On receiving Mrs Oon's letter, Tan Cheng Lock discussed the matter with his colleagues and it was agreed to send an invitation to Dr Purcell and Francis Carnell to visit Malaya as honorary MCA advisers, and shortly afterwards they arrived in Malaya on a short visit from 20 August to 20 September 1952. However, much occurred during their short visit, and it was little realized at the time how contentious it would be.

REACTIONS TO PURCELL'S AND CARNELL'S VISIT

Not long after their arrival, the UMNO Perak Branch concluded an annual two-day meeting behind closed doors to express its concern about the visit and it issued a press release as follows:

> This assembly views with concern the intention to instigate an investigation by Dr Purcell into the conditions of the Chinese in this country without at the same time investigating the conditions of other communities. This assembly resolved that it is not proper for Dr Purcell who is in receipt of a pension from this country to visit this country in the direct interest of a section of the people. The assembly resolves that any report confined to the conditions of one community only will prejudice the position of other communities here in the eyes of the world and will lead to racial disharmony.[2]

If anything, this reaction brings out how essentially fragile the relationship was between UMNO and MCA, or to put it another way, the Malays and the Chinese communities, although the personal relationship between the leaders of the two communal parties, Tunku Abdul Rahman and Tan Cheng Lock, was good.

The MCA immediately issued a statement to clarify the situation and said that the UMNO Perak Branch had completely misunderstood the situation and Tan Siew Sin, Tan Cheng Lock's son and Chairman of the MCA's Central Publicity Committee, explained that the main purpose of

Purcell's visit was to promote better cooperation between the Chinese and the Malays and it was in no sense a "mission", and its main purpose was to "enable its honorary adviser [the emphasis was on Purcell rather than Carnell, who was not so well known in Malaya] to inform himself of the up-to-date position in Malaya so he could correct on his return to the United Kingdom any misunderstandings that may have arisen".[3] In a personal note to Tan Cheng Lock on 21 August, the day following Purcell's arrival, Tunku Abdul Rahman wrote to say that he had seen in the newspapers reports of the arrival of Purcell and Carnell in Singapore and he was rather concerned as

> many Malays including myself consider that Mr Purcell, to say the least, is hardly sympathetic to the Malay people.... We have endeavoured to the best of our ability to strike up an alliance with the Chinese people of Malaya and in certain directions we have succeeded.

The Tunku added that it was

> his greatest hope that Malays and Chinese in Malaya would come to a complete understanding of each other and that without knowing the purpose of the MCA in inviting Purcell and his political adviser to Malaya, he was concerned that Purcell's visit would create misunderstanding between our two peoples

which he had so far tried to avoid.[4]

Tan replied by return that he had sent a telegram to Purcell to ask him to reassure the Tunku of his good intentions in coming to Malaya and that his main purpose was to advise the MCA on the best way to achieve "our aim of affecting the best cooperation between our two communities and between the Chinese and the governments of the Federation of Malaya and Singapore". He added that he had already had a talk with Mohammed Sopiee on the subject on 23 August and had given an interview about Purcell's and Carnell's visit to the Malay press.[5] He said that Purcell was a Professor at Cambridge University and had been invited to Malaya to obtain up-to-date information for his work in the United Kingdom on behalf of the MCA. He had known him for twenty-eight years, and that Purcell spoke Malay as well as Chinese, and he did "not think he was anti-Malay at all".[6]

Purcell himself said he had come to Malaya in a purely private capacity at the invitation of the MCA and that he and Carnell were

> not confining themselves to obtaining information as to the opinions of one section of the community but are interested to ascertain the views of

every section. We are therefore meeting the Malay, Chinese and Indian party leaders wherever they may be and government officials.[7]

But all the various explanations that were necessary at the beginning of Purcell's visit only served to reinforce the fragile nature of ethnic relations that existed in Malaya at the time. Purcell's and Carnell's visit to Malaya as honorary advisers to the MCA undoubtedly brought about many problems in its wake involving Tan Cheng Lock and the MCA with General Templer, as well as the relationship between the MCA and many of Templer's senior Government officials, which came to a head with the interview Purcell and Carnell later had with General Templer at King's House, Kuala Lumpur. It was at this meeting that Purcell was to allege that General Templer transgressed the normally accepted boundaries of good manners and courtesy and was extremely unpleasant and rude to him. Purcell was clearly greatly incensed at his treatment and never forgave General Templer for the discourteous way in which he alleged he had been received. He complained to Tan about it, too, and on his return to the United Kingdom, he attacked Templer in the press and various magazine articles. Purcell used his book, *Malaya: Communist or Free?*, published in 1954 in the United States by Stanford University Press under the prestigious auspices of the Institute of Pacific Relations, which rolled off the press just as Templer left Malaya, to criticize Templer and his policy in Malaya, and though in parts it may be coloured by Purcell's animus, it cannot be disregarded.

PURCELL'S AND CARNELL'S MALAYAN REPORT

After visiting Bangkok, Rangoon, Calcutta and Rome on his way back to Cambridge, Purcell wrote to Tan Cheng Lock on 7 October 1952 to thank him for the warm welcome that had been extended to him and Carnell by the MCA, and for being invited to Tan's Malacca home which he described as "one of the stately homes of Malaya". But he said that as regards the "general situation [in Malaya], Carnell and myself were definitely depressed" by what they had seen and that further detailed impressions would be sent to Tan by "safe hand".[8]

Their subsequent report was sent to Tan some time later after their return to the United Kingdom, and it may be appropriate to examine it at this stage as it provides an interesting account of their month-long visit to Malaya, their impressions and comments on what they had seen, as well as an account of their meeting with General Templer at King's

House, Kuala Lumpur, where they allege they were so rudely received by him.

In their report, they said their visit had been excellently arranged by the MCA and they had received a warm welcome throughout their stay in Malaya from the Chinese community.[9] They had had a "unique opportunity to meet representatives of several Malayan [sic] communities and ascertain by personal observation the present state of the country and at the same time provide the Chinese with an opportunity to take stock of their own situation". They went on to say: "We cannot presume to influence MCA policy, which is purely a matter for their own members, but we can indicate the probable effect of alternative lines of policy on opinion in Britain and overseas generally." Their main impression was that the

> Chinese community is vital and active as ever and likely to retain in future a [more] leading position in the Malayan economy than it has enjoyed in the past. In spite of some controversial issues, the Chinese are more united than either the Malays or Indians. The MCA discharges a vital function especially in the Federation in providing a communal organisation for the discussion of matters of political, social and economic interest and for representing the Chinese point of view to the Government and public. So long as Malaya remains communally divided and as long as other communal bodies exist MCA will have an important part to play in Malaya's life.[10]

They then commented on what they regarded as "certain disturbing features" which they had noticed during their time in Malaya, and provided an account of matters that had been taken up during their interview with General Templer.

THE CONSTITUTION

In general, Purcell and Carnell had formed the view there was "a lack of opportunity [for the Chinese] to participate in the administration, an inequality of citizenship and land tenure, and the fundamental principle of equality in citizenship had not yet been accepted".

They considered that the method of increasing citizenship by defining "subjects of Sultans" [sic] was open to serious objection as it tended "to perpetuate state boundaries and reinforce the theory that Malaya is primarily a 'Malay country'". Though in voting for the National Federation Bill, Chinese members showed compromise, and Purcell and Carnell considered "they would have been justified in walking out of the Chamber".

From their conversations with General Templer and some leading Malays, they obtained the impression that this "concession to the Chinese was expected to satisfy them [the Chinese] indefinitely". General Templer had made it clear to them that "any concessions made by the Malays to the Chinese were insisted on by him as a major political expediency in order to assist in the end of the Emergency". He said he "was not interested in long-term objectives" and he showed "a complete lack of sympathy with Chinese aspirations, and that while the Federal Constitution was undoubtedly as bad as it could be [that is, an obstruction to his administration], he would not have a finger laid on it since it might offend the Malays who are bearing ninety-eight per cent of the brunt in fighting the Communists". He added: "if we give the Chinese an inch they will take all." It was clear, Purcell and Carnell contended, that "whatever promises he [Templer] may make, Chinese have little to hope for from the present High Commissioner and his statements should be treated with circumspection and reserve."[11]

THE SQUATTERS

Purcell and Carnell said they had visited a number of New Villages in Selangor, Negri Sembilan, and Kedah during their stay, and Purcell visited, too, Permatang Tinggi in Province Wellesley. They said that conditions varied in relation to the qualities of the resettlement officers and the length of time the New Villages had been established. While Chinese-speaking MCS (Malayan Civil Service) officers and the "better resettlement officers" were able to understand the problems of the villagers and make friends with them, the administration as a whole was largely out of touch with them. This problem was partly due to the lack of Chinese-speaking European officers and the failure to appoint persons of Chinese race to the MCS. Though no doubt Templer would insist on the appointment of a few Chinese, they felt that the Government Chinese-language school at Cameron Highlands [which provided short courses in spoken Hokkien and Cantonese] could do little to improve the situation, and "although General Templer may appoint a few Chinese to the MCS this is unlikely to take place on a scale that will make any real difference as long as the Federal Constitution remains in force", leaving the power and the bulk of the administration in the hands of the Malays, and "the grievances of the Chinese are likely to continue". Aside from ignorance or prejudice on the part of Malay district officers and police, "it is too much to expect they will of their own accord allocate to the Chinese squatters land of quality and quantity that will suffice for their needs".

The MCA is doing work of high importance in the New Villages and this work should be extended and developed.[12]

PUNITIVE MEASURES TAKEN BY GENERAL TEMPLER

Purcell and Carnell doubted whether the harsh punitive measures imposed by Templer were justified, such as the imposition of curfews, the cutting back of food supplies, and the closing of schools, in various villages especially Tanjong Malim, Permatang Tinggi, Broga, and Pekan Jabbi where the villagers were suspected of helping the Communist terrorists and withholding information from the Government. But in their view Templer was fortunate that his punitive action, which attracted intense public disquiet, was supported by Lyttelton, the Colonial Secretary in London, who in reply to a question raised by a member of the House of Commons, described them as being "most useful" and that Templer had acted with his full support.[13] Lyttelton said that by imposing curfews the security forces were aided in their operations, and the cutting back of rice supplies and strict rationing prevented rice from being supplied to the Communist terrorists. Lyttelton described "Operation Question", introduced by General Templer, which required villagers to complete a questionnaire form to provide information in complete confidence to the authorities about Communist terrorists in their locality, as being "successful". However, the usefulness of this method was disputed by senior Colonial Office officials such as T.C. Jerrom, a Principal Secretary, who minuted to J.D. Higham, Assistant Secretary, Head of South East Asia Department, that the questionnaire method used by Templer had been a "flop" [sic] and "no useful information had been provided". Moreover, it did not seem to have been realized by Templer that most of the Chinese villagers were in any case illiterate and not able to read or write and, even if they had wanted to, they would not be able to complete the questionnaires they had been given.[14]

Collective punitive measures were first used by Templer at Tanjong Malim in March 1952, not long after he arrived at Malaya, when a party led by the Assistant District Officer, Michael Codner, which was on its way to repair the village water supply pipeline, was ambushed by Communist terrorists and Codner was killed. Codner was one of the heroes of the "Wooden Horse" escape from a German prisoner-of-war camp in World

War II. Templer visited the village under a heavy army escort, lashed out at its inhabitants, and imposed a twenty-hour house curfew, the confiscation of all surplus rice, and the introduction of a strict rice rationing scheme, which remained in force for thirteen days.[15]

At Permatang Tinggi, a small village in Province Wellesley, where a Chinese Resettlement officer had been shot dead in a coffee shop by Communist terrorists, Templer had used the ultimate collective punishment imposed by the Government under Regulation 17D of the Emergency Regulations, which allowed for collective detention followed by deportation to China. When he visited the village in an armoured car under heavy army escort on 22 August 1952, he harangued its sixty-two inhabitants and gave them three days in which to provide information about the killing. He said:

> None of you will leave your houses. If you want food, you can ask the policeman to buy it for you. ... if you have not given the information in your possession by next Monday, I shall apply Emergency Regulation 17D to every inhabitant in this village.... Maintain your silence and you will go into detention — everyone, man, woman and child.[16] If you cooperate, but are afraid of communist vengeance, we will resettle you elsewhere. It is your duty to help your Government.

The Police visited each house during the curfew period but no one would talk and the questionnaire forms left with each family were returned blank.

On 25 August, the inhabitants were removed to the Ipoh Detention Camp, and their houses and shophouses were razed to the ground. At the end of the year, however, a number of the detainees were released and thirty-nine of them who wished to do so were resettled in a model New Village a short distance away from the former Permatang Tinggi.[17]

Purcell said he had made careful enquiries of what had happened at Permatang Tinggi and the general belief among Chinese of nearby Penang and Province Wellesley was that it was an "inside job". Purcell said this could not be proved either way but assuming it was true, no threat of detention would persuade villagers to convict themselves of the crime.[18]

As Templer's biographer points out, Templer cancelled Emergency Regulation 17D in his speech to the Legislative Council on 18 March 1953.[19] This may well have been due to questions being asked in the House of Commons about such punitive measures but it is noticeable that thereafter Templer used milder forms of collective punishment even in "bad" villages.

On 23 August 1953, A.M. MacKintosh, an Assistant Secretary in the Colonial Office, minuted that the abolition of Regulation 17D of the Emergency Regulations (for mass detention) should help to rebut further the charges of a "military regime in Malaya and of personal ruthlessness on the part of General Templer which are so often levelled out of ignorance or malice". Nevertheless it was difficult to allay the widespread impression the imposition of punitive action had already made.[20]

MEETING WITH GENERAL TEMPLER AT
KING'S HOUSE, KUALA LUMPUR

According to Purcell's and Carnell's report of their meeting with General Templer, which is corroborated by Cloake's account of what happened, Templer summoned Purcell and Carnell to see him at King's House, Kuala Lumpur, and "took an instant dislike to them and he lashed out at them" for what they were doing in Malaya and accused them of meddling in local politics.

According to Cloake, Templer told Purcell that "he had done more harm in a few days than all the Communists and enemies of this country put together, in so far as things I have been attempting to achieve since my arrival are concerned".[21]

Purcell was taken to task by Templer, too, for making statements that were taken up by the local press that the Chinese were being discriminated against and that they should stand up for the own rights against the threat of Malay domination. Carnell, for his part, had proposed a new political model for Malaya which involved dividing the country into three separate states, two of which would have clear Malay majorities and the third a clear Chinese majority.

Purcell asked Templer why he did not deport him if he was such a harmful influence and Templer replied that if he did so, it would have the effect of giving more importance to him than he deserved.[22]

Alec Peterson, Secretary General of the Government Information Services, asked Templer later whether as Purcell claimed, he had descended to crudities by describing Purcell as looking like "a fat white pig", and Templer gave a "roguish look" and replied, "Of course, I didn't — but he *did* look like a fat white pig, didn't he?"[23]

It is apparent, however, that Templer must have been disturbed by Purcell's and Carnell's visit, as he wrote to Lyttelton, the Colonial Secretary in London, as follows:

> The press in Malaya, both British and vernacular, was full of mischief as a result of the arrival of these two gentlemen [Purcell and Carnell]. The many articles and letters [written by Purcell after he returned to the United Kingdom] contained more vitriol in the shape of inter-communal trouble between Malays and Chinese than during the whole of the six and-a-half months I have been here.[24]

But the crux of the matter was that the "chemistry" between the two men was not good. Yet if things had been different they could perhaps have sorted out their disagreements as they both shared attributes in common. Purcell, like Templer, had been an infantry officer and had fought in World War I in France where he had been badly wounded twice and had become a prisoner-of-war of the Germans; he had also served again in the army during World War II, so army ways were not alien to him. There is little doubt that each in his own way had the welfare and political future of Malaya at heart but it was unfortunate that they approached the problem from different perspectives — Templer perhaps as an "imperialist" and Purcell as a sinologue — which made it difficult for their views to converge.

There is no doubt, however, that Templer had made an intractable enemy of Purcell and when Purcell and Carnell returned to the United Kingdom after their fact-finding visit to Malaya, Purcell embarked on a series of articles which were published in the press and leading magazines that were extremely critical of Templer and his administration.[25] Hogan, the Malayan Attorney General, whom Templer had asked to consider whether what Purcell had written about him in *Twentieth Century* constituted libel, offered the view that it contained "seventy-seven different lies or libels" but although Templer asked the Colonial Office to obtain counsel's opinion with a view to taking legal proceedings against Purcell, there is no record of any further action being taken.[26]

As a political scientist, Carnell's visit provided him with ample material for a series of academic papers he wrote , such as, "Communalism and Communism", "The Malayan Elections", and "Constitutional Reforms and Elections in Malaya", all of which appeared in *Pacific Affairs* (University of British Columbia) between June 1953 and December 1955, and several other articles.

TEMPLER'S RELATIONS WITH THE PRESS

Templer does not appear to have had an easy relationship with the press and he was inclined to treat reporters as if he was an army officer providing an

Tan Cheng Lock (President, MCA), Tunku Abdul Rahman and David Marshall (Chief Minister, Singapore) at the Baling Talks (28 December 1955). Courtesy of National Archives of Malaysia.

Dinner given for General Templer by Tan Cheng Lock at his ancestral home at Heeren Street, Malacca, in 1952. Front row: Tan Cheng Lock, General Templer, Lady Templer, Mrs Tan Cheng Lock. Courtesy of National Archives of Malaysia.

Dr Han Suyin presenting a cheque for M$4,000 to Tunku Abdul Rahman for a Malay student studying engineering at the University of Malaya (22 November 1966). Courtesy of National Archives of Malaysia.

Dato' Onn bin Ja'afar (1952). Courtesy of National Archives of Malaysia.

Sir Donald MacGillivray presiding over a Federal Legislative Council meeting, Kuala Lumpur (1955). Courtesy of National Archives of Malaysia.

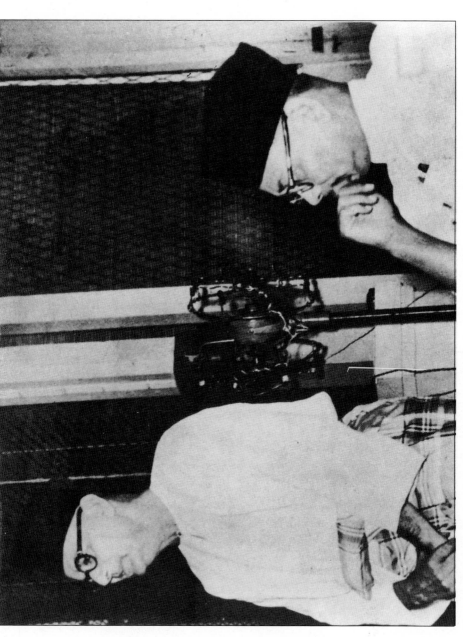

Dato' Onn bin Ja'afar (standing) and Tunku Abdul Rahman at the Majestic Hotel, Kuala Lumpur, when Dato' Onn resigned the Presidency of UMNO (1951). Courtesy of National Archives of Malaysia.

Plenary Conference for Constitutional Proposals for Malaya, King's House, Kuala Lumpur (20 November 1946). Centre front row: Malcolm MacDonald (Governor General, Malaya, and later Commissioner General for the United Kingdom in South East Asia) with Sir Edward Gent (Governor of Malaya) on his right, with Malay Sultans and other senior administrators. Courtesy of National Archives of Malaysia.

HRH The Duchess of Kent and her son HRH The Duke of Kent and General Sir Gerald Templer, King's House, Kuala Lumpur (5 October 1952). Courtesy of National Archives of Malaysia.

Kinta Valley Home Guard on firing range near Batu Gajah (1952). Courtesy of National Archives of Malaysia.

Launch of Tunku Abdul Rahman's book, *Viewpoints*, at the E & O Hotel, Penang (1978). On the Tunku's left, Leon Comber and General Tan Sri Tunku Osman Tunku Mohammed Jewa, first Malaysian Armed Forces Chief of Staff. Courtesy of *The Star*.

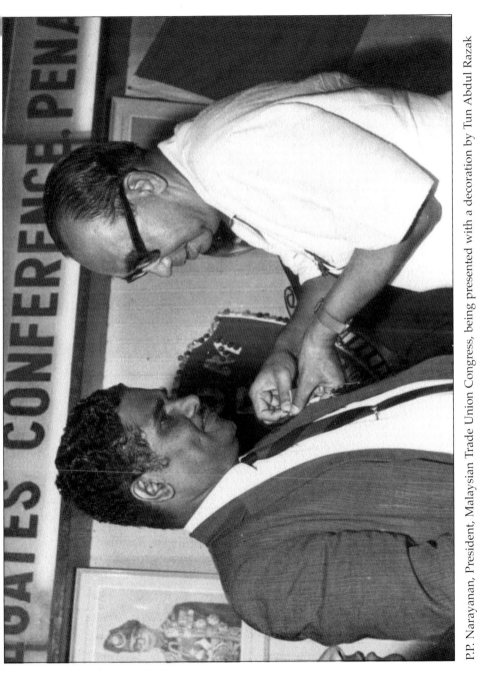

P.P. Narayanan, President, Malaysian Trade Union Congress, being presented with a decoration by Tun Abdul Razak (1966). Courtesy of National Archives of Malaysia.

Lieutenant General Sir Harold Briggs, the originator of the Briggs Plan. Courtesy of The Royal Malaysian Police Retired Officers Association, United Kingdom.

Lee Meng (Lee Tien Tai), the "Grenade Girl". A member of the CPM's Perak State Committee, whose arrest and sentencing to death became an international *cause célèbre*. Courtesy of Department of Information, Kuala Lumpur.

official briefing of a military operation. For instance, when S. Rajaratnam[27] passed stricture on him in an editorial he wrote for the *Singapore Standard* on 28 March 1952 and criticized him for the harsh punitive action he had imposed on inhabitants of Tanjong Malim for failing to provide information about Communist terrorists, General Templer summoned him from Singapore to Kuala Lumpur to explain what he had written.[28] According to Rajaratnam, Templer kept him waiting for two hours outside his office before seeing him and then proceeded to lambast him for what he had written. "There were no niceties and not even a chair to sit on", Rajaratnam recalled, and during their conversation Templer rested his foot on the open drawer of his desk in which he had conspicuously placed a revolver. Rajaratnam tried to explain that he was a journalist and not a Communist and that he had not written with any malicious intent. But he was left in no doubt that his anti-colonial views were not acceptable to Templer.[29]

The Observer (London) reported on 22 June 1952 under the heading "His Excellency" that after having spent four-and-a-half months in Malaya in tackling a situation what was at once both political and military,

> Sir Gerald Templer still insists that he is a soldier. The half-hour statement he made at the Colonial Office last week to his packed press conference (the biggest ever held at the Colonial Office) was like an eve-of-action briefing. But he struggled manfully to rid himself of his soldierly dislike of the press, one of his functional drawbacks when he was first appointed High Commissioner. He has not yet learned, however, the good politician's technique for dealing with hostile questions. When the *Daily Worker* man asked loaded questions about the "Liberation Army" (meaning the Communist terrorists), Mr Lyttelton, sitting next to Templer, at once smiled round for the conference's support. Templer, on the other hand, went for his opponent, wrapped his knuckles on the table, as if he had been personally insulted. Templer's emotions (he is a very highly strung man) have plainly become involved in Malaya's plight. However sound his political judgement may prove to be, this general can certainly evoke admiration and sympathy from an audience of press men.[30]

Perhaps another indication of General Templer's dealings with the press may be obtained from the following excerpt from a statement he made to the Malayan press on 4 July 1952 July on his return to Kuala Lumpur from one of his visits to London.

I have been given to understand that, as a result of the first meeting
of editors which I held a very few days after my appointment last
February, you came to the conclusion that either I was trying to muzzle
the press or alternately, that I was the sort of person who would be
likely to attempt to do so. I can assure you that I am not, and I hope
now that I have been here a few months longer that you realise it.
I have, however, one request to make to you today. It may occasionally
happen (it has, in fact, happened on one or two occasions since I have
been out here) that something about which I and the Government feel
strongly is misrepresented in the press or in a certain newspaper or
newspapers, perhaps through lack of proper understanding of the real
facts of the case. In such a case, it may be that we feel so strongly about
it that we wish our case to at least to be printed. In such a position, the
Chief Secretary would send to the paper or papers concerned a short
statement and ask that it be published. In these cases, and I think they
would arise extremely seldom, I would ask you to do what we want.
How you comment on that statement, whether in an editorial or not, is
then of course entirely your affair, but from the Government's point of
view it has ensured that our point of view has at the same time been
printed. I don't think I am unreasonable in what I ask.[31]

Yet in the following year, Templer treated Abdul Aziz bin Ishak, a
journalist, in some aspects in rather a similar fashion to what he had
done to Rajaratnam. Aziz was the brother of Yusof bin Ishak, who became
Singapore's first Yang di Pertuan Negara (Head of State),[32] and had been
invited to attend the coronation of Queen Elizabeth II in London as a
representative of the *Utusan Melayu,* the most important Malay-language
newspaper in Malaya and as a member of the Federal Legislative Council.
In the article Aziz wrote for the *Utusan Melayu* after his return from London,
he commented on Winston Churchill, the British Prime Minister, sitting
down on two occasions when he should have been standing, and he made
other critical comments about members of the British establishment who
were attending the coronation.

On his return to Kuala Lumpur, Templer summoned him to King's
House to explain what he had written, and when Aziz attempted to clarify
that he only wrote what he observed, he gave him a tongue lashing and
called him "a rat, and a rotten journalist whose name stinks in Southeast
Asia".[33] Templer challenged him to publish what he had said and Aziz
did so in the *Singapore Standard.* Templer afterwards explained that he was
referring to Aziz as a journalist and not as a Legislative Councillor but Aziz

became something of a Malay folk-hero on account of his confrontation with Templer.[34]

But the matter did not rest there. On 6 July 1953, the matter was raised in the House of Commons by Maurice Edelman, Labour MP for Coventry North, who asked Lyttelton, the Colonial Secretary, whether "the abusive and intemperate language used by General Templer was considered fitting and designed to promote a liberal attitude in Malaya". Lyttelton replied that "a High Commissioner could not, when provoked, be expected to use parliamentary language."[35]

RELATIONS WITH THE MALAYS

In their report, Purcell and Carnell considered that UMNO was far from being representative of the Malays as a whole. They were probably referring to the party IMP formed by Dato' Onn who had relinquished the leadership of UMNO after unsuccessfully attempting to change it into a multi-ethnic Party. Purcell and Carnell said they regarded Malay opinion as "confused and divided" and commented that the Mentris Besar and their staffs they had met privately "confessed to us the ineffectiveness of UMNO". Purcell and Carnell did not seem to realize, however, that the function of Mentri Besar was to reflect the views of their Sultans, some of whom regarded UMNO as a threat to their status as hereditary rulers. According to Purcell and Carnell, the real danger was that if British control was removed, the country would be ruled by the Armed Forces and the Police who were predominantly Malay and not multi-ethnic, "and Malays would obtain a share of the economic growth which they have been unable to obtain in economic competition with the Chinese".

FUNDAMENTAL CHINESE WEAKNESSES

Purcell and Carnell did not have much new to offer in their report under this heading that had not already been said elsewhere. They referred to the under-representation of the Chinese in the security forces for which in their opinion one of the reasons was that the rates of pay offered did not match what they could earn in the private sector.

The MCA's plans for assisting the Government to encourage the Chinese to join the Armed Forces and Police were announced after Purcell and Carnell had left Malaya but, rather surprisingly, they did not refer to Tan Cheng Lock's plan to "use Chinese to fight Chinese" which he had submitted to Lyttelton and the former High Commissioner, Sir Henry Gurney, before Templer's arrival. Perhaps they were rather off the mark, too, when they suggested in their report that "the Kinta Valley Home Guard to which the basic Government pay is augmented by Chinese associations were not likely to go far towards solving the problem". As will be described in the next chapter, the Kinta Valley Home Guard received financial and material support from Templer to supplement the funding provided by the Kinta Valley Chinese tin miners who were in the main MCA members, which did have some effect in bringing about at least the beginning of an understanding between Templer and his Government, and the MCA.

CHINESE EDUCATION

Purcell and Carnell said they had studied the Barnes and Fenn-Wu Reports and the Report of the Committee of the Federal Legislative Council on Education Policy and supported the fear of the Chinese that the teaching of Chinese in Malayan schools was endangered by the Government's policy, and shared their resentment about the unequal salaries that were paid to teachers in English and Chinese schools. Perhaps Purcell may have elaborated further under this heading, however, as he had had valuable experience as a Chinese Affairs officer attached to the Education Department to supervise Chinese schools during his earlier career in Malaya and was well placed to give his views from this perspective. It was correct, however, that in Malaya's plural society, education and language have always been important aspects of cultural distinctiveness and any attempt to take responsibility from the Chinese community for them was regarded as a threat to their cultural identity.

CHINESE POLITICAL OBJECTIVES IN MALAYA

Purcell and Carnell considered it highly important that the MCA should continue to "conciliate the Malays" and in their view MCA policy in Malaya "should be directed towards the creation of a Malayan nation based on a strong assertive Malayan consciousness to bring about a democratic self-governing Malaya". An underlying problem which perhaps Purcell and Carnell could have mentioned too, was that Templer's policy which tended to favour Malays over other ethnicities in business, appointment to the Civil Service, and politics, was probably based on his interpretation of the Directive he had been given by the British Government, though they did not seem to have had the opportunity to discuss this with him.

In general, as Purcell and Carnell commented, Onn's IMP had not succeeded in attracting either Malay or Chinese support and they did not consider it a potent political force, and they added "neither had Communism made any inroads in winning over Malay support".

In regard to a suggestion that Tan Cheng Lock had made to them, Purcell and Carnell said they did not recommend it was necessary for the MCA to establish a representative office in London at this stage but they considered, if and when it was necessary to do so, a very appropriate person to fill the appointment would be Chang Min-Tat, a Malayan Chinese, who had recently graduated from Oxford.[36]

They confirmed that the only expenses they contemplated for the immediate future were secretarial and incidental ones, and the sum they had in hand for these expenses was sufficient for the time being.

The Purcell and Carnell report illuminates the political situation as they saw it during their visit to Malaya as honorary MCA advisers, as well as providing details of their unfortunate *contretemps* with General Templer. In some aspects, however, considering Purcell's background, he was perhaps understandably pro-MCA and critical of UMNO and Malay aspirations, which would tend to bear out the reservations about their visit expressed earlier by the UMNO Perak Branch and Tunku Abdul Rahman himself in his letter to Tan Cheng Lock referred to earlier.

Meanwhile, Alec Peterson, Director General of Information Services, in the first of several official reactions to Purcell's and Carnell's visit, wrote to Tan Cheng Lock on 20 December 1952 to take up with him several matters that were contained in a series of articles that Purcell had written for *The Times* (London) and the *Daily Telegraph* which were highly critical of New Villages in Malaya. T.H. Tan, the Secretary General of the MCA, replied on behalf of Tan Cheng Lock on 29 December to say that "Dr Purcell did not consult the MCA in formulating his views and these views cannot necessarily represent the views of the MCA: they represented his personal opinion," and pointed out that "Dr Purcell is not described [in them] as our Honorary Adviser in the U.K.".[37]

It was clear, however, that Tan Cheng Lock's reply did not satisfy Templer, and R.H. Oakley, the Acting Secretary for Chinese Affairs, wrote to Tan again on 5 January 1953 to say that he had been instructed by General Templer to take up with him a recent letter "Dr Purcell, Honorary Adviser to the MCA" had written to *The Times* (London) dealing with the resettlement of villagers in Malaya. He said that the Government "was anxious that resettlement in the New Villages should be regarded as a success as the Government had been pouring money into them to improve them and provide them with the necessary amenities." He continued that he was "surprised that the MCA, which has been an ally of the Government", and providing funds to improve the New Villages, should so "belittle the Government's efforts", especially as the New Villages had been provided with piped water, electric light, and police protection, and Red Cross and other social workers had been assigned to them to alleviate the lot of the New Villagers.

Oakley went on to ask whether Tan could

> consider writing a letter to *The Times* describing the progress that had been made in the New Villages and the part the MCA had played in it which would help to remove the general impression created by Dr Purcell's letter that the MCA and its distinguished President supported the local Communist propaganda and that New Villages are nothing more than detention camps.[38]

It would appear that Tan did not immediately reply to Oakley's letter but instead sent a copy of it to Colonel H.S. Lee for his comments. Lee replied that he was not in Malaya at the time of Purcell's visit but he gathered there were "some unfortunate feelings and personal disappointment in Purcell's mind which probably resulted in certain parts of his letter to the London *Times*". He referred, in particular, to Purcell writing that "relations between Chinese and Malays have recently deteriorated" and "if they refuse to help the terrorists they will probably be shot: if they fail to help the Government they may be put into a detention camp which is probably not noticeably worse than the villages they are already in". However, Lee felt that there were portions of Purcell's letter "which make very good reading". Lee thought it would be undiplomatic and undesirable for Tan to write to *The Times* contradicting Purcell "because of his position as Honorary Advisor to the MCA, and [sic] which may also create the impression to the public that the MCA is having its own internal trouble". On the other hand, Lee said that it was correct that the Government has spent tens of millions of dollars and the MCA has spent more than one million dollars in assisting the squatters and "one cannot deny that Templer's policy to improve welfare and protect squatters is gradually, though slowly, taking effect." He suggested that Tan might write to Purcell to provide him with the background for the unsatisfactory state of affairs of the squatters that he [Templer] had seen in the first phase and inform him of the improvements that had taken place since then. He said this may induce Purcell to write to *The Times,* and at the same time "you may write a reply to the Acting Secretary for Chinese Affairs that you have now given the true facts to Dr Purcell and you trust he will write again to the London *Times* to give the true picture in Malaya as it now appears."

Colonel Lee said admittedly the present position was unsatisfactory both from the MCA's and the Government's points of view and something should be done about it.[39]

Meanwhile, Tan wrote to acknowledge Oakley's letter of 5 January and confirmed that Purcell had published his article in the *The London Times* in his private capacity, and he did not refer to himself as an "Honorary Adviser to the MCA". He said that Purcell was entitled to his own opinion, and "I do not consider it is fair that I should be called upon to interfere with the expression of that opinion" and added that "insofar as the MCA is concerned, we have regarded resettlement as an experiment of the greatest value and effect in fighting the Emergency", and that Purcell in formulating his views did not consult the MCA "and therefore those views cannot necessarily express the views of this association nor, I can assure you, was Dr Purcell ever requested by us to write the article in question."[40]

Tan then wrote to Purcell on 26 January to acknowledge receipt of his letters of 7 October and 5 December 1952, and said it was a great pleasure to meet and entertain him and Carnell while they were in Malaya and the Chinese in Malaya greatly appreciated the work they were doing on their behalf in London. "We are convinced you have the cause of the Chinese community at heart. We have so many enemies here. My own policy is to win over the Chinese in Malaya to be loyal citizens of Malaya within the British Commonwealth." He then informed Purcell that he had been asked "by a Government official" to write to *The London Times* to contradict what Purcell had written about the New Villages and the Emergency, and he had replied that it was impossible for him to do so and "your views were written in your personal capacity and cannot necessarily be those of the MCA." He was sending to Purcell a letter indicating what the Government considered objectionable in his articles and ignored the good work the Government was doing. Tan said he was very annoyed with the article "Mr Douglas" had published in *Look* magazine which "blackguarded the

Chinese in Malaya" and "we should be grateful if you could publish a full correction to refute all his false statements about the Chinese in Malaya to American newspapers and magazines and write something to the same effect to the *New York Times* too."

The correspondence between Tan Cheng Lock, Government officials, and Purcell continued in a similar vein for some time, with Brian T.W. Stewart, the Secretary for Chinese Affairs, Malacca, becoming involved too, and although Stewart took a somewhat more conciliatory and tactful stand, the matter was clearly becoming increasingly heated.

Meanwhile, a letter Purcell wrote to Tan on 8 February is worth noting as it perhaps crystallizes Purcell's point of view in response to the Government criticisms that had been levelled against him. It was, in fact, not until Tan responded to Oakley on 11 February in a somewhat more forthright manner to the correspondence he continued to receive from him [seemingly written at General Templer's instigation] that some semblance of calm was restored, although the exchange of correspondence could not have done anything to improve the rapidly deteriorating relations between the MCA and the Government.

In his letter of 8 February, Purcell said that the MCA should register a protest with General Templer about the offending article about the Chinese in Malaya that Mr Douglas has contributed to *Look* magazine and enquire whether it represented Templer's opinion of the Malayan Chinese, and "if not, will he say so publicly". He continued that on 28 August last year (1952):

> General Templer greeted Carnell and me with gross and gratuitous offensiveness. This was an affront not only to ourselves but to the MCA on whose behalf we were interviewing him. He said that the MCA had no right to appoint me as their adviser, and being a pensioned civil servant, I had no right to represent them. He further told us that he had no opinion of the Chinese and "if you gave them an inch they would take an ell" .... he added that "he would have no amendment to the Constitution in favour of the Chinese since it might offend the Malays on whom he relied for 98 per cent of his support. Carnell and I are prepared, if necessary, to state that this is a true account of General Templer's remarks."

Purcell continued that he proposed to publish an account of this interview with General Templer and in a footnote to it he would state that he was writing in his personal capacity and not as an adviser to the MCA.

The article will probably provoke violent reaction on the part of General Templer's friends and the MCA will probably be asked to dissociate themselves from what I say. This they will scarcely be able to do without repudiating the testimony of Carnell and myself as to the fact of the General's remarks. If this request is made to you I suggest that you should inform the High Commissioner accordingly and ask him whether he is in a position to refute what I say. [The] only other person at the interview besides Carnell and myself was Godsall, the acting Chief Secretary, who would, I am sure, confirm the truth of what I say. Godsall is now in England on retirement.[41]

In a further letter Purcell sent to Tan, he explained that his article which appeared in *The Times* on 15 December 1952 was extracted by the staff of the newspaper from three articles he had sent them as background to the problems of the Chinese in Malaya as there was not sufficient space to print all that he had written. In so doing, the section he had written on New Villages which was based on what he had seen himself and had been told by others, was greatly cut down and he could not agree with the Government's contention that it conveyed the impression that the New Villages "are little Belsens". He continued that he "bitterly resented" Oakley's insinuations that he was repeating Communist propaganda, and he had written of "good villages which the spirit and energy of devoted resettlement officers had turned into human habitations", and in any case his real criticism was "directed against the arrogant and coercive tactics of the High Commissioner" which would tend, in his opinion, to transform even the finest model village into a concentration camp. He had no wish to belittle the work of men who are trying to improve the conditions of the New Villagers and whenever possible he would give publicity to the facts mentioned by Tan Cheng Lock.

On 9 February 1953, Oakley again wrote to Tan Cheng Lock and said that he had been instructed by General Templer to find out whether or not the MCA agreed with the views expressed by Purcell. He wrote:

As the High Commissioner is pressing me for a reply to this question, please let me know how I am to reply. I gather from your final paragraph that you agree with some of what he says but I do not wish to reply to the High Commissioner that you agree with it all without making sure that this is, in fact, the position.'[42]

Tan was obviously incensed by the correspondence he had received from Oakley, and he wrote to him rather curtly on 11 February:

... as I read it you seemed to insinuate with veiled impertinence that I supported some sort of Communist propaganda. At first I simply did not believe you meant what you had written. However, your latest letter of 9 February seems to indicate that I agree with all of what Dr Purcell said — an unequally unwarrantable conclusion. I therefore much regret to have to tell you that unless you are prepared to withdraw and apologise, I must ask you not to address me personally in the future on any matter whatsoever. I am writing to the High Commissioner concerning the substance of your enquiries but shall not mention the strong objections which I hope I have made clear to you.[43]

Purcell wrote to Tan on 19 February 1953 that

The principal object of my indignation and wrath is General Templer, who as I have shown and hope to show further, has brought this retribution on himself by his tactics of force and his anti-Chinese policy.... I believe the facts I adduce are irrefutable. Carnell says I give a plain unvarnished account. I went to Malaya in August with the firm intention of bringing an influence for moderation and negotiation. It was the High Commissioner and not I who made this impossible. I never dreamt that in 1952 a Briton would receive us in such a barbarous fashion. The attempts being made in this country to discredit me are of such a nature that you, I have no doubt, would be roused to anger if you knew of them. I cannot for obvious reasons say any more in a letter but I can assure you I shall use all the vigour and resource I possess to counter them — and England unlike Malaya is still a free country.... General Templer is in complete ignorance of the Chinese character in using the strong arm alone... my obligation is to the people of Malaya, and in particular, the Chinese and the MCA.[44]

Meanwhile, in the midst of this rather heated correspondence, it did not particularly help matters that General Templer had provided a blurb to a book written by Major Arthur Campbell about his experiences as a company commander of the Suffolk Regiment in the Emergency, which Templer had described as "authentic".[45] In his book, Campbell had described the Chinese as "bastard Chinks who should be sent back to where they came from".[46] As soon as the book came to the attention of the MCA, it issued a press release calling upon all Chinese in Malaya to boycott the book, and on taking up the matter with the publishers, the book was withdrawn from the market until some sixteen passages in the book which were considered offensive were deleted.[47]

On 11 February 1953, Tan Cheng Lock wrote directly to General Templer that the Acting Secretary for Chinese Affairs had been writing to him concerning certain articles written in England by Dr Purcell and in his last letter had specifically "enquired on your behalf whether or not the MCA agrees with the views expressed". Tan went on to summarize the great help that the MCA had given the Government in resettling Chinese squatters and thanked Templer for his help.

> As for the MCA, our report for 1952, published on 14 January 1953, has already made our position quite clear ... Dr Purcell is a friend of mine and I have already written to him in the way I think would be most calculated to help him modify his views. I do not think it is necessary to contradict him in public ... Would you please write to me if there is any particular remarks of his own on which you require the views of the MCA and I will have enquiries made among the members.[48]

In replying to Tan's letter, Templer said that he was aware of the assistance given by the MCA to the Government and that as Purcell is an unpaid political adviser to the MCA he was at perfect liberty to write what he likes to the English press but

> The fact remains that whoever is interested in the matter and who reads his articles in the London *Times* presumably thinks that he is enunciating the official opinions of the MCA. ... I care nothing about personal attacks on myself. I care very deeply about misrepresentations of the situation in Malaya to the general public in the UK especially when this is done by your Political Adviser.[49]

However, the whole imbroglio was now slowly winding down and coming to an end.

Purcell wrote to Tan on 19 February that "for tactical reasons" he had decided to hold up publication of his interview with Templer and Tan replied on 3 March that he hoped Purcell would insert a note in whatever he wrote for the press in future which could be construed as being critical of the Malayan administration that he was writing in his "personal capacity and not as the MCA's Political Adviser" and his views were not necessarily those of the MCA. He said he was glad to hear that Purcell would not publish an account of his interview with Templer as this would only exacerbate the feelings of bitterness on both sides and might embarrass the Chinese community and the MCA in Malaya.[50]

In summing up, however, there is no doubt that the whole episode helped to sour relations between the MCA and the Government which were already at a low ebb, and it would take some time before they were restored to a more even keel.

Notes

1. ISEAS Library, Singapore, Tun Sir Henry H.S. Lee Private Papers Collection, HSL.8.036, "Letter dated 12 June 1952 from Mrs B.H. Oon to Colonel H.S. Lee". Victor Purcell, CMG, PhD, D. Litt., (1896–1965) was educated at Trinity College, Cambridge. He served as an officer in the Green Howards in France in World War I, was twice wounded, and became a prisoner-of-war. In 1921 he was appointed as a Cadet in the Chinese Protectorate of the MCS in charge of Chinese vernacular education. Thereafter he was Protector of Chinese in Penang; Kedah; Selangor; Pahang; Immigration Officer; Director General of Information, Malaya; and had become a Colonel in his old regiment during the British Military Administration when he was Principal Adviser on Chinese Affairs. He was a Consultant to the UN on various postwar commissions in Asia during 1946–48, and in 1949 he became a Reader in Far Eastern History, Cambridge University. Some of his books include *The Chinese in Malaya* (Kuala Lumpur: Oxford University Press, 1967 and 1978); *The Chinese in South East Asia* (London: Oxford University Press, 1965); and *Malaya: Communist or Free* (Stanford: Stanford University Press, 1954). His obituary in the *Journal of the Royal Asiatic Society*, London (Vol. 97, Issue No. 1, January 1965, p. 39), was written, as a nice touch, by Sir Richard Winstedt, who had been his contemporary in Malaya as the doyen of Malay Studies.
2. ISEAS Library, Singapore, Tun Sir Henry H.S. Lee Private Papers Collection, HSL.4.022/10, quoting the *Malay Mail*, 26 August 1952.
3. ISEAS Library, Singapore, Tun Sir Henry H.S. Lee Private Papers Collection, HSL.8.063, MCA Central Publicity Sub-Committee Press Statement No. 8/52, 25 August 1952, re. fact-finding mission of Victor Purcell and Francis A. Carnell.
4. ISEAS Library, Singapore, Tan Cheng Lock Private Papers Collection, TCL.6.2, 21 August 1952, "Letter to Tan Cheng Lock from Tunku Abdul Rahman".
5. Datuk Mohammed Sopiee (1924–2002) was educated at St. Xavier's Institution, Penang. He was a journalist and founder member of UMNO. He had a distinguished career as a diplomat and politician, and was a member of the Organising Committee of IMP (1951), UMNO Youth Leader (1952), Chairman of the Pan-Malayan Labour Party (1952), and Director of the Information Department, Kuala Lumpur. He was later appointed Malayan High Commissioner in Ceylon (Sri Lanka), India and Pakistan, and Malaya's Deputy Representative to the United Nations.
6. ISEAS Library, Singapore, Tan Cheng Lock Private Papers Collection, TCL.6.3, 25 August 1952. "Tan Cheng Lock to Tunku Abdul Rahman, President UMNO".
7. ISEAS Library, Singapore, Tun Sir Henry H.S. Lee Private Papers Collection, HSL.4.022/10, quoting *The Singapore Standard*, 26 August 1952.
8. ISEAS Library, Singapore, Tan Cheng Lock Private Papers, TCL.10.1, "Purcell to Tan Cheng Lock, 7 October 1952".

9. ISEAS Library, Singapore. Tan Cheng Lock Private Papers Collection, TCL.6.1.1, "Report on Visit to Malaya 20 August–20 September 1952 at invitation of MCA by Victor Purcell and Francis Carnell".

10. Ibid. See also Heng Pek Koon, *Chinese Politics in Malaysia: A History of the Malaysian Chinese Association* (Singapore: Oxford University Press, 1988), p. 107.

11. ISEAS Library, Singapore, Tan Cheng Lock Private Papers, TCL 6.1.1, op. cit.

12. Ibid. See also Heng, op. cit., pp. 136–39, "The Transition of the MCA into a Political Party".

13. General Templer's imposition of collective punishment upon villages that refused to cooperate with the Government provoked both protest and approval in Britain, and towards the end of November 1952, Jo Grimmond, Chief Whip of the Liberal Party in the House of Commons, wrote to Lyttelton for further information about it. He was reassured by Lyttelton's reply which he said "was most useful and made quite an impression on a good many people who obviously know nothing about conditions in Malaya". See A.J. Stockwell, ed., *Malaya: Part II The Communist Insurrection 1948–1953* (London: HMSO, 1995), p. 424.

14. CO 1022/54, Jerrom to Higham, 21 May 1952.

15. CO 1022/56, no. 35, 10 December 1952, [Collective punishment]: Letter from Lyttelton to Grimmond in support of Templer's methods.

16. Emergency Regulation 17D allowed the Government to detain collectively a whole village for failing to cooperate with the authorities and deport the inhabitants to China.

17. Cloake, op. cit., pp. 272–73.

18. ISEAS Library, Singapore, Tan Cheng Lock Private Papers, TCL 6.1.1, "Report on visit to Malaya 20 August–20 September 1952 at invitation of MCA by Victor Purcell and Francis Carnell".

19. Cloake, op. cit.

20. Stockwell, op. cit., p. 470, fn. 3.

21. Cloake, op. cit., p. 307.

22. Ibid., pp. 307–309.

23. Ibid., p. 308. If Templer had actually used the words he is alleged to have said, it is understandable they would have caused offence. Perhaps a more polite description of Purcell, whom the author had met, was that he was rather "portly".

24. Ibid., p. 307, quoting a letter Templer sent to Lyttelton on 2 September 1952.

25. See, for example, *The Times* (London) 15 December 1952; *The New Statesmen and The Nation,* 17 January 1953; and *The Spectator,* 5 February 1953.

26. Cloake, op. cit., p. 309.

27. S. Rajaratnam, as related previously, was then a journalist but he became a leading member of the PAP.

28. Irene Ng, *The Singapore Lion: A Biography of S. Rajaratnam* (Singapore: Institute of Southeast Asian Studies, 2010), pp. 128–32.

29. Ibid.

30. *The Observer* (London), 22 June 1952.

31. CO 1022/492, "Federal Press Statement D.INF.7/52/20 (HC), 4 July 1952".

32. Yusof bin Ishak became the first President of Singapore on 9 August 1965 when Singapore separated from the Federation of Malaysia to become the Republic of Singapore. Yusof's portrait appears on Singapore currency notes to this day (2015).

33. Purcell, op. cit., p. 238. Aziz had a chequered career. He had been a newspaper reporter in Singapore for three years (1934–36), Editor of the *Utusan Melayu* (1948–51), a member of IMP, a Federal Legislative Councillor, and Minister for Agriculture and Cooperatives (1955–62). He had incurred Sir Henry Gurney's displeasure previously in 1951 when he had moved a motion in the Federal Legislative Council opposing the dispossession of Malays from land that was needed by the Government's Fisheries Research Station at Penang, and in 1957 after Malaya's independence, he introduced a motion in the Federal Legislative Council opposing the location of British military bases in Malaya (See CO 537/7262, no. 51 (Executive and Legislative Council) "Letter from Sir Henry Gurney on recent constitutional innovations, 28 April 1951", and Stockwell, op. cit., p. 289). In 1962, long after Templer had left Malaya, Aziz was expelled from UMNO, dismissed as a Minister, and detained under the Emergency Regulations during confrontation with Indonesia.

34. See Karl von Vorys, *Democracy without Consensus, Communalism and Political Stability in Malaysia* (Princeton, New Jersey: Princeton University Press, 1975), p. 171.

35. Purcell, op. cit.

36. Chang Min-Tat (subsequently Tan Sri Chang Min Tat) (1916–2007), who had recently come down from Oxford, was educated at Raffles College, Singapore, and had graduated in English Language and Literature at Exeter College, Oxford, in 1952. He was admitted to the Bar (Inner Temple) in 1953. He rose to become a Judge of the High Court of Malaya. He was born in Ipoh, the fourth son of Chang Yin Fatt, tin miner, philanthropist, and founder president of the Chinese Chamber of Commerce, Perak.

37. ISEAS Library, Singapore, Tan Cheng Lock Private Papers, TCL.190.13, "Secret letter dated 29 December 1952 from Tan Cheng Lock to Director-General of Information Services, Kuala Lumpur".

38. ISEAS Library, Singapore, Tan Cheng Lock Private Papers, TCL.10.4, Secret, "Letter from Acting Secretary of Chinese Affairs (R.H. Oakley) to Tan Cheng Lock dated 5 January 1953".

39. ISEAS Library, Singapore, Tan Cheng Lock Private Papers TCL 10/6/1 Strictly Secret, "Letter from H.S. Lee to Tan Cheng Lock, 9 January 1953".
40. ISEAS Library, Singapore, Tan Cheng Lock Private Papers, TCL 1.7a, Strictly Confidential, "Tan Cheng Lock to Oakley" (undated).
41. ISEAS Library, Singapore, Tan Cheng Lock Private Papers, TCL.10/14/1, "From Purcell to Tan Cheng Lock, 8 February 1953". In August 1952, W.D. Godsall was acting Chief Secretary of Malaya and later in November he became Financial Secretary.
42. ISEAS Library, Singapore, Tan Cheng Lock Private Papers, TCL. 10.15, "Letter dated 9 February 1953 from Oakley to Tan Cheng Lock".
43. ISEAS Library, Singapore, Tan Cheng Lock Private Papers, TCL.10.17, "Letter from Tan Cheng Lock to Oakley".
44. ISEAS Library, Singapore, Tan Cheng Lock Private Papers TCL.10.17.1 "Undated handwritten letter from Purcell to Tan Cheng Lock".
45. Arthur Campbell, *Jungle Green* (Boston: Little Brown & Co, 1953).
46. Kumar Ramakrishna, *Emergency Propaganda: The Winning of Malayan's Hearts and Minds, 1948–55* (London: Curzon, 2002), p. 135.
47. Victor Purcell, *Malaya: Communist or Free?* op. cit., pp. 129–30.
48. ISEAS Library, Singapore, Tan Cheng Lock Private Papers, TCL.10.19/1, "Letter dated 11 February 1953 from Tan Cheng Lock to Templer".
49. ISEAS Library, Singapore, Tan Cheng Lock Private Papers, TCL. 10.23, "Templer's reply to Tan Cheng Lock, 25 February 1953".
50. ISEAS Library, Singapore, Tan Cheng Lock Private Papers, TCL. 10.23a, "Letter from Purcell to Tan Cheng Lock dated 19 February 1953" and TCL.10.24/1 "Letter from Tan Cheng Lock to Purcell dated 3 March 1953".

5

GENERAL SIR GERALD TEMPLER, THE MCA, AND THE KINTA VALLEY HOME GUARD (1952–1954)[1]

The Kinta Valley Home Guard (KVHG) was established by the MCA-controlled Perak Chinese Tin Mining Association (PCTMA), Ipoh, with the backing and support of General Templer soon after he arrived in Malaya in February 1952.[2] It was an all-Chinese Home Guard, aside from a few senior European officers. Some 4,000 members were recruited and trained by the Government. According to General Templer's biographer John Cloake, it was what he himself described as his "biggest gamble". Many of his detractors thought it would be a disaster to supply arms to what was to be a large Chinese Home Guard dominated by the MCA for the defence of what were predominantly Chinese tin mines, and referred to what had happened to some of the weapons supplied by the British to the Communist Malayan Peoples Anti-Japanese Army (MPAJA) in World War II, many of which were secretly hoarded at the end of the war to be used later against the British in the Emergency. Nevertheless, General Templer gave his support to the KVHG, which was often described as a "Chinese private army" because of its close connections with the KMT which had been prescribed by the colonial government in Malaya on 9 May 1949,[3] and he played an important role in its funding, organization, training, and deployment. By 1954, when Templer left Malaya, it was reported that there were 323 tin mines defended by the KVHG which remained operational until the end of the Malayan Emergency in July 1960.[4]

THE MALAYAN ECONOMY

The tin and rubber industries then constituted the main sources of revenue for the Malayan Government. They were, in fact, by far the most important sources of U.S. dollars in the whole of the British colonial empire, and the Kinta Valley in Perak, covering some 1,035 square kilometres, was one of the richest tin mining areas in Malaya and accounted for the major part of Malaya's tin exports to the United States.[5]

Templer was concerned that the revenue earned from the export of both tin and rubber, mainly to the United States, was vital for Malaya's economy not only to build up the prosperity of the country but to continue to finance the ever-escalating costs of the counter-insurgency operations that were being carried out against the CPM.[6] It was in recognition of this need that the Government appointed a Rubber Fact Finding Mission under Sir Francis Mudie, which in its report published on 1 October 1954 drew attention in the strongest possible terms to the necessity for a massive and rapid rubber replanting programme. At the same time, the Government took measures to support a proposed international Tin Agreement, which was then awaiting ratification by a sufficient number of countries, to stabilize the fluctuating price of tin, and furthermore, with regard to the broader aspects of the economy, made arrangements during the early part of 1954 for a three months' visit by a team of experts from the International Bank for Reconstruction and Development to help develop an overall development plan for the country.[7]

However, when Templer arrived in Malaya early in 1952, the economy appeared to be good shape and the Malayan financial reserves were replete with funds. Malaya had benefited enormously from the stockpiling of rubber and tin by the U.S. Government at the outbreak of the Korean War (1950). It undoubtedly helped too that the jungle war against the Communist insurgents seemed to be taking a turn for the better as a result of the Briggs Plan, which was making it more difficult for them to obtain food and other supplies from the New Villages and caused them to reduce contact with the security forces and concentrate on building up their own supply bases deep in the jungle.[8]

But when the demand for tin and rubber decreased after the end of the Korean War, the effect on the Malayan economy was dramatic. For instance, the price of tin had reached a high of M$526.58 per picul in 1951 but by 1954 it had fallen to M$353.59.[9] Revenue earned from the export of rubber was similarly affected when a high of M$3,785.60 per ton in 1951 dropped to M$1,530.67 in 1954 (see Table 2). By the end of 1953 it was clear that Malaya was faced with a serious economic problem.

Even as revenue dropped, funds still had to be provided to cover the costs of the Emergency and by the end of the year it became evident that unless drastic measures were taken, there would be insufficient funds available for Malaya's continued development and maintaining of pressure on the Communist insurgents.[10]

The serious economic downturn was exacerbated, too, by the determined efforts of the CPM to damage the economy by attacking tin mines and damaging tin dredges and other expensive tin mining equipment of mines where the owners refused to pay protection money. The official *1952 Malayan Annual Report* refers to ninety-eight attacks on tin mines during the year with the loss of twenty-one lives, and tin production was reported to have dropped to 70 per cent of its pre-war level, with there being little likelihood of an improvement in the situation until the country was sufficiently peaceful to permit further prospecting for new tin deposits.[11]

Templer adverted to the dire economic situation when he visited the Colonial Office in June 1952 and said that Malaya faced an unprecedented

TABLE 2
Tin and Rubber Prices, 1950–54

Year	Tin $ per Picul	Rubber $ per Ton
1950	366.92	2,419.20
1951	526.58	3,785.60
1952	480.08	2,116.05
1953	363.72	1,500.80
1954	353.59	1,530.67

Adapted from Francis Loh Kok Wah, *Beyond the Tin Mines. Coolies, Squatters and New Villagers in the Kinta Valley, Malaysia c.1880–1960* (Singapore: Oxford University Press, 1988), p. 140.

and serious reduction in its budget estimates for the year.[12] In the following year (1953), the situation deteriorated further on account of the continuing downturn in the prices of rubber and tin especially when it became evident there was little prospect of expansion in earnings from other alternative sources of revenue. The stark reality of the situation struck home when it was felt that tin, unlike rubber, was a "wasting asset", and a great many tin mines were nearing exhaustion. Prospecting for new sources had been disrupted by the Communist insurrection, though the Government hoped that the decrease in open CPM terrorist activities (referred to earlier) would enable prospecting to start again.

In his address to the Malayan Legislative Council on 19 November 1953, General Templer said that at the beginning of the 1953 financial year, the fiscal deficit was estimated to be M$97 million but by the end of the year, the annual deficit was estimated to amount to M$146 million, which he attributed mainly to increased government expenditure on account of the Emergency and a decrease in the world prices of tin and rubber.[13] He announced there would have to be a reduction in the strength of the Home Guard from 220,000 to 210,000, and a slower expansion of the Malayan security forces. He ordered a 10 per cent cut in the establishment of the regular Police and said that he would consider a further reduction in 1954. However, he explained that the reduction in the strength of the regular police was due to a "decline in the Communists' striking power" and said that the Police, on account of their improved training, would be able to protect the public from Communist terrorism with fewer men.[14] He said that M$100 million of the deficit for 1953 would be financed from a security loan which had been floated by the Government in the course of the year, augmented by funds from the Government's General Revenue account, and that the British Government, in implementing a promise made in 1949, would grant M$51.5 million in 1954 towards the cost of the Emergency. He added that it was fortunate, too, that the State of Brunei had approved a M$40 million loan to Malaya and on 24 November 1953 the Singapore Government had approved a M$30 million loan, with an interest-free period of ten years.[15] In addition, development was being financed by M$34 million from the Colonial Development and Welfare Funds.[16]

In view of the serious downturn in the economy, it became increasingly clear that drastic action would be required urgently to strengthen the protection of existing tin mines in the Kinta Valley area to counter the threat posed by the Communist terrorists, and this was what Templer set out to do soon after his arrival at Kuala Lumpur in February 1952.

FORMATION OF KVHG

General Templer referred for the first time to the formation of the KVHG at the Malayan Executive Council Meeting on 25 March 1952 when he spoke about the unsatisfactory state of affairs regarding the security of tin mines in the Kinta Valley, 75 per cent of which were owned by Chinese. He stated that he would be introducing a scheme for handing over protection of the mines to a "fully-armed Home Guard, the members of which would be sponsored by the Perak Chinese Tin Mining Association. There would be the equivalent of about two battalions of these [sic] Home Guard with three British officers in charge." When they had been trained in their duties, "the existing Special Constables would be withdrawn for training. The present Police Stations would remain and a working relationship would have to be devised between the Police and the Home Guard." General Templer ended his remarks by saying that "this was an experiment in which he had every confidence".[17]

The Special Constables had been recruited by the Perak Chinese Mining Association soon after the outbreak of the Emergency in June 1948, using its own funds, to protect Chinese tin mines and workers from the Communists.[18]

There does not appear to have been any debate about Templer's proposals in the Council, most likely because the members were fully aware of the seriousness of the situation and the attention that was then being given to the overall reorganization of the Malayan Home Guard, which led to the announcement by Templer on 31 March 1952 of the appointment of a retired British Army General, Major General E.P. de Fonblanque, CBE, CB, DSO, as Inspector General of the Malayan Home Guard.[19]

Though Templer's decision to authorize the formation of an all-Chinese Home Guard in the Kinta Valley was the first time a "Chinese Home Guard" of this size had been formed in Malaya, it was undoubtedly a courageous step as it was criticized in some quarters as bringing into existence what was virtually a "Chinese Army" made up mostly of KMT (Kuomintang) supporters, with some Chinese secret society supporters too, as will be referred to later. In fact, most of the MCA leaders in Perak had close connections with the KMT including Lau Pak Kuan, who first headed the MCA Perak State branch, and Leong Yew Koh, who had been a Major General in the KMT Army in China in World War II. As Templer himself admitted, "I realise quite well in the Kinta area we are inevitably handing ourselves over to the KMT but one has got to try something."[20]

In fact, for some years, the control of the lucrative tin mines in the Kinta Valley had been fought over by contesting Chinese groups made up of elements of the CPM, the KMT, and Chinese secret societies each with its own "dreams of power".[21]

Though plans proceeded at a fast pace after Templer's announcement at the Executive Council of the decision to enrol recruits for the KVHG with the help of the Perak Chinese Tin Mining Association because he wanted the force to be trained and operational as soon as possible, the Secretary of Chinese Affairs issued a note of warning about some of the problems involved. In a review dated September 1952, he adverted to recruitment for the KVHG being carried out by the Perak Chinese Tin Mining Association in Penang, as well as Perak and other parts of Malaya, which he said interfered with the recruitment of Chinese candidates for the Police. He referred, too, to a power struggle taking place between "twenty [former] KMT officers, who received a secret subsidy of M$20 per month from the Perak Chinese Tin Mining Association, who are trying to drive out other non-KMT officers, who have contacts with Government officials and speak English".[22]

OLIVER LYTTELTON'S RECOMMENDATIONS

Meanwhile, it may be opportune at this stage to summarize the situation in regard to the Home Guard and place it in its wider perspective, especially as the reorganization and strengthening of the Home Guard was singled out by Oliver Lyttelton in the report he submitted to the British Government after his mission to Malaya in November 1951 prior to Templer's arrival.

In 1951, General Briggs, then Director of Operations, had instructed the Civil Defence Department to coordinate and assist in the formation of the "Malay Kampong Guards [which were raised primarily for the defence of Malay kampongs] and the Chinese Home Guard [which were raised primarily for the defence of Chinese New Villages]", and had instructed the Police to assume responsibility for their training. However, this duality of responsibility between the Civil Defence Department and the Police did not prove to be entirely satisfactory as the organization of the Home Guard was still in a rudimentary stage and the Malay States were reluctant to relinquish control to an overall Federal authority. Moreover, in the Malay States, it was alleged that the Home Guard State Inspectors, who were mostly Malays, were inclined to neglect the development of the Chinese Home Guard.[23]

After his mission to Malaya in November 1951, Lyttelton had come to the heart of the matter when he decided that the time had come for Kampung and Home Guards to be reorganized and placed on a proper footing, and on his return to London, he made a number of important recommendations dealing with the matter in his report to the British Cabinet. He advocated that the Chinese element of the overall Home Guard organization should be strengthened and enlarged as a first step to gaining increased Chinese support in the fight against the Communist insurgents.[24] He hoped this would have a twofold effect and lead to an increase in the flow of intelligence to the Special Branch from Chinese sources and, moreover, encourage Chinese to enlist in the regular uniformed branch of the Police.[25]

It was this state of affairs that General Templer turned his attention to soon after his arrival at Kuala Lumpur when he announced the appointment of Major General de Fonblanque as Inspector General of the Malayan Home Guard.

APPOINTMENT OF GENERAL DE FONBLANQUE AS INSPECTOR GENERAL HOME GUARD

By 1 June 1952, under the new arrangements made by Templer and de Fonblanque, the administration of the Home Guard was functionally separated from the Civil Defence Department and Police, and reorganized on a State or Settlement basis under the respective State and Settlements War Executive Committees (SWECs). De Fonblanque as the newly appointed Inspector General of Home Guard and his staff would coordinate the rearrangements to bring this about by working closely with the Department of the Secretary of Defence. Thus General de Fonblanque became responsible for all aspects of Home Guard organization and training. However, he was not responsible for the operational use of the Home Guard which remained with the security forces.[26]

De Fonblanque authorized through SWECs the issue of arms and equipment to the Home Guard. One shotgun was issued to every three Home Guards and he arranged for an order from the United States of 10,000 semi-automatic Browning shotguns and 2,000 semi-automatic carbines for operational use and for certain static defence purposes.

The Home Guard officer establishment was approved and each State or Settlement would have Grade A and Grade B officers in charge of the State/

Settlement Home Guard, who would be supported by District Home Guard officers, Home Guard Inspectors and Kampung Home Guard officers.[27]

In each State/Settlement, SWECs would be responsible for the formation and efficiency of the Home Guard organization in accordance with general instructions issued by the Home Guard Inspector General. This responsibility would be exercised through the State/Settlement Home Guard officer, who was a member of SWEC and commander of the Home Guard in the State/Settlement concerned.

At a district level, the District Officer commanded all Home Guards in his district and he was in some cases supported by a District Home Guard Officer who would be the District Officer's deputy in all Home Guard matters. Additionally, there would be Home Guard Inspectors responsible for training, with other officers being appointed to assist unit commanders in administration and training.

The Malayan Home Guard was now beginning to take shape as a properly organized force.[28] It was a very large quasi-military force to organize and equip amounting to some quarter of a million men who after they had been trained, fully armed and equipped, would cooperate with the Police and the Army not only in a static role but on operational jungle patrols too.[29]

It should be noted that Lyttelton's recommendations referred to earlier may well have been influenced by a confidential memorandum that Tan Cheng Lock, President of the Malayan Chinese Association, had submitted in May 1950 to Creech Jones, the Colonial Secretary, and John Strachey, the Secretary of State for War, who were then visiting Malaya, where he had advocated the greater use of "Chinese to fight Chinese". As stated, Tan's proposals were not taken up by the Government at the time probably on account of the concern of the Malayan Special Branch that by doing so, an irregular Chinese force would thereby be formed which would be separate from the regular Army and Police and heavily influenced by political factors. In simplest terms it would most likely have provided an opportunity for former KMT officers and soldiers then living and working in Malaya to participate in and form a "Third Force" to fight the Communists which might well have caused political problems as Britain had by then recognized the Communist People's Republic of China in January 1950.[30] According to Special Branch intelligence, the KMT in Malaya had already had considerable success in penetrating the Malayan Auxiliary Police and it was reliably reported that many of the 2,300 members making up the

Auxiliary Police in 1951 were KMT members. It was known that many of the alumni of the KMT Central Chinese Military Academy that had been based in Chungking during World War II were scattered throughout Malaya and Singapore including a former KMT Major-General, three former Colonels, six Lieutenant Colonels, twelve Majors, fifty Captains, forty Lieutenants and twelve Second Lieutenants, and there may have been others, too, who had escaped the Special Branch network.[31]

It is quite likely that General Templer's decision to support the Kinta Valley Home Guard was influenced by both security and economic-political factors as he wanted to ensure not only that the Kinta Valley tin mines did not fall under Communist control but that the output of tin from them still played an important part in earning revenue for Malaya. It became clear that he treated the Kinta Valley Home Guard, although forming part of the overall Home Guard organization for Malaya, somewhat differently from other Home Guard units. Its uniqueness and the financial arrangements that were made for it by General Templer to ensure that its operating expenses and administration were shared between the Government and the Perak Chinese Tin Mining Association, with the latter recruiting most of its members and paying part of their salaries, will be described later.[32]

COLONEL H.S. LEE

With his tin mining, banking, and other business interests, especially in Perak, and as one of the top leaders of the MCA, Colonel H.S. Lee (subsequently Colonel Tun Sir Henry H.S. Lee, SMN, KBE, JP), was closely involved in the establishment of the Kinta Valley Home Guard and the Force Commander, KVHG, reported to him, although credit for its establishment is often given to Dato Seri Lau Pak Kuan, a wealthy Perak tin miner, who was one of the leading Chinese MCA and community leaders in Perak and Tun Leong Yew Koh, another prominent MCA and Perak Chinese business leader, and there is no doubt that all of them played an important part in the formation of the KVHG.[33]

Lau Pak Kuan, who had been appointed a Justice of the Peace (JP) by the Sultan of Perak in 1936, and was a prominent member of the Perak Chinese Advisory Council, maintained close connections with China, which he visited in 1940 as part of the Nanyang Overseas Chinese Save China Fund Raising Committee. During the Japanese invasion of Malaya in World

War II, he escaped to Burma [Myanmar], and eventually to Chungking, which was the capital of wartime China. He owned some twenty tin mines in Perak, and was President of the Perak Chinese Tin Mining Association, Chairman of the Perak Chamber of Commerce, and President of the Perak branch of the MCA, and a former KMT leader in Perak.[34]

Leong Yew Koh, who was well known as a lawyer in Ipoh, had held high office in various departments under the KMT Central Government in China in the 1930s. After he moved to Malaya, he became Vice-President of the Perak Branch of the MCA and a member of the Malayan Federal Legislative Council.[35] He was a friend of Lau Pak Kuan, and Khoo and Lubis in their study of the Kinta Valley refer to Leung holding honorary KMT military rank and enlisting some of the former KMT guerrillas from the Lenggong area of Perak into the KVHG.[36]

Nevertheless, it is evident that Colonel Lee's role in the establishment of the Kinta Valley Home Guard was crucial as he was based in Kuala Lumpur the Federal capital, where he was on good terms and maintained close relations with many of the senior British colonial officials including the High Commissioner, General Templer.[37] He was, as previously noted, a member of the official reception party of senior officials who welcomed Templer when the latter first arrived at Kuala Lumpur on 10 February 1952 to take up his appointment as High Commissioner and Director of Operations.

As one of the leading Chinese community leaders in Malaya, Colonel Lee was highly regarded by the British colonial authorities. He had been educated at Hong Kong University, an old-established colonial university, and subsequently at Cambridge University. His services were sought after in many official capacities.[38] He maintained, too, a close connection with the KMT in Malaya resulting from his service in World War II with the KMT Army in India and Burma and his long-standing family connections with the KMT in south China. During the Japanese Occupation of Malaya, the British colonial authorities evacuated Lee and his family to India. He was appointed a Colonel in the KMT Army and played an important part as a liaison officer between the Kuomintang (KMT) and the British army in the Burma-China border region.

Lee was not only a prominent and wealthy Chinese tin miner in his own right in Perak, but politically active in Chinese guilds and clan associations after he moved to Kuala Lumpur from Hong Kong in the mid-1920s to take over his family's tin mining business in Perak, Selangor, and Negri

Sembilan. He had inherited wealth and came from a large, distinguished, and prominent family in Guangdong Province, China, where his great-grandfather had been appointed a mandarin during the reign of Emperor Tongzhi (1856–75) of the Qing dynasty. His grandfather, too, was a famous Chinese scholar, while his father became a prominent businessman and founded Kam Lun Tai, the flagship company of the Lee family business. One of his uncles was Secretary of the Treasury in Guangdong Province and a close friend of Generalissimo Chiang Kai-shek, President of the Republic of China, whom Colonel Lee had met.[39]

Some idea of his influence in Malaya may be obtained from the many senior appointments he held. He had been Adviser of the Malayan delegation to the International Tin Study Group since 1947, and was the Mining Representative on the Selangor War Executive Committee, the Government body concerned with the direction of counterinsurgency operations in Selangor against the CPM insurgents, and was Chairman of the Associated Chinese Chambers of Commerce in Malaya and Singapore.[40] He was one of the founder members of the MCA, which represented the interests of the Chinese community in Malaya in its dealings with the colonial Government and played a leading role in the Malayan independence movement.[41] He was appointed a member of the Malayan Legislative Council, and subsequently became Malayan Minister for Transport (1955–57). After Malayan independence in 1957, he became Malaya's first Finance Minister in the UMNO-MCA-MIC National Alliance headed by Prime Minister Tunku Abdul Rahman, whom he accompanied to London in 1956 as one of the signatories of the independence agreement with the British Government, and Financial Chairman for the Board of Commissioners of Currency Malaya (1956–61). After his retirement, his activities continued unabated, and he established in Malaya the Development and Commerce Bank, which became a major bank in Malaya. He was knighted for his services to Malaya and the United Kingdom by both governments.

KUOMINTANG

It was well known in Malaya at the time that many members of the MCA and the Chinese Chamber of Commerce were supporters of the Kuomintang Party, and as the MCA became recognized by the British colonial Government as representing the interests of the Malayan-Chinese community, just as UMNO and the MIC represented the interests of the

Malays and Indian communities respectively, there was often a certain amount of ambivalence on the part of the British officials about the position of the KMT, especially as there had been KMT consular offices in Singapore, Kuala Lumpur, Ipoh and Penang before Britain recognized the People's Republic of China and the KMT branches in Malaya were officially closed down in 1949.[42]

On 2 September 1952, (Sir) John Nicoll, then Governor of Singapore, wrote a secret personal letter to General Templer in which he adverted to Templer's Member for Home Affairs "pressing my Secretariat for a statement on our policy regarding the Kuomintang", and he said that he preferred to write to Templer personally on the issue as he did not know how his Member for Home Affairs would take up the matter "as the Singapore Executive Council did not wish to make it a live issue". The gist of what he wrote to Templer was that it was the Singapore Government's policy "not to preclude the use of individuals who might belong to the KMT but our point is that we will not use the KMT as such [as a Party]."[43]

Yet another view was presented by Malcolm MacDonald, then British Commissioner General in South East Asia, who held the view that as the KMT was staunchly anti-Communist and had been engaged in an internecine struggle in China with the Chinese Communist Party until it was driven into exile in Taiwan, its members could be used as a "Third Force" to fight the Communists in Malaya.[44] However, this view did not find favour with many officials in the local colonial Malayan and Singapore Governments.[45] While General Templer could not have been unaware of the continuing existence of KMT supporters in Malaya when he decided to support the KVHG, it is not at all clear whether he was aware of the full extent of the KMT's ramifications and how well entrenched it was in the top echelons of the Malayan-Chinese business world and, in particular, the MCA, even though one of his most senior officials, the Chief Secretary, had sent a secret and personal letter to Colonel H.S. Lee on 8 March 1954 advising him that the Malayan Special Branch had been concerned for some time that the KMT was trying to penetrate and control the MCA.[46]

ORGANIZATION OF KVHG

The organization of the KVHG is well brought out in various reports by J.C.H. Brett, Force Commander, KVHG, to Lee, in which he described the security situation in the Kinta Valley in 1951 and early 1952 as "serious" on account of the Communist menace. Chinese mines were frequently sabotaged and the small formations of Special Constables employed to guard them were frequently overrun by the Communist guerrillas. Consequently, a scheme was proposed by members of the Perak Chinese Tin Mining Association to raise "an armed force of Chinese" to protect their tin mines which would be financially supported by a levy of M$8 per picul on tin ore produced by those mines coming within the scheme. This was the scheme that was subsequently approved by Templer in face of what Brett referred to as "considerable official and unofficial opposition". The main principle of the force was to protect the mines by employing a mobile force of Chinese Home Guards as opposed to Special Constables who were formerly employed in a static role, and it was this force that became known as "The Kinta Valley Home Guard".[47]

The PCTMA established recruiting centres in various parts of the country and as many as 200–300 recruits were selected at a time. It was perhaps inevitable with the speed at which the force was formed that undesirable elements including Chinese secret society members who supported the MCA/KMT were recruited. The initial training for recruits was limited to three weeks but when this proved to be insufficient as the standard of marksmanship remained low, Templer agreed that it should be extended to six weeks, which provided the Police with sufficient time to catch up with the backlog of fingerprint and security checks of new recruits. Further, a reduction in the establishment of the KVHG in the mid-1950s for reasons of economy provided an opportunity to remove many of the remaining undesirable recruits.[48]

Meanwhile, thousands of scattered inhabitants in the Kinta Valley were regrouped into thirty-four New Villages and twelve new towns which were surrounded for security purposes by barbed wire fences. Additionally, KVHG platoon bases and section posts were established in those areas where there was the largest concentration of tin mines.[49]

The force was divided into three groups situated at Ipoh, Batu Gajah and Kampar under the central command of force headquarters at Ipoh. Each group was commanded by a group commander, assisted by an assistant group commander (usually a police lieutenant on secondment from the Malayan Police), an adjutant, with the rank of lieutenant in the Home Guard, who was responsible for discipline, training and general supervision of the group, an administrative officer and a clerical assistant. Eight of these officers were European.

Under arrangements agreed to by Templer, the "operational establishment" of the Home Guard was jointly funded by the Federal Government and the Perak Chinese Tin Mining Association. The Government paid each Home Guard irrespective of rank M$120 per month with the PCTMA paying M$45 per month, of which M$40 was regarded as a ration allowance. The eight European officers were paid for by the Federal Government. The strength of the KVHG was reduced from 1,650 in mid-1953 to 900 for reasons of economy and, at the same time, the Training Centre at Batu Gajah was abandoned and training concentrated at the Perak State Home Guard Training Centre.[50]

In addition, the PCTMA paid M$210 p.m. to 3 Lieutenants, M$180 p.m. to 36 Second Lieutenants, M$70 p.m. to 25 Sergeants, M$50 p.m. to 35 Corporals, and M$30 p.m. to 118 Lance-Corporals. It was agreed that the Government should provide uniform, ammunition and transport costs as well as the capital costs for constructing defence works and maintenance costs for platoon bases with the PCTMA being responsible for the construction and repair of barracks, bathrooms, kitchens, latrines and the provision of water supplies. The Government assumed responsibility for lighting costs.[51]

The MCA provided funds for the KVHG too. At the Fifth Cabinet Meeting of the MCA held in Kuala Lumpur on 3 October 1952, several matters concerning the financing of the KVHG by the MCA were discussed. Payments had been made previously to the KVHG out of the MCA Welfare Fund but it was now suggested that payments should be made from the MCA's General Fund, as it was considered inappropriate that the Welfare Fund should be used in this way. It was decided that the MCA General Fund could be recompensed for this by reducing the commission paid to MCA branches from the MCA Lottery from 10 per cent to 8 per cent and crediting the other 2 per cent to the MCA General Fund.

Tun Leong Yew Koh, the Vice-President of the Perak State MCA who attended the meeting, said that the Kinta Valley Home Guard must be supported in the interests not only of the tin miners but in the "grand interests" of the "Chinese community as a whole". He said that the KVHG had been successfully organized and the Malayan Government had supported it as a special case by paying a monthly subsidy of M$200,000.[52]

Some idea of the important and significant contribution the Government made to the KVHG may be obtained by the entry in the Government's annual estimates for 1955 that the Government allocated 15.4 per cent, or M$1,600,000, to the Kinta Valley Home Guard out of a total amount of M$10,388,143 budgeted for the Malayan Home Guard for that year.[53]

CONCLUSION

On 9 August 1952, General Templer toured the Kinta Valley area with a distinguished visitor from the United States, Justice William C. Douglas, a judge of the U.S. Supreme Court, and visited the M$100,000 Kinta Valley Home Guard Training Centre near Batu Gajah, which had been established two months previously with Government funds. During this short period, over 40 officers and 120 non-commissioned officers had been trained and there were currently 300 officers and men under training. General Templer told Justice Douglas that some of the Chinese officers who were being trained there had seen service during World War II against the Japanese Imperial Army in Malaya with the clandestine British Force 136. "There was nothing here in June — not even a hut. Now you will see a well-laid out camp," he told his visitor. "The camp was built in record time by a Malay contractor". General Templer then addressed the 300 trainees, and told them:

> The Communists want to stop the whole thing and create chaos and unemployment for everyone. A few thousand Communists are trying to wreck the economic life of Malaya. They like to get hold of the tin and rubber industry in order to create chaos and gain economic control of the country. We are not allowing them to do it. So it is determined [sic] to start the Kinta Valley Chinese Home Guard. You are formed for a special purpose — to defend the Kinta Valley .... We will kill Communists in Kinta Valley. I will come and see you at your posts..... Shoot straight and accurately — one shot, one bandit.[54]

This is pure "vintage Templer", who was well known for his brusque military manner of speech and for not mincing his words but in a wider context, it is a good example of his determination to intervene and protect the Kinta Valley tin mines where the bulk of Malaya's tin was produced from the attacks of the Communist insurgents, without having regard to the political undertones. By providing his personal support for the KVHG and substantial Government financial backing, Templer averted the spin-off effect a further downturn in the economy would have had on Government revenue, the tin industry and tin mine workers, as well as the prosecution of the counterinsurgency operations against the CPM's armed uprising.

The risks he took paid off. The steps taken prevented the Communists from dominating the Kinta Valley area. It succeeded in spite of Templer's detractors who were concerned about the involvement of the Kuomintang, Chinese secret societies and other undesirable elements. It allowed Templer, too, a breathing space to continue with his socio-political plans for Malaya's progress towards self-government, and perhaps gain greater support from the Chinese, especially the MCA, for his political plans.

However, General Templer's support for the KVHG still gave rise to serious unease in some circles, including the Special Branch, who were concerned that the Government was perceived to be cooperating, if indirectly, with the KMT, then an illegal association in Malaya, and Chinese secret society elements.[55]

Notes

1. An earlier version of this chapter appeared in *The Journal of the Malaysian Branch of the Royal Asiatic Society* 85, Pt 1, no. 302 (June 2012), pp. 45–62. The Malayan Film Unit (MFU) made a film about the KVHG (see paper by Abdul Muthalib "The End of Empire: The Films of the MFU in 1950's British Malaya", in Lee Grieveson and Colin McCabe, eds., *End of Empire: Cultural Histories of Cinema* (London: British Film Institute, 2011), pp. 69–89.
2. Cloake, op. cit., p. 248.
3. Lee Su Yin, *British Policy and the Chinese in Singapore, 1939–1955. The Public Service Career of Tan Chin Tuan* (Singapore: Talisman Publishing, 2011), p. 77.
4. ISEAS Library, Tun Sir Henry H.S. Lee, Private Papers Collection, HSL 20.042, Confidential, "Report on Kinta Valley Home Guard, J.G.H. Brett, Force Commander, KVHG, to Colonel H.S. Lee, CBE, JP, 29 October 1954". See also Heng Pek Koon, *Chinese Politics in Malaysia: A History of the Malaysian Chinese Association* (Singapore: Oxford University Press, 1988), p. 123. It is believed that some of Lee's private papers are held in his family archives in Xinyi, his family hometown in south China, but they probably relate to his time in China before he moved to Malaya in the mid-1920's, and it has not been possible to consult them.
5. Robert Heussler, *British Rule in Malaya 1942–1957* (Kuala Lumpur: Heinemann Educational Books (Asia) Ltd, 1983), pp. 169–71, and CO 1022/187, Secret, "Paper by Combined General Staff Intelligence on CPM's Finance, 27 November 1953". The CPM was reliably reported to be levying a monthly tax on tin mines throughout Malaya as a form of "protection money". See also *Federation of Malaya Annual Report 1952* (Kuala Lumpur: Government Printer, 1953), p. 14,

and Salma Nasution Khoo and Abdul-Razzaq Lubis, *Kinta Valley. Pioneering Malaya's Modern Development* (Ipoh: Perak Academy, 2005), pp. 7–15.

6. Curriculum Development Institute of Singapore, *Social and Economic History of Modern Singapore* (Singapore: Longman Singapore Publishers, 1986), p. 56.
7. *Federation of Malaya Annual Report, 1954*, Her Majesty's Stationery Office, London, 1955, p. 6.
8. Chin Peng, the Secretary General of the CPM, referred to the serious impact the Briggs Plan had on the CPM's source of food supplies from New Villages in his closed-door seminar "My Views on the Emergency" held at ISEAS on 7 October 2004. See also Richard Stubbs, "Counter-insurgency. The Impact of the Korean War Prices Boom on the Malayan Emergency", ISEAS, Occasional Paper no. 19, February 1974, and A.J. Stockwell, "Insurgency & Decolonization during the Malayan Emergency", *JCCP*, 23 (1987), p. 75.
9. A picul is a Chinese and Southeast Asian unit of weight equal to 133 1/3 pounds (about 60 kilos).
10. *Federation of Malaya Annual Report 1952* (1953: xii) and Heussler, op. cit., pp. 169–71. See also CO 1030/174, "Sir Donald MacGillivray's Dispatch No. 94/55 to Lennox Boyd, Secretary of State for the Colonies", referring to the serious drop in tin and rubber prices.
11. *Federation of Malaya Annual Report 1952* (Kuala Lumpur: Government Printer, 1953), p. 148.
12. CO 1022/461, "Extract from press statement by General Templer in London, 14 June 1952".
13. The Malayan financial year corresponded to the calendar year.
14. CO 1022/100, "General Templer's Speech from the Chair, 19 November 1953".
15. CO 1022/35, Minutes of the Federal Executive Council, 25 November 1953, pp. 748–53 and Lee Su Yin, *British Policy and the Chinese in Singapore, The Public Service Career of Tan Chin Tuan* (Singapore: Talisman Publishing, 2011), p. 108.
16. National Archives of Australia, NAA: A816, Malaya — File 3, "High Commissioner's Budget Speech", 20 December 1954, from Australian Commissioner, Singapore, to Department of External Affairs, Canberra.
17. CO10 22/35, "Extract from Malaya Federal Executive Council Meeting", 25 March 1952.
18. Francis Loh, op. cit. p. 166.
19. *Federation of Malaya Annual Report 1953*, op. cit., p. 346. The Inspector-General of Home Guard was responsible for the Home Guard organization but not its operational deployment. Before taking up his appointment, Major General de Fonblanque was Assistant Director of Civil Defence, Penang. See also CO 1022/35, Federal Government Press Statement D.INF.3/52/264 (DEF),

30 March 1952, "Reorganisation of Home Guard" and CO 1022/35, Malayan Home Guard Reorganisation. ("Best Use of Force", *Glasgow Herald*, 31 March 1952).

20. Khoo and Lubis, op. cit., p. 310.

21. Heussler, op. cit., pp. 169–72; ISEAS Library, Tun Sir Henry H.S. Lee, Private Papers Collection HSL 20.046C, Secret, "Home Guard in 1954", Director of Operations Combined Emergency Planning Staff Paper No. 49, 6 October 1954, in which the Chinese secret societies were identified as the Ang Bin Hoey (spelling in romanized form according to the Hokkien dialect) and the Wah Kee (spelling according to the Cantonese dialect). The first name is sometimes spelt in romanized form as "Hung Min Hui" and the latter as "Hua Chi" (see Leon Comber, *The Triads: Chinese Secret Societies in 1950's Malaya and Singapore* (Singapore: Talisman Publishing and Singapore Heritage Society, 2009), pp. 67–71). The major Chinese secret societies, and the most powerful ones in the Ipoh/Kinta Valley area who were reportedly behind the MCA were the Ang Bin Hoey Triad secret society and the "108" and "08" gangs (Karl von Vorys, *Democracy without Consensus: Communalism and Political Stability in Malaysia* (Princeton: Princeton University Press, 1975), p. 291, fn. 3). In fact, Lau Pak Kuan, the Perak tin mining magnate mentioned above, was often seen in the company of Chiam Ai Hua, said to be the triad liaison officer for north Malaya (see Malayan Security Service, Secret, *Political Intelligence Journal*, Serial No. 14/1947, 1 September 1947, p. 331). One of the concerns of the Malayan Special Branch at the time was that General Templer was not fully aware, if aware at all, of the triad connection with the KVHG which he was supporting. See also Leon Comber, *Malaya's Secret Police 1945–60: The Role of the Special Branch in the Malayan Emergency* (Singapore: Institute of Southeast Asian Studies/Monash University Press, 2008), p. 55, fn. 95, and *New York Times*, 28 July 1952, Tillman Durdin, "Chinese Organise Malayan Army Unit in Tin-Rich Kinta Valley". Tillman said "Pro-Nationalist China elements [i.e. KMT] are predominant not only among the officers but also among the rank and file".

22. CO 1022/36, "The Kinta Valley Home Guard", Extract from *Chinese Affairs Review*, September 1952.

23. AIR 20/7777, "Briggs Report 15 May 1950–30 September 1950" and Directive No. 6, "The Home Guard Scheme", p. 18, called for each village and resettlement area to establish and train a Home Guard to help in its defence. The Home Guard would be issued with a proportion of shotguns, and operate with and under the control of the Police in the area. (See CO 1022/35, "Home Guard", minute dated 19 February 1952 by P.F. Jerrom, Colonial Office).

24. See Federal Government Press Statement, 31 March 1952. "Reorganisation of the Home Guard".

25. CAB 129/48 (C) 51 59, Malaya, Secret. "Lyttelton's Cabinet papers re. Mission to Malaya, Appendix IX, Intelligence Services & Related Counter-Measures". See also "Lyttelton Stresses Govt's Trust in Chinese" in the *Singapore Standard*, 12 December 1951.

26. Federal Government Press Statement, D.INF. 3/52/264 (DEF), 31 March 1952, "Reorganisation of the Home Guard and Appointment of Major General EP de Fonblanque, CB, CBE, DSO as Inspector General of 246,978 Home Guards".

27. CO 1022/35, "Home Guard. Organisation and Training", Extract from Lord Munster's Brief. House of Lords Debate, 27 February 1952.

28. ISEAS Library, Tun Sir Henry H.S. Lee, Private Papers Collection, HSL 20.046C/1, Secret. "The Home Guard in 1955, Director of Operations Combined Emergency Planning Staff Paper 49, Appendix A to Director of Operations Committee Meeting 38/54". According to this Staff Paper only 12 per cent of the Home Guards serving in operational sections were Chinese compared with 85 per cent Malays in 1955. Most of the Chinese Home Guards were employed in guarding Chinese New Villages and towns, and some of them were reported to be keeping the peace by making "unofficial payments" to the Communists.

29. CO 1022/35, "Home Guard".

30. See CO 825/74/3, "Monthly Political Reports from Federation of Malaya", minute dated 30 August 1949, p. 15, in which reference is made to a suggestion that the MCA provided a cover for the KMT. In May 1949 the KMT officially ceased to exist in Malaya as a legal organization, and in January 1950 Britain recognized the Communist People's Republic of China. But in a paradoxical way in the neighbouring British colony of Hong Kong the KMT was allowed to exist with the tacit approval of the British colonial Government as it was in a good position to provide intelligence about Communist activities in the colony. (See Keith Jeffery, *MI6: The History of the Secret Intelligence Service 1909–1949* (London: Bloomsbury Publishing, 2010), pp. 700–701). Like the Chinese Communists, the KMT was not particularly well disposed towards the British. It was a Nationalist Party but it faced with the British a common enemy in Communism. For an interesting account of KMT activities in Singapore (1937–41), see Lee Su Yin, op. cit., pp. 36–47.

31. Comber, *Malaya's Secret Police*, op. cit., p. 118.

32. See ISEAS Library, Tun Sir Henry H.S. Lee, Private Papers Collection, HSL 20.046C, Secret, "Director of Operations Combined Emergency Planning Staff Paper 49, The Home Guard in 1954", p. 36. The authors of the Staff Paper clearly regarded the Kinta Valley Home Guard as *sui generis* and different from other Home Guard units in Malaya.

33. He was awarded an OBE by the British government in 1956 and in 1966 was conferred with the title "Dato Seri" by the Sultan of Perak.

34. MSS, Secret. "Who's Who", *Political Intelligence Journal*, Serial No. 38, P.F. No. 1/430.

35. ISEAS Library, Tun Sir Henry H.S. Lee, Private Papers Collection, HSL 4.009, "MCA Supports General Templer's Call for Chinese Youths to join Police, 2 April 1952".

36. Khoo and Lubis, op. cit., pp. 309–10.

37. Cloake, op. cit., p. 301.

38. H.S. Lee was one of the most successful Chinese businessmen in Malaya, and President of the Associated Chinese Chambers of Commerce, the bastion of Chinese capitalist interests in Malaya (see Heng, op. cit., p. 207). Although he had been educated at the old colonial-established Hong Kong University and at Cambridge University where he read law and politics (King George VI was one of his contemporaries there), he spoke English with quite a heavily accented Cantonese accent (author's notes).

39. *Tun Sir Henry H.S. Lee.* Muzium Negara, Kuala Lumpur, 19 November 1988, and author's notes.

40. ISEAS Library, Tun Sir Henry H.S. Lee, Private Papers Collection, HSL 18.007 (undated), "Mining Representative, Selangor State War Executive Committee".

41. ISEAS Library, Tun Sir Henry H.S. Lee, Private Papers Collection, HSL 21/04/1, "Colonel HS Lee, Member Federation of Malaya War Council, 1952". See also ISEAS Library, Tun Sir Henry H.S. Lee, Private Papers Collection, HSL 18.007, "Selangor War Executive Committee" and <http://en.wikipedia.org/wiki/Henry_Lee_Hau_Shik> (accessed 1 August 2011).

42. Comber, *Malaya's Secret Police*, op. cit., p. 54, fn. 86.

43. CO 1022/198. "Secret letter dated 2 September 1952 from Sir J.F. Nicoll to General Templer". See *The Scotsman*, 19 August 1952 (Rawle Knox, Special Correspondent, Singapore), "Kuomintang Appeal to Overseas Chinese to Fight Communism".

44. It is possible that MacDonald's view was influenced by the use made by MI6 in neighbouring Hong Kong, then a British colony, of the KMT as a "counter-Communist force" (see Jeffery, op. cit., pp. 700–701).

45. Comber, *Malaya's Secret Police*, op. cit., p. 40. While it was correct that the KMT was anti-Communist and willing to support the Malayan Government in its war against the CPM and to this extent its aims coincided with the Government's, its loyalty lay with China and not Malaya.

46. ISEAS Library, Tun Sir Henry H.S. Lee, Private Papers Collection, HSL 11.099/1, "Secret & Personal letter, 8 March 1954, from the Malayan Colonial Secretary to Colonel H.S. Lee".

47. ISEAS Library, Tun Sir Henry H.S. Lee, Private Papers Collection, HSL 20.042a, "Report on Kinta Valley Home Guard" by J.C.H. Brett, Force Commander, KVHG.

48. Ibid.

49. CO 1022/36, "Chinese Organize Malaya Army Unit. Anti-Reds Forming New Force to Combat Communism in Tin-Rich Kinta Valley", *New York Times*, 30 July 1952. According to this article, thirty-six Chinese officers were enlisted and were participating in the training programme, and pro-KMT elements were prominent not only among the officers but among the rank and file.

50. ISEAS Library, Tun Sir Henry H.S. Lee, Private Papers Collection, HSL 20.042a, Confidential, "Report on Kinta Valley Home Guard" by J.C.H. Brett, Force Commander, KVHG, to Colonel H.S. Lee, CBE, JP.

51. ISEAS Library, Tun Sir Henry H.S. Lee, Private Papers Collection. HSL 20.042a, ibid.

52. ISEAS Library, Tun Sir Henry H.S. Lee, Private Papers Collection. HSL 15.24, Secret. "MCA HQ Kuala Lumpur, 5th Cabinet Meeting, 3 October 1952".

53. ISEAS Library, Tun Sir Henry H.S. Lee, Private Papers Collection. HSL 20.042, Confidential. "Letter dated 29 October 1954 from J.G.H. Brett, Force Commander, Kinta Valley Home Guard, Perak, to Colonel H.S. Lee, enclosing a copy of the Malayan Government draft budget for 1955, together with his report on the KVHG which he had prepared for a meeting of the Perak State War Advisory Council".

54. CO 1022/36, "General Templer's Visit to Kinta Valley", Federal Government Press Statement, Kuala Lumpur, (D. INF. 8/52/99 (HG), 9 August 1952.

55. See note 11 *supra*, and author's notes. CO 1022/35, "Extract from Malayan Federal Executive Council Minutes, 25 March 1952"; ISEAS Library Tun Sir H.S. Lee Private Papers, HSL 20.04c, Secret, "Home Guard in 1954"; Heussler, op. cit., pp. 169–72, and W. Blythe, *The Impact of Chinese Secret Societies in Malaya* (Kuala Lumpur: Oxford University Press, 1969), p. 441.

6

THE CASE OF LEE MENG —
A CAUSE CÉLÈBRE:[1]
The System of Justice in Malaya
(1952)

One of the most dramatic incidents of General Templer's proconsulship occurred in 1952, which had the makings of a serious misunderstanding between the Malayan people and the British colonial Government. It brought into question various aspects of the legal system under the Emergency Regulations which were in force during General Templer's proconsulship that were of serious concern to the general public. It involved the trial, which was given wide publicity, of Lee Tien Tai (usually known as Lee Meng), an attractive twenty-six-year-old Chinese (Cantonese) woman senior cadre of the Communist Party of Malaya, running the important Communist courier link between Chin Peng's CPM Central Committee in south Thailand and Singapore, who was arrested and sentenced to death in 1952 for being in possession of a hand grenade contrary to Regulation 4(1)(b) of the Emergency Regulations 1948.[2]

The case received considerable publicity at the time in the Malayan, Singapore and the international press, as it brought to light several disturbing features about the Malayan legal system, which attracted considerable public criticism during General Templer's proconsulship that will be discussed in due course in this chapter. It eventually involved not only the Malayan Government but also the British and Hungarian Governments. Several other prominent persons became involved too, such as the British Prime Minister Winston Churchill; Malcolm MacDonald; P.G. Lim; Tan Cheng Lock; Tunku Abdul Rahman; and the Sultan of Perak, Sir Yussuf 'Izzudin Shah.

The Lee Meng's case is still remembered by the Malayan Chinese community. As recently as 21 February 2014, Dato Seri Ong Ka Chuan, Secretary General of the Malayan Chinese Association, referred to it in an interview he gave to *The Star Online* in which he recollected the important part played by the MCA's first President, Tan Cheng Lock, in drawing up a petition to seek clemency from the Sultan of Perak for Lee Meng who had been sentenced to death.[3] Dato Seri Ong said the way in which her case was handled by the British colonial authorities came in for considerable criticism at the time and that the Chinese community was angry at what they perceived as "blatant persecution" on the part of the British colonial officials to ensure that she was convicted. It was widely felt at the time that General Templer and Malcolm MacDonald could have intervened more actively in responding to the accusations that she had been unfairly tried under the legal system then in existence.

In his autobiography, the CPM's Secretary General, Chin Peng, described Lee Meng as the "head courier" operating under the direction of the CPM's Central Committee.[4] However, aside from controlling a high-level Communist courier network , she was on Special Branch record as being a member of the CPM's Perak State Committee who had held several important positions in the Communist organization in Perak including the leadership of the notorious "Kepayang gang" in the Ipoh district that was responsible for much of the violence in that area.[5] For a short time, at the beginning of the Emergency, she was Secretary of the CPM's District Committee responsible for the main Chemor–Kuala Kangsar Road area in Perak before she moved to Ipoh as Secretary of the CPM's Ipoh Town Committee.[6] As one of the top Communists in Malaya, the Government had placed a reward of M$120,000 on her head.[7]

LEGAL SYSTEM IN THE MALAY STATES AND STRAITS SETTLEMENTS

The development of legal procedures in the Malay States and the Straits Settlements of Singapore, Malacca, and Penang followed different paths. From 1900, in the Straits Settlements, serious criminal cases were tried by a judge and jury but in the Malay States it was found impractical to empanel a sufficient number of peers with competency in English to participate in the trial of persons charged with a capital offence, and capital cases where the maximum penalty was death were tried by a judge and two assessors. Under this system, three assessors were chosen from ordinary people who were conversant in English and the presiding judge would select two of them to serve as assessors, including one who spoke the language of the accused.

At the time of Lee Meng's trial, cases in the Malay States with the maximum penalty of death under the Emergency Regulations were tried by a judge assisted by two assessors. While assessors did not have the same powers as a jury, their functions were not simply advisory and the judge had to be in agreement with at least one of them in order to arrive at a verdict. Under the assessor system, however, Europeans had the right of trial by two assessors of their own race but the same right did not extend to Asian defendants who could be tried by European assessors, and this was one of the grievances of the opposition to the assessor system. If, however, a judge disagreed with both assessors as to the innocence or guilt of the accused, he could order a retrial. At the conclusion of Lee Meng's trial, when the two Asian assessors found Lee Meng not guilty, the judge Justice J. Thomson followed this procedure and announced that he did not agree with the verdict and ordered a retrial under different assessors. This was perceived by many members of the general public as trying her twice for the same offence.

The view of the British colonial Government at the time, which General Templer supported, was that Malaya "was not yet ready for the introduction of a jury system owing to the shortage of suitable jurors with a sufficient knowledge of English and a sufficient degree of public responsibility".[8] In an off-the-record interview he gave on 3 October 1953 to Ian Hamilton, Public Relations Officer, Australian Commission in Kuala Lumpur, he opined that 85 per cent of the Asian population of Malaya, Chinese, Malays and Indians, "completely lacked political consciousness".[9]

Nevertheless, although the assessor system had been quietly followed for many years until Lee Meng's trial, it seemed that the catalyst of the international attention it now aroused, had the effect of bringing to the forefront the inherent shortcomings and problems of the system.[10]

LEE MENG'S ARREST AND TRIAL

Lee Meng was arrested in Ipoh on 24 July 1952 for being in possession of Communist documents, as the result of months of skilful and painstaking investigation by the Malayan and Singapore Special Branches leading to her arrest. After her detention, as she was not eligible for bail, she was detained in Taiping Prison to await trial.

On 6 August 1952, she was arraigned before the Assize Court, Ipoh, with Justice Thomson presiding [who was later to become Malaysia's first Lord President], assisted by two assessors, a Chinese and an Indian. The case for the Crown was led by M.G. Neal (Deputy Public Prosecutor). Lee Meng was represented by S.P. Seenivasagam, a prominent Ceylonese (Sri Lankan) barrister in Ipoh, and she pleaded not guilty to the offence.

S.P. Seenivasagam and his barrister brother D.R. Seenivasagam, who assisted him in his law firm, were both prominent members of the People's Progressive Party (PPP) which was regarded as the political voice of the Chinese and Indian electorate in Ipoh at that time.[11]

The case was adjourned for hearing until 28 August when according to press reports, hundreds of people gathered at every possible vantage point in and around the Court in order to catch a glimpse of Lee Meng and strong security measures had to be taken with armed members of a police jungle squad posted in and around the building.[12]

In opening the case, the DPP said that it had been decided not to proceed against her for possessing Communist documents but to charge her with three other offences under the Emergency Regulations each carrying the death penalty. The charges were, firstly, that she was armed with a pistol between August 1948 and September 1951 in the Kepayang area of Ipoh; secondly, she carried a hand grenade at the same time; and thirdly, she consorted with persons who were carrying firearms and acting in a manner prejudicial to the maintenance of law and good order. It seems that her position as the controller of the vitally important CPM courier link stretching southwards from the CPM's Central Committee in south Thailand to the CPM's Singapore Town Committee in Singapore was not disclosed so that the CPM's Central Committee would not be aware, at least for the time being, of what the authorities knew about her.

The DPP announced, too, that he intended to arraign her on a fourth charge of carrying a Browning automatic pistol during the two-month period prior to her arrest. However, he said that while this would remain in the record, he was only proceeding against her on the charge of possessing a hand grenade at five different places in the Ipoh area between 15 July 1949 and September 1951, which was a capital offence punishable by death under Regulation 4(1)(b) of the Emergency Regulations 1948.[13]

The charge, however, was unusual as Lee Meng had not been arrested in possession of a hand grenade or a firearm and it was clear that the prosecution case would have to rest on the evidence of a group of nine surrendered Communist terrorists (SEPs) — eight Chinese and one Tamil, who claimed to have been in the jungle with her when she was armed with a hand grenade; a Chinese woman who had been abducted by the Communist terrorists and detained in their camp who stated she had seen Lee Meng there armed with a hand grenade; and a Chinese Special Branch inspector who had participated in an attack on the camp, who could identify Lee Meng as being one of the Communist guerrillas present in the camp. As supporting evidence, the Police produced photographs purportedly showing Lee Meng wearing Communist terrorist uniform and carrying a rifle and hand grenade, which the police had recovered from an attack on a Communist hideout in a cave on the outskirts of Ipoh. Lee Meng, however, strongly denied she was the woman in the photographs. Nevertheless, on the face of it, there appeared to be a strong *prima facie* case against her.[14]

Not unexpectedly, the line taken by the defence at the trial was that the evidence provided by the SEPs was tainted and unreliable, and the witnesses were committing perjury in order to obtain a free pardon. Lee Meng did not call any witnesses for her defence and declined to give evidence on oath. However, she made a statement from the witness box, for which she could not be cross-examined, in which she said that she had intended to call her friend Cheow Yin as a witness on her behalf but her counsel S.P. Seenivasagam had told her that she had committed suicide while in police custody. She denied that her name was Lee Meng, as some of the witnesses had stated, and said that it was Lee Tien Tai. She stated that she had formerly lived in Ipoh for many years but had stayed with her married sister in Singapore from 1948 to 1950. After her sister had died, she moved back to Ipoh and stayed with her friend Cheow Yin, whom her counsel had told her had committed suicide.[15] Lee Meng claimed that while she was in Ipoh, she stayed most of the time at home looking after two young children, whom she claimed were her nephew and niece.[16] However, according to Special Branch records, they were either the children of CPM's Central Committee member Kah Sim, who had been killed in December 1949 by the security forces in the Chemor area of Perak, or of the CPM's Central Committee member Yong Chan Meng (alias Ah Loo), who was then in the jungle in charge of the CPM's North Malaya Bureau.[17]

To the dismay of the prosecution, after Mr Justice Thomson had summed up the case for seventy minutes, the two Asian assessors assisting him, after retiring for twenty minutes, returned to present a verdict of "not guilty". Mr Justice Thomson said that he disagreed with them, and used his prerogative under the assessor system to order a retrial.[18] He addressed Lee Meng as follows: "Both assessors are of opinion that you are not guilty. How, as reasonable men, they can come to that opinion, I have no means of knowing. I disagree with their opinion and order a retrial."[19]

RETRIAL OF LEE MENG (10 SEPTEMBER 1952)

At Lee Meng's retrial on 10 September 1952 before Mr Justice Pretheroe, the assessors were a European, E.W. Woolfendon, and a Chinese, Tan Yew Hock. The selection of a European assessor was considered unusual as it was, in fact, the first time that a European had been selected from the assessors' panel to serve on a trial of an Asian in the Perak High Court for offences against the Emergency Regulations.

Lee Meng, speaking in Cantonese from the dock, objected to the appointment of a European as an assessor, and told the Judge: "One of the assessors and you are European, and only one is Chinese." However, when her comments were translated to Justice Pretheroe, he informed her that her objection was overruled and advised her to keep quiet as she would only prejudice her case.[20] However, her subsequent remarks "that she feared, as she was being accused of associating with people alleged to have killed Europeans, a European assessor would be prejudiced against her", were not translated.[21]

At the end of trial, the two assessors were divided. The European found her guilty and the Chinese not guilty. Mr Justice Pretheroe, however, agreed with the European assessor's verdict and found her guilty and thereupon passed the mandatory death sentence on her.

As P.G. Lim subsequently commented in her book *Kaleidoscope: The Memoirs of P.G. Lim*: "There were disturbing aspects to the case which were a subject of concern as her trials had been conducted under the assessor system then prevailing in the Malay States, whereas in the British Settlements of Penang, Malacca and Singapore trial by jury applied in all criminal cases involving the death penalty."[22] The *Straits Times*, the leading English-language newspaper which usually supported the Government line, came out, too, in favour of trial by jury, and reported that the Federation of Malaya Government and the local Bar Council were considering the introduction of trial by jury as the assessor system was unsatisfactory in many ways. In nearly every case it resulted in the judge disagreeing with the assessor who had found the accused not guilty and ruling in favour of the assessor who found the accused guilty, thus resulting in a large number of retrials.[23]

APPEALS IN MALAYAN COURT OF APPEAL, KUALA LUMPUR, AND PRIVY COUNCIL, LONDON

Lee Meng's counsel S.P. Seenivasagam then lodged an appeal in the Malayan Court of Appeal in Kuala Lumpur against his client's conviction and sentence, and the appeal was argued on 14 November 1952 before three judges making up the Court: the Chief Justice of the Federation of Malaya, Mr Justice Mathew; the Chief Justice of Singapore, Sir Charles Murray-Aynsley; and Mr Justice Whitton. However, the appeal was rejected and the Court dismissed it by a two-to-one verdict with Sir Charles Murray-Aynsley, the Singapore Chief Justice, dissenting. In his view the charge was "defective in law" as no facts had been adduced to show that Lee Meng was in possession of a hand grenade at the five different places alleged.[24]

S.P. Seenivasagam then lodged an appeal to be heard by the Privy Council in London which was the supreme court of appeal for both civil and criminal cases in the United Kingdom and the British Empire, and was able to obtain the services of P.G. Lim (then known as Mrs Wee Phair Gan Lim but usually referred to by her unmarried name of P.G. Lim), who was living in London at the time and came from a well-known Penang Malayan-Chinese Peranakan family, to assist him in recommending a senior barrister who could take up the case and prepare a petition in *forma pauperis* to argue the appeal to the Privy Council.[25]

P.G. Lim suggested H.C.L. Hanne & Co., a well-known firm of London solicitors, and as a result Mr Dingle Foot, QC, an eminent U.K. barrister, agreed to take up Lee Meng's case, with P.G. Lim assisting him as his junior counsel, on a *pro bono* basis.[26] Seenivasagam immediately sent by airmail the necessary documents to enable them to present a petition for special permission to appeal in *forma pauperis* against Lee Meng's death sentence which was duly lodged with the Privy Council in London. On 17 February 1953, Dingle Foot, with P.G. Lim assisting him as his junior counsel, appeared to argue the case before the Judicial Committee of the Privy Council consisting of Lords Porter, Tucker and Asquith. However, their Lordships, after retiring for deliberation, refused permission for the case to proceed on the grounds that it did not fall within their terms of reference.[27]

As P.G. Lim wryly remarked:

> We lost the battle on a point of law which could have been tilted on one side or the other ... the result did not come as too much of a surprise [to Foot and herself] and one has to take into account that the Privy Council exercised a very special and limited jurisdiction in criminal matters and is not, as such, a Court of Criminal Appeal at all.[28]

Dingle Foot commented that: "[Lee Meng's] case might well be fair but was not seen to be fair, given that no Asian, sitting in judgement, had found her guilty."[29] And S.P. Seenivasagam, in discussing the matter, criticized "the pernicious nature of the Malayan assessor system where the accused was tried and retried until the 'desired verdict' was reached."[30]

COMMUTATION OF SENTENCE

Meanwhile, the indefatigable Seenivasagam, in anticipation of the outcome of the Privy Council appeal, had instructed Hanne & Co. to prepare a petition to be sent to the Sultan of Perak[31] to exercise his prerogative of mercy in Lee Meng's case and commute her death sentence to life imprisonment. In those days, the Sultan of a Malay State had the right to exercise clemency to commute a death sentence.[32]

Arrangements were made too for Dingle Foot and P.G. Lim to address a group of distinguished and prominent parliamentarians of both Houses of Parliament of their concern about Lee Meng's case, and a petition of clemency was drafted and sent to the Sultan of Perak. Some of the more noteworthy of a large group of well-known MPs who signed the petition were Harold Wilson, a future British Prime Minister; Tony Benn, a well-known Labour MP; Jennie Lee, Minister of the Arts and founder of the U.K. Open University; and Elwyn Jones, QC, a former British Attorney General. The petition was signed by sixty MPs and appealed to the Sultan to "grant free or conditional pardon to Lee Tien Tai alias Lee Meng". The petition was airmailed on 19 February 1953 to the Attorney General (Hogan) in Kuala Lumpur for transmission to the Sultan of Perak and another copy was sent to the Mentri Besar of Perak.[33]

Tan Cheng Lock, who had himself been wounded by a grenade in a Communist attack while he was addressing an MCA meeting in Ipoh in 1949, entered a plea on Lee Meng's behalf, too, in which he argued that racial prejudice had been shown at Lee Meng's trial in that while Europeans had a right of trial by two assessors of their own race, the same right was denied to Asian defendants.

HUNGARIAN GOVERNMENT OFFER

In the meantime, on 2 March 1953, there was a completely unexpected and dramatic twist to the case when the Communist Hungarian Government contacted Robert Hankey, the British Minister in Budapest, with an offer to release a British businessman, Edgar Sanders, who was serving thirteen years' imprisonment in Budapest for espionage, in exchange for Lee Meng.

Edgar Sanders, who was then forty-three years old, had come to Britain from Leningrad when he was eleven, was the cousin of George Sanders, a well-known film star, and had served as a captain in the British Army during World War II. He was employed in Hungary by the American-owned International Telegraph and Telephone Company and had been arrested on espionage charges with his business associate Robert Volger, an American national, and Imre Geiger, a Hungarian. At their trial, all the defendants were found guilty of spying. Geiger was executed, Volger was sentenced to fifteen years' imprisonment, and Sanders to thirteen years. The British Government had been denied access to Sanders after his arrest and he was refused the assistance of legal representation at his trial and was not provided with any facilities to communicate with his wife and children in England. Volger's counsel was denied a visa. Volger, however, was released from prison early on as the U.S. Government made what were described as "diplomatic concessions" to the Hungarian Government, whereas the Labour Government in Britain had broken off trade relations with Hungary.[34]

The unusual features of Lee Meng's case attracted widespread local and international interest. There was public reaction, too, in Malaya at the way the case had been handled by the British colonial authorities and, in the opinion of many people "thoroughly deserved critical remarks [were made] about British justice not only in Malaya but also in Britain".[35]

There was a mixed reaction to the Hungarian offer. Some resentment was expressed in Malaya at what was described as "outside interference and cynical opportunism" by the Hungarian Government. Even the redoubtable S.P. Seenivasagam regarded the offer as "political propaganda" and doubted whether it was made on "humanitarian grounds", and opined it would be a pity if it interfered with the "sincere petitions" for clemency that had been sent to the Sultan of Perak.[36]

A British MP, Ernest Davies, asked the British Prime Minister, Winston Churchill, in the House of Commons, if he could announce the decision that had been made on the Hungarian Government's offer, and Churchill replied that "after earnest consideration Her Majesty's Government have decided that they cannot entertain the proposals made by the Hungarian Government." And there the matter seemed to rest for the time being.

Tan Cheng Lock's petition, as mentioned earlier, drew attention, too, to the commonly held perception that Europeans in the Malay States were being treated differently from Asians. Various levels of critical remarks were in fact embedded in this simple narrative but there were many lawyers, journalists and members of the public who were critical of General Templer for his acceptance of the assessor system that they considered to be defective.[37] As Tunku Abdul Rahman related a few years later after he became Prime Minister of Malaya, whether or not Lee Meng was guilty, her trials did disclose a glaring defect in the legal system that was being followed in Malaya at the time which should have been rectified by the British colonial Government.

COMMUTATION OF LEE MENG'S DEATH SENTENCE AND RELEASE OF EDGAR SANDERS

In the meantime, petitions for clemency that had been sent to the Sultan of Perak were considered at the weekly meeting of the Perak State Executive Council on 9 March 1953 and the Sultan decided to commute Lee Meng's death sentence to penal servitude for life.

Lee Meng was then moved out of the condemned cell at Taiping Prison where she had been held since she had been sentenced to death and informed by the prison superintendent, W.J. Burton, that her death sentence had been commuted to life imprisonment. She apparently showed no emotion. She was, however, to serve for another eleven years in prison before she was quietly released by the Malaysian Government and deported to China in 1964. She was thirty-six years old at the time.

Meanwhile, the British Cabinet had discussed the Hungarian Government's offer and various arguments were advanced for and against the offer to exchange Sanders for Lee Meng. General Templer and Malcolm MacDonald, for instance, had themselves raised serious political objections to the exchange along the following lines:

- Lee Meng's release would be exploited by Communist propaganda as indicative of Communist power and its world influence.
- The CPM would claim that an exchange of the two prisoners demonstrated the power and influence it wielded in the Communist world.
- The Hungarian offer had already provided considerable encouragement to the CPM and its sympathizers.
- The two cases of Lee Meng and Sanders were not on par but if the proposed exchange went ahead, it would be assumed that both parties had been unjustly convicted.
- Malayan public opinion would resent any interference with a judicial sentence on political grounds.
- The reputation of British justice would suffer.[38]
- In support of these arguments, General Templer referred to a letter he had received from Yap Mau Tatt, Secretary General of the MCA, predicting a serious upsurge in terrorism in Malaya if the exchange took place.[39]

Their arguments in support of accepting the Hungarian Government's proposed exchange of prisoners were as follows:

- Sanders had already served three years of his sentence and his health had deteriorated.
- The British Government could argue that the trade ban imposed on Hungary had so hurt the Hungarian economy that Hungary had

decided after obtaining "permission from Moscow" to make the exchange offer.
- The way would be open for Britain to resume trade with Hungary.[40]

It is interesting, nevertheless, that no mention appears to have been made of the humanitarian aspects of the case and the likely effect the continued detention of Sanders would have had on his wife and family who had not seen him for more than three years.

In the meantime, the Hungarian Minister for Foreign Affairs confirmed with the British Minister in Budapest there would be no objection if Lee Meng was banished to China rather than to Hungary as originally proposed.

On 5 August, Mrs Sanders took the matter out of the hands of the British Government and was granted an interview with Imre Horvath, the Hungarian Minister in London, and in a press statement the Minister gave after the interview, he said that when he returned to Hungary on 11 August, he would take a letter from her to the President of the Hungarian People's Republic pleading for her husband's release. Events moved fast after that. On 17 August, Wireless Budapest announced that the Hungarian Government had pardoned Edgar Sanders and he had been expelled from the country.[41]

The Hungarian Foreign Ministry stated that the Presidium, which in People's Democracies fulfils the functions of a President, had granted Mrs Sanders' petition asking for clemency for her husband after taking into account "her grave health conditions and their children".[42]

On Lee Meng's sentence being commuted, the Malayan Special Branch requested permission to transfer her to the secret Special Branch Holding Centre in Kuala Lumpur for three months to interrogate her further concerning her knowledge of Communist courier routes and other matters, such as, for instance, the arrangements she had been making for the confinement of pregnant wives of high-ranking Communist terrorists in Perak in the houses of their relatives. One such person was Wong Pik Lin, the wife of CPM Perak State Committee member Chong Chor, who was staying with a relative at Gopeng. The Special Branch was aware, too, that while Lee Meng was in Taiping Prison, she had attempted to pass a message to Chin Voon, the CPM's Branch Secretary in the Gunong Rapat area of Ipoh, asking him to endeavour to recover on her behalf a substantial amount of party funds she had invested with a relative of a senior Perak State Committee member who was in the real estate business.[43]

It seems likely, however, that the Special Branch request to move her to the Special Branch Holding Centre in Kuala Lumpur was not acceded to on account of the considerable public interest being shown at the time about allegations that the Special Branch was using "strong-arm methods" to obtain information from detained persons and it would be difficult to convince the public that Lee Meng would not be treated in this way if she was transferred to Kuala Lumpur.[44]

In his biography Chin Peng writes that she contacted her lawyer, S.P. Seenivasagam, before her departure to China to ask him to purchase for her a sewing machine, two bicycles, and some clothes.[45] According to P.G. Lim, Seenivasagam gave her a wristwatch too.[46]

When Lee Meng returned to Guangzhou, she was reunited with her mother whom she had not seen for fourteen years since her mother had been banished to China from Malaya in 1950. Lee Meng resumed, too, her acquaintance with Chen Tian, a prominent member of the CPM's Central Committee under Chin Peng whom she had known in Malaya before he moved back to China from the Malayan-Thailand border area, and they were married in 1965.[47]

Many years afterwards, in August 2007, when Lee Meng visited Malaysia from Guangzhou where she was then living, she and some friends called on P.G. Lim, and after saying it was somewhat belated, she presented her with an enormous bouquet of red roses and an autographed copy of her biography (*Ma Gung qi nü zi*) to thank her for "her release" as she put it.[48]

As a postscript to the Lee Meng saga, Chin Peng wrote in his autobiography that Lee Meng and her husband intended to move to south Thailand after the end of the Emergency to live in one of the CPM villages that had been established there under the supervision of the Thai authorities. Chin Peng had set aside a house for her in one of these "Peace Villages" but Lee Meng did not avail herself of the offer as by that time, her husband Chen Tian had died and she was left to care for her ageing mother who had gone blind. She finally moved into a "government middle-cadre residence" that the Chinese authorities had made available for her in south China.[49]

From the security point of view, although the Special Branch felt that Lee Meng's arrest had dealt a serious blow to the main CPM communication links in Malaya, the Special Branch became aware one year after her release that courier links between Perak and Kedah had already been resumed by the brother of a Communist guerrilla operating with the 26th Platoon MNLA, who was living in Sungei Buloh New Village, Sungei Siput, Perak. Some relatives of Chin Voon, a Branch Committee Secretary mentioned earlier, were also known to be operating as couriers. The problem was that Ipoh, where Lee Meng operated, was an important CPM centre, and many high-ranking Communists, including Chin Peng himself, Lee Meng's husband Chen Tian, and Ng Thin Ong, a member of the CPM's Perak State Committee, had family ties and close friends living there. It was evident that the Communist hold over the Ipoh area was still deep-rooted, widespread, and difficult to eradicate in spite of the strength of the security forces arrayed against it, and it was clear too that the end of the Emergency was still a long way off.[50]

To revert to the Lee Meng case and the assessor system, according to the historian Anthony Short, there was a second case not long after Lee Meng's involving an eighteen-year-old girl, Lee Ah Tai, who was sentenced to death for consorting with armed Communist terrorists, which showed that the Government had not learned very much from the inherent weaknesses of the "trial by assessor system" as demonstrated in the Lee Meng case, nor indeed had it shown any scruples about sentencing women guerrillas to death.[51]

OPPOSITION TO TRIAL BY ASSESSOR SYSTEM

In the meantime, the trial by assessor system continued to attract a considerable amount of criticism which reflected adversely on the colonial Government, as a result of the Lee Meng case.

The *Straits Times* on 21 February 1953 reported that the assessor system was unsatisfactory and when it breaks down it is "an offence to justice. The system is well out of date.... There can be little doubt that the High Commissioner [Templer] and the Chief Justice would respond to public pressure." *The Times* (London) took a similar line on 7 March 1953 and referred to the *Straits Times'* report which together with other newspapers had commented on the weakness of the assessor system. It agreed there was full provision in the Criminal Procedure Code for a system of trial by jury to be introduced into the [Malay] States without further legislation. However, while it considered that "the High Commissioner and the Chief

Justice would respond to public pressure", it asked why it was necessary to wait such a long time for them to do so.

On 30 May 1953, twenty-one leading advocates and solicitors of Malaya sent a joint submission to the Registrar of the Supreme Court, Kuala Lumpur, to advocate that all offences punishable by death or by ten years' imprisonment or more should be tried by jury, and they pointed out the advantages and disadvantages of trials by jury that had already been fully discussed in the local press. Lee Meng's lawyer S.P. Seenivasagam submitted a long memorandum on the mode of trial of criminal cases in the High Court of the Malay States, and urged *inter alia* that:

- The assessor system should be abrogated forthwith and trial by Jury introduced in all criminal cases tried in the High Court.
- All criminal cases — capital and non-capital — in the High Court should be tried by jury.
- Sections 185 and 201 of the Criminal Procedure Code [referring to the appointment of European assessors for cases involving Europeans], which appears to be based on racial discrimination, should be repealed.
- All cases during the Malayan Emergency should be tried by jury to avoid discrimination.

CRIMINAL PROCEDURE CODE
(AMENDMENT) BILL 1953

As public agitation against the assessor system mounted and the repercussions from the Lee Meng trials gathered momentum, on 22 April 1953 General Templer set up a Committee under the Chief Justice, Charles Mathew, to enquire into the system and make recommendations as to the desirability of replacing it by trial by jury. The Committee deliberated for three days, and then rather surprisingly advised against introducing the jury system and unanimously recommended that the assessor system should be retained with some minor alterations.[52] A Bill entitled the Criminal Procedure Code (Amendment) Ordnance 1953 was prepared embodying the controversial conclusions of the Committee. P.G. Lim who was, as she put it, "drawn into the activities relating to the case" commented that the turn of events "had taken everyone by surprise", and she was prominent in the protests which gathered strength against the passing of the Bill.[53]

The *Straits Times* of 7 January 1954, too, came out strongly against it:

..... the proposed revision of the system of trial has shocked many people
because it is a retrogressive step..... The Committee was prejudiced .....
The Bill which is before the Federal Council ought not, we believe, to
become law despite the amendment it has undergone.[54]

The "amendment" or "improvement" to the assessor system referred to
provided for a judge to be at liberty to disagree with both the assessors
at the trial and if the judge convicted as a result of such disagreement the
case would automatically go to the Court of Appeal. For the purpose of
recording the opinions of the assessors the judge would be required to
ask them for their opinions and reasons on such issues of fact that the
judge might specify although he would not be bound by them. As P.G.
Lim commented, this meant that "only the judge had the power to decide
on the guilt or innocence of the prisoner."[55]

In view of the continuing widespread public disquiet with the
Government's legal system, P.G. Lim organized a mass rally and public
meeting in the Kuala Lumpur Town Hall on 16 January 1954 to call for
the Government's Bill to be overturned and the assessor system to be
replaced by trial by jury. It was an unprecedented move in Malaya's legal
history, more especially so as the country was in the throes of a Communist
uprising, and the Emergency Regulations that were in force provided the
Government with almost unlimited powers of arrest and detention for
holding unauthorized public meetings, but presumably in this instance
permission had been obtained. A formidable body of well-known speakers
led by Tan Cheng Lock took the stage to address the meeting, and the Bill
before the Legislative Council was attacked and a motion unanimously
adopted in favour of trial by jury. A petition was prepared along these
lines signed by over 3,000 persons which was read out to members of the
Legislative Council before the start of Council business on 27 January.[56]

When the Bill came up for hearing, Tunku Abdul Rahman, supported
by Tan Cheng Lock, and S.M. Yong (who later became Justice Dato S.M.
Yong), tabled a motion in the Legislative Council, which was seconded
by Abdul Aziz, that the assessor system in the Malay States should be
replaced by the jury system and that the former system was inequitable
in allowing an accused person to be tried and retried until "the desired
verdict" had been obtained by the Government.[57]

Two days of intense debate ensued, which was opened by the Attorney
General, J.P. Hogan, who moved the adoption of the Report of the Select

Committee.[58] He skilfully argued that trial by jury and the administration of justice had nothing to do with self-government and if the Criminal Courts are to be used for "a sort of training ground for democracy, a school for self-government or something of that sort, we will pervert and divert the stream of justice, which we want to keep as clear as we possibly can".

However, the Attorney General's speech did not seem to deal directly with the widespread objections against trial by assessor that had been voiced publicly in the local press as well as by most of the non-official Legislative Council, and he once again emphasized the lack of civil consciousness in Malaya, which seemed very much to be a reflection of the views already expressed by the British colonial Government and General Templer, as mentioned earlier. The Mentri Besar of Trengganu seconded his motion.

Tunku Abdul Rahman then rose to oppose the adoption of the Bill and said: "for a long time there has never been a Bill that has been discussed so much as this Bill is being discussed, nor has any Bill been so strongly opposed by the public" and he said he completely disagreed with the Attorney General's

> idea in not introducing a jury system in this country because there is a lack of civic responsibility in this country ... there are other countries with less, and yet there is a jury system established in those countries.... The demand for the introduction of the jury system was made quite rightly as a result of Lee Meng's case. The principle of the case was this. Lee Meng was tried and was charged — wrongly or rightly — it is not material on this particular issue. The fact was that she was tried twice. The first time two assessors found her not guilty. The judge ordered a retrial. The second time she was again tried and one of the assessors found her guilty. Therefore the result of that case was that there were three persons out of four who found her not guilty and one found her guilty and she was convicted. This case went to the Privy Council, and it was as a result of certain adverse comment by members of the public that the demand was made for the introduction of a jury system. His Excellency then appointed a Committee to go into this question ....

The Tunku went on to refer to

> the peculiarities of Asian people [that] are not very well understood by those judges who have just arrived in this country. Men on the jury would be able to assist them. .... No new legislation would be required to introduce the jury system. As long ago as 1927 there is embodied in Chapter 22 of the Criminal Procedure Code, Sections 200 and 235, which

made provision for trial by jury. The time has come to implement this
chapter. .... I do not wish to confuse the issue but I very strongly oppose
the Bill on the grounds that it is inconsistent with the trends of thoughts
today and [the] principle of democracy.'[59]

However, the rhetoric of the Attorney General, who was well known
for his oratory and often perceived to be the official mouthpiece of
General Templer, won the day, and the adoption of the Bill was passed
by all official Malay States and Settlement members of the Legislative
Council who formed the majority of the Council members, as well as
some unofficial members. When the vote was taken, there were 48 votes
in favour of passing the Bill, 14 "no's", and 3 "abstaining".[60] P.G. Lim
commented that "as we left the council lobby, I heard one Englishman
remarking to another about the Tunku that 'he can never be elected as
Prime Minister'."[61]

But Tunku Abdul Rahman still had the last word. In his book *As a
Matter of Interest* he wrote

> ... we were more or less driven out of the Council; certainly we were
> jeered and laughed at by those on the government benches. That was the
> only time we walked out, and as I was leaving the Council chambers,
> I turned round to my good friend, the late Tun Dr Ismail, saying: "Let
> them laugh. We will win one day and when the victory is won, I will
> show them what we will do; and that is exactly what our party did."[62]

When Malaya gained independence in 1957 and Tunku Abdul Rahman
became Prime Minister, his new Government passed a law to introduce
trial by jury in capital offences, and the Malayan Criminal Procedure Code
was amended accordingly.[63] A year later local juries sat in court to hear
such cases for the first time in the Malayan States.[64]

Trial by jury in Malaya lasted thirty-eight years and it was only brought
to an end on 17 February 1995 by the Criminal Procedure (Amendment)
Act 1994, which cited the danger of "lay jurors delivering judgements
coloured by emotions or popular perceptions", and under the present
system a single judge hears and decides almost all cases. However, at the
time of the passing of the Bill, the Malayan Bar Council and other NGOs
complained that they were not consulted by the Government before the
tabling of such an important amendment to the law but there the matter
seems to have rested.

Notes

1. Earlier accounts of the Lee Meng case by the author appeared in "The Weather has been Horrible: Malayan Communist Communications during the Emergency (1946–1960)", *Asian Studies Review* 19, no. 2 (1995), pp. 37–57, and in *Malaya's Secret Police 1945–60: The Role of the Special Branch in the Malayan Emergency* (Singapore: Institute of Southeast Asian Studies/Monash University Press, 2009) (reprint), pp. 228–37. Since then, however, much new information has become available which has been incorporated in this account from a biography of Lee Meng in Chinese by Zhèng Zhào Xián, *Ma Gung qi nü zi. Chen Tian fu ren. Li Ming kou su li shi* (A Woman of the Communist Party of Malaya. Mdm Chen Tian. An Oral history of Lee Meng) (Petaling Jaya: Strategic Information & Research Development, Zhèng Zhào Xián Centre, 2007); P.G. Lim, *Kaleidoscope: The Memoirs of P.G. Lim* (Petaling Jaya: Strategic Information & Research Development Centre, 2012); and Courtesy of ISEAS Library, Singapore: P.G. Lim Private Papers Archives Collection, Folios 5 and 14.

2. Lee Meng (b. 1926 in Guangzhou) joined the CPM in Ipoh in 1942 at the age of sixteen years, and even at a young age was active in the Party's resistance movement against the Japanese in the Ipoh area during the Japanese Occupation. At the age of twenty-two years, she became a member of the CPM's Perak State Committee. She was at one time a teacher in a Chinese school in Teluk Anson (now Teluk Intan). See Zhèng, op. cit., which provides a full account of her life and trials under the assessor system that was then in force in Malaya; the commutation of her death sentence by the Sultan of Perak to life imprisonment; her eventual release from Taiping Prison; and her repatriation to Guangzhou in 1963, where in 1965 she married Chen Tian, former head of the CPM's Central Propaganda Department and a former member of the CPM's Central Executive Committee. Chen Tian, together with Rashid Maidin, a Malay senior CPM representative, had accompanied Chin Peng, the CPM's Secretary General, in December 1955 to the Baling Talks with Tunku Abdul Rahman, David Marshall, Singapore's Chief Minister, and Dato Sir Cheng Lock Tan, President of the Malayan Chinese Association.

3. *The Star ePaper*, "Ong : MCA is a rational voice" by Yuen Mei Keng, 21 February 2014, p. 1.

4. Chin Peng, *Alias Chin Peng: My Side of History* (as told to Ian Ward & Norma Miraflor) (Singapore: Media Publishers, 2003), p. 348.

5. *The Times* (London), 10 March 1953, p. 7.

6. Ibid., 18 February 1953, p. 11; 2 March 1953, pp. 7–8; 10 March 1953, p. 7; 12 March 1953, p. 5; 19 March 1953, p. 6; Yuen Yuet Leng, *Operation Ginger* (Kuala Lumpur: Vinpress Press Sdn. Bhd., 1988), p. 57; Anthony Short, *The Communist Insurrection in Malaya 1948–60* (London: Frederick Muller Ltd., 1975), pp. 383–85.

7. Yuen, ibid.; *The Times* (London), 10 March 1953, p. 7; 13 March 1953, p. 3. In his account of Lee Meng in *The War of the Running Dogs: The Malayan Emergency, 1948–60* (London: Fontana Books, 1973) (3rd impression), Noel Barber describes her as "the virtual boss of the Communist courier network". According to Special Branch records, her mother had been arrested early on in the Emergency for Communist activities and had been banished to China in 1950. *The Times* (London), 10 March 1953, p. 7.

8. CO 1022/3/146, File SEA 75/02, p. 18, and *The Times* (London), 18 February 1953, p. 11.

9. National Archives of Australia, NAA: Confidential, A816/58, Item: 19/321/18PR/891/53, "Off-the-record Interview with General Templer on 3 October 1953", Australian Commissioner, Singapore, to Department of External Affairs, Canberra.

10. See Zhèng Zhào Xián, op. cit., p. 65.

11. See Barbara Watson Andaya and Leonard Y. Andaya, *A History of Malaysia* (London: Macmillan Press Ltd., 1982), p. 280.

12. *Straits Times*, 30 August 1952.

13. Yap Yok Foo, *Berita Harian*, 11 March 2003.

14. ISEAS Library, P.G. Lim Private Archives Collection, Folios 5 and 14.

15. *The Times* (London), 18 February 1953, p. 11.

16. ISEAS Library, P.G. Lim Private Archives Collection, Folio 14, PGL/014/014/001, enclosing copy of the *Straits Times*, 29 August 1952. It was subsequently determined, when Lee Meng's lawyer SP Seenivasagam enquired about the children's whereabouts, that they had been moved by the Government to a Social Welfare Children's Home in Kuala Lumpur (Short, op. cit., p. 385, fn. 51).

17. Yuen Yuet Leng, op. cit., p. 57.

18. CO 1022/3, "Representations Against Sentence of Death Passed on Lee Tien Tai (Lee Meng) in Federation of Malaya". The *Nanyang Siang Pau* (Singapore, 1 December 1952) described the Malayan colonial government's attitude in pursuing Lee Meng's conviction as "ruthless". See also *Straits Times, 19 February 1953*, and Noel Barber, *The War of the Running Dogs: The Malayan Emergency 1948–60* (London: Fontana Books, 1973) (3rd impression), p. 158.

19. Chin Peng, op. cit., p. 343, and Barber, op. cit., p. 158.

20. P.G. Lim, op. cit., p. 137 and Chin Peng, op. cit., p. 342.

21. See ISEAS Library, P.G. Lim Private Archives Collection, Folio 14, PGL/019/025/001, enclosing a letter dated 11 February 1953 from S.P. Seenivasagam to H.C.L. Hanne & Co., Solicitors at the Inns of Court, London.

22. P.G. Lim, op. cit., p. 136.

23. *Straits Times,* 20 February 1953 and P.G. Lim, op. cit., p. 146.

24. P.G. Lim, op. cit., p. 138, and *The Times* (London), 15 November 1952, p. 5.

25. Tan Sri Phair Gan Lim (P.G. Lim) (1915–2013), MA (Cantab), Barrister-at-Law (Lincoln's Inn) and Advocate and Solicitor (Malaysia), subsequently had a long and distinguished career both as a lawyer and diplomat, and helped to introduce the trial-by-jury system to Malaya in 1954. As a diplomat, she served as Malaysian Ambassador and Deputy Permanent Representative of Malaysia to the United Nations (1971–73), Ambassador to Yugoslavia and Austria (1973–77), Ambassador to Belgium and the European and the European Economic Commission (EEC) (1977–80). She was honoured by the award of Panglima Setia Mahkota (PSM), which carried the title "Tan Sri" by the Yang di-Pertuan Agong (the Malaysian King) on 8 June 2011.

26. See Yap Yook Foo, "The Assessors. Precursors to the Jury System", *Berita Malaysia*, 11 March 2003. Sir Dingle Mackintosh Foot, QC, PC (24 August 1905–18 June 1978) was a barrister, politician and Labour Government Minister. He was educated at Balliol College, Oxford University, and was President of the Oxford Union (1928). He was called to the Bar (1930), and knighted and appointed a P.C. in 1964.

27. CO 1022/3, "Representations against Death Sentence passed on Lee Tien Tai (Lee Meng) in the Federation of Malaya." According to an unsigned note on this file, part of the minutes and enclosures had been transferred on 20 February 1953 to a "Top Secret Annex", and were not available for consultation. See also a letter by Leslie Plummer, Labour MP, in *The Statesman* discussing the case; *The Times* (London), 18 February 1953, p. 11; Short, op. cit., pp. 383–85; and Yuen, op. cit., pp. 57–58.

28. Yap, op. cit.

29. Ibid.

30. Ibid.

31. H.H. Paduka Sri Sultan Sir Yusuf 'Izzuddin Shah ibni Al-Marhum Sultan Abdul Jalil, KCMG, OBE.

32. *The Times* (London), 18 February 1953, p. 11.

33. *The Times* (London), 20 February 1953, p. 1. Copies of the petition left London by Comet aircraft which was the first jet aircraft flying the London-Singapore route.

34. Chris Hale Website, Writer/producer/director, "Britain's Wars in Malaya", <http://Malayanwars.blogspot.sg/2012/11/the-pretty-communist--and-the-hollywood-star-html>; CO 1022/6, Top Secret, "Representations against Sentence of Death Passed on Lee Tien Tai (Lee Meng) in Federation of Malaya"; CAB 129/59, Secret, "Sanders/Lee Exchange. Memorandum by the Minister of State, 11 March 1953; and Sanders/Lee Exchange. Memorandum by the Secretary of State for the Colonies", 13 March 1953; and Telegram dated 13 March 1953 from General Templer to Secretary of State for the Colonies.

35. See Yap Yook Foo, op. cit., and P.G. Lim, op. cit., pp. 141–42.

36. *The Times* (London), 2 March 1953, p. 7, and 10 March 1952, p. 7.

37. P.G. Lim, op. cit., p. 137.

38. CAB 129/59, Secret, "Sanders-Lee Exchange Memorandum by the Minister of State, 11 March 1953"; "Sanders-Lee Meng Exchange. Memorandum by Secretary of State for the Colonies, 13 March 1953"; and Telegram dated 13 March 1953 from High Commissioner for the Federation of Malaya to Secretary of State for Colonies.

39. Ibid. Yap Mau Tatt, then Secretary General of the MCA, had been a prominent leader of the KMT in Malaya before it was officially proscribed in 1949 and was known to hold extremely anti-Communist views. Although the British colonial Government at the time was concerned about the consequences of pro-KMT activities still being carried out by some MCA leaders, it is not clear whether General Templer was aware of Yap's political background. (Heng Pek Khoon, *Chinese Politics in Malaysia: A History of the Malaysian Chinese Association* (Kuala Lumpur: Oxford University Press, 1988), pp. 89–90 and 91.

40. Ibid. Telegram dated 13 March 1953 from High Commissioner for the Federation of Malaya to the Secretary of State for the Colonies.

41. The *British Movietone News* recorded Sanders' arrival at Croydon Airport from Budapest, where he was met by his wife and daughters and gave a short press conference. He was described as a tall, distinguished-looking man who bore a striking resemblance to his cousin, the Hollywood film star George Sanders. Apparently, he found it difficult to find employment in austerity Britain and he became a bus driver at Clacton. Although the British Government had insisted throughout his trial that he was innocent of all charges, he admitted on his return to England, that he had passed on information to the British military attaché at Budapest. During his imprisonment in Budapest, his wife, Winifred, had worked at a café at Frinton-on-Sea in Essex to make ends meet for her three children while he was in prison (See Chris Hale Website, Writer/producer/director, op. cit.).

42. *The Times* (London), 18 August 1953, p. 6.

43. Yuen, op. cit., p. 58. CPM cadres of State rank and above were allowed to conduct business on behalf of the Party.

44. Comber, *Malaya's Secret Police*, op. cit., pp. 58, 83–84; Short, op. cit., p. 385, fn. 51; and Chin Peng, 2003, op. cit., p. 502.

45. Chin Peng, 2003, op. cit., p. 350.

46. P.G. Lim, op. cit., p. 151.

47. Ibid. See also Leon Comber, review of *Alias Chin Peng: My Side of History* in *Intelligence and National Security* 19, Part 1 (2004).

48. P.G. Lim, op. cit., p. 152.

49. Chin Peng, op. cit., p. 502.

50. Yuen, op. cit., p. 57.

51. Short, op. cit., p. 385.
52. Minutes of the Legislative Council with Council Papers for the Period (Sixth Session), March 1953 to January 1954, Kuala Lumpur, Government Printer, 1954, pp. 1–18.
53. P.G. Lim, op., cit., pp. 145–46.
54. Ibid.
55. Ibid.
56. *Minutes of the Legislative Council of the Federation of Malaya with Council Papers for the Period (Sixth Session) March 1953 to January 1954* (Kuala Lumpur: Government Press, 1954), "Petition re. Criminal Procedure Code", pp. 1087–91.
57. It is rather strange that no one referred to Secretary of State Lyttelton's reply in which he poured scorn to a proposal made by European planters when he visited Malaya in November 1951 that he should dispense with normal procedure and speed up the administration of justice through drumhead courts. He said: "We stand for law and order ... Never will I agree to suspend the processes of law ... the principles must remain intact." (Short, op. cit., p. 332).
58. Ibid. "The Criminal Procedure Codes (Amendment) Bill 1953", 27 January 1954, pp. 1144–63. Sir Michael Joseph Hogan, CMG, QC, served in a number of British colonies as a senior government lawyer. He was Solicitor-General Malaya (1950) and Attorney-General (1950–55), where he worked closely with General Templer and often seemed to act as his spokesman. After leaving Malaya, he was appointed Chief Justice Hong Kong (1955–70).
59. *Minutes of the Legislative Council of the Federation of Malaya with Council Papers for the Period (Sixth Session) March 1953 to January 1954* (Kuala Lumpur: Government Press, 1954), "Petition re. Criminal Procedure Code", pp. 1163–71.
60. Ibid., p. 1238 and ISEAS Library, P.G. Lim Private Archives Collection, Folio 14, PGL/014/022/001, "P.G. Lim's letter to the *Straits Times* dated 18 July 1968".
61. P.G. Lim, op. cit., p. 150.
62. Tunku Abdul Rahman, *As a Matter of Interest* (Kuala Lumpur: Heinemann Asia, 1981), p. 56.
63. See The Criminal Procedure Code (Amendment) Bill 1957, Federal Legislative Council, 5th Meeting of the 2nd Session, 14 November 1957 ("Trial by Jury").
64. ISEAS Library, P.G. Lim Private Archives Collection, Folio 14 (ISEAS), op. cit.

7

THE ROAD TO SELF-GOVERNMENT:
"The Pistols are Out"

In furtherance of his political plans to defeat the Communist uprising, General Templer realized that it was important to obtain the support of the Indian population in Malaya, as well as the other communities, and he took an active interest in improving the social conditions of the Tamil rubber tappers and labourers throughout Malaya which had often been neglected. One way he did this was by enlisting the cooperation of P.P. Narayanan, a Federal Legislative Council member, a powerful trade union leader, and the first President of the Malayan Trades Union Congress and General Secretary of the National Union of Plantation Workers. Narayanan had formerly headed the Negri Sembilan Indian Labour Union with H.K. Choudhury. Both had been officers in the INA (Indian National Army) formed by Subhas Chandra Bose in Singapore during the Japanese Occupation with the support of the Japanese to fight alongside the Japanese Army in its advance on India. After the Japanese surrender and the return of the British colonial power to Malaya in September 1945, several INA personnel took the lead of forming Indian sections of the trade union movement and as many of them were anti-British, they were attractive candidates for recruitment by the Communist Party of Malaya but Narayanan was anti-Communist.[1]

The National Union was an amalgamation of five unions and as it formed one of the most powerful trade union groups in Malaya representing in 1953 close to 79,000 members, the majority of whom were Indians, its support for the Government's cause would be of great value.[2]

An approximate breakdown of employees' unions by ethnic groups at the time was Indian 78,984; Malay 15,869; Chinese 12,912; and Others 1,792, from which it can be seen that Indian rubber plantation workers provided an important platform for shaping the direction of the Malayan trade union movement.[3] Templer was shrewd in making this move as according to secret CPM instructions issued just before the outbreak of the first Malayan Emergency, "the progressive mass organisations of the various Trade Unions in Malaya ... youth organisations, women's associations" should all come under the direct leadership of the Party "and efforts should be made through Communist-controlled trade unions to create labour unrest ... Labour unions could be strengthened as they could be Communists' strongest weapons."[4]

The five plantation state-based unions making up the National Union were the Plantation Workers Union of Malaya (formerly the Negri Sembilan Indian Labour Union); Malayan Estate Workers Union (formerly the Perak Estate Employees Union); Johor State Plantation Workers Union (formerly the North Johor Indian Labour Union); the Malacca Estate Workers Union; and the Alor Gajah Labour Union (in Malacca). The amalgamation or merger of these five trade unions had the backing of the British colonial Government and the influential International Confederation of Free Trade Unions. John Brazier from the British Trade Union Council, a senior British trade union leader, was sent out to Malaya from Britain as Trade Union Adviser, to advise trade union leaders to eschew militant (Communist) trade unionism and create a trade union movement that would be acceptable to the British colonial government, and he played a vital role on the formation of the National Union.[5]

Narayanan, who was to dominate the Malayan trade union movement for several decades, was a towering figure in the trade union movement in Malaya and internationally, became on good terms with Brazier and benefited greatly from his support. He was anti-Communist and a supporter of Dato' Onn's IMP and, aside from anything else, these attributes and the fact that the trade union movement was one of the strongest forces working for a Malayan nation, undoubtedly stood him in good stead in his relations with Templer.[6]

Brazier developed a close personal relationship not only with Narayanan but also with other English-educated anti-Communist trade union leaders who played a key role in forming the National Union of Plantation Workers of which Narayanan became the General Secretary. Brazier worked closely, too, with the Malayan Special Branch in identifying trade unions that were left-wing or under Communist control. Two trade union leaders, Rayal Jose and K.P.C. Menon, who disagreed with his policy — and what they perceived as P.P. Narayanan's close relationship with General Templer — were detained by the Special Branch under the Emergency Regulations.[7]

It is interesting to speculate whether General Templer's view of Narayanan would have been different if he had known that Narayanan had been an officer in the Japanese-sponsored INA which had supported the Japanese Imperial Army in Burma and the Japanese attempt to liberate India from British rule and was only stopped by British and British/Indian Army units in the desperate fighting which took place at Kohima and Imphal in Manipur State.[8]

Trade union leaders had criticized Templer for the absence of any reference to trade unions or labour in his speech to the Federal Legislative Council on 19 March 1952, and they had requested an interview with him to discuss the strike of the North Eastern Transport Workers at Kota Baru, Kelantan. He met their delegation which was led by Narayanan, accompanied by V.M.N. Menon and two Malay trade union leaders, Nasurridin bin Rais and Mohammed Yusoff, at King's House, Kuala Lumpur, on 27 March. Brazier, the Trade Union Adviser, was in attendance. At the meeting, Templer told them that his non-reference to trade unions in his speech was unintentional and gave them an assurance that he would encourage the trade union movement as long as it opposed Communism.[9] This was probably the first time that Templer had met Narayanan on a one-to-one basis.

The Tamil labour force was very much a depressed class in Malaya, and with the Emergency and the Communist menace in Malaya, its importance assumed a new significance. An estimated 150,000 Tamils were employed on rubber estates, and nearly 60 to 70 per cent of the clashes between the security forces and the Communist insurgents took place on or close to rubber estates where Tamil labourers were employed.

The plans which Templer worked out with Narayanan for improving the lot of the Tamil labourers and winning them over to the Government's side were quite extensive and impressive. They included the developing of facilities for primary school education for the children of Tamil labourers on rubber estates; the improving of estate hospitals and rural health services; the providing of assistance to Tamil labourers, many of whom kept cattle, with their animal husbandry needs; the improving of kitchen and washing facilities in labour lines on the rubber estates; the building of proper crèches for their children; and as a security measure, the wiring in of labour lines and the improving of lighting around the labour lines against Communist infiltration. He planned, too, to establish a team of Tamil-speaking Eurasians to work closely with the Tamil work force so that they could be kept in regular and close contact with Government activities. The records do not show whether such a team ever came into existence and, if so, how it would fit in with the work of the Labour Department of the Malayan Civil Service which traditionally worked closely with Tamil plantation workers.[10]

Meanwhile, the Communities Liaison Committee (CLC), referred to earlier, which had played an influential behind-the-scenes role in quietly working away towards the establishment of a non-communal Malayan nation, had closed down just before Templer's arrival. As Karl von Vorus states, it ceased to function when it became apparent that its Chinese members could not (or would not) agree to the best way in which the MCA could help to improve the economic lot of the Malays.

In its earlier days, the CLC had in a sense assumed an unofficial advisory role with the Malayan Government, not only on matters connected with the Malayan Emergency but also on the political moves then gradually taking place towards self-government though it was not an official body. General Templer's apparent disinterest in the CLC might well have been because he had never had an easy relationship with MacDonald who was behind the CLC. However, when Templer arrived, he did not seem to have paid much attention to it. It had the backing of a number of prominent Malayans including Dato Thuraisingham, Tan Cheng Lock, Dato' Onn and Dato' Panglima Bukit Gantang, the Mentri Besar of Perak (1948–57), who was Onn's old friend. Dato' Panglima had formerly been a member of UMNO when Onn was President, and he had swung his support behind Onn when the latter formed IMP.[11] He was well known as a Malay nationalist from the Malay-elite dominated Perak, and he had come to notice when he was Chairman of the Perak State Squatter Committee for objecting to Chinese squatters being permitted to settle in Perak. However, there is no doubt that he later played a prominent part in the move towards Malaya's self government and independence, which will be referred to later.[12]

Nevertheless, the CLC undoubtedly played a useful part in bringing together political leaders from different ethnic groups to discuss informally a number of contentious issues between the Malay and Chinese communities, especially citizenship and inter-community issues. MacDonald, in fact, claimed that the CLC accomplished a great deal in helping the Government prepare the way for a national education system, a unified Malayan citizenship, and the holding of elections, and his claim probably had some substance to it.[13]

Although Templer and MacDonald did not always see eye-to-eye on official matters and Templer disagreed too with MacDonald's flamboyant lifestyle and the close relations he maintained with the local Asian community, they both favoured the establishment of non-communal politics in Malaya which reflected the British official policy at the time.[14] According to Templer's biographer John Cloake, General Templer was quite forthright in his criticism of MacDonald and said he had "little respect" for him, and that he was given "to public behaviour unsuited to a senior representative of the British government".[15]

There is little doubt that Templer's views were enhanced by some scandalous and perhaps libellous remarks circulating in the 1950s about MacDonald and what were referred to by MacDonald's biographer, Clyde Sanger, as "his Chinese girl friends", including the photographer Christina Loke (the wife of Loke Wan Tho, the Cathay Cinema chain magnate), the doctor-novelist Han Suyin, and several Singapore university students. It could not have helped matters, too, that when in 1955 the British Government announced the extension of his term of office as Commissioner General for South East Asia, a photograph of him hand-in-hand with two bare-breasted Iban maidens, Sioh and Sani, the daughter and niece respectively of Chief Jugoh, conducting him to a reception in Sarawak, was given prominent coverage in both local and overseas' newspapers.[16]

It was perhaps because of the criticism that MacDonald faced in Britain that Lord Munster, Under-Secretary for the Colonies, felt it necessary to tell the House of Lords during a debate on Malaya:

> We are satisfied that Mr Malcolm MacDonald has done a good job of work.... It was particularly unfortunate that "savage and bitter" attacks should have been made against him in the British press. He was not in a position to reply and had had no direct responsibility for the conduct of operations in Malaya.[17]

Oliver Lyttelton told the House of Commons, too, that MacDonald did not exercise any executive functions within colonial and protected territories, but it was his duty to promote the coordination of policy and administration between their governments and for this purpose, he may convene conferences of Governors and High Commissioners. He outlined, too, the following numerous responsibilities that MacDonald held:

(a) He is required to advise the Secretary of State from time to time on the question of closer political cooperation between these territories.

(b) He represents civil and political interest of the territories and is on the British Defence Coordination Committee, of which he is Chairman.

(c) He has special responsibilities in the sphere of external defence of Southeast Asia.

(d) In the field of foreign affairs he holds the personal rank of Ambassador and in consultation with Her Majesty's representatives in the foreign countries of Southeast Asia is responsible for advising Her Majesty's Government on general problems of foreign policy in the area.[18]

However, as MacDonald's biographer Sanger puts it, "there were still some polite fights over jurisdiction and turf." Sir Anthony Abell, then Governor of Sarawak, recalls Malcolm's resistance to being indirectly dictated to by Templer about security matters at Bukit Serene, Johor Bahru, one of the Sultan of Johor's palaces, where MacDonald was staying at the time during what Abell referred to as "a royal visit".[19]

Abell was, no doubt, referring to the visit of Her Royal Highness Marina, The Duchess of Kent, in October 1952, who was MacDonald's guest during her visit to Singapore and Malaya. MacDonald, who had written a long Foreword for the novel, *A Many Splendoured Thing*, written by the author's wife and was well known to the author who was then a Special Branch officer at Johor State headquarters, told him that Templer had written to him to complain that he should have been consulted before the Duchess had been invited to stay at Bukit Serene, as it had been reported that the daughter of one of his Chinese cooks had joined the Communist guerrillas in the jungle. General Templer felt the Duchess was exposed to a serious security risk that he was not prepared to shoulder. MacDonald said that he was already well aware of the facts of the case and he had spoken to the cook, who was a very loyal and long-serving member of his staff, and had reported the matter to the local army and police commanders so that they could take whatever extra security precautions they thought necessary. He nevertheless asked the author to address in Malay his assembled domestic staff to inform them that he had complete trust in them and he expected them to be on their best behaviour during the Duchess's visit to ensure that her stay was both pleasant and safe. He said that he proposed to send Templer a photograph of the Duchess with the cook and his family, and he would write to Templer to inform him that he would take full responsibility for her during her stay at Bukit Serene.[20]

PANGLIMA BUKIT GANTANG: NATIONAL CONFERENCE

Meanwhile, on the political front, in order to counter the latest UMNO-MCA plans to accelerate the holding of State and Federal elections which did not fit in with the Government's own timetable, Dato' Onn encouraged his friend Dato' Panglima Bukit Gantang to convene a National Conference to discuss the road to self-government and independence. A series of closed meetings under the chairmanship of the Panglima were held at Kuala Lumpur, Penang, and Ipoh, and plans were made to convene the conference on 27 April 1953. The Panglima had the support of Dato E.E.C. Thuraisingham (Ceylonese lawyer, former Chairman of the CLC, Member for Education in the Federal Legislative Council); Yong Shook Lin (Legislative Councillor, and formerly a senior MCA member); G. Shelley (President of the Eurasian Association); Heah Joo Seang (Penang Chinese business magnate); P.P. Narayanan (Legislative Councillor and trade union leader); Chin Swee Onn (Chinese tin magnate); J.C. Kang (Chinese businessman); and W.N. McLeod (European accountant), all of whom were former CLC members.[21]

Meanwhile, Dato' Panglima Bukit Gantang proposed to put out feelers to the UMNO-MCA Alliance leaders to see whether they would be agreeable to becoming affiliated with the National Conference, which he felt was essential in any move that was likely to affect their position. He proposed, too, if the Alliance was unwilling to join the Conference, to take steps to win over certain elements of UMNO that he had known when he had been a member to support his plan. Similarly, if the MCA did not wish to participate in the National Conference, he intended to see whether Yong Shook Lin and Heah Joo Seang, who had close MCA connections, would be agreeable to forming a breakaway group from the MCA to support him. The Panglima arranged, too, for invitations to be issued to the following political groups to nominate two representatives each to attend the Conference: Straits Chinese British Association; Malayan Indian Congress; Ceylon Federation of Malaya; Eurasian Association of Malaya; Pan-Malayan Labour Party; Malayan Trades Union Council; Federation of Indian Organizations; All-Malaya Islam Association; and Peninsular Malays Union.[22]

The UMNO-MCA Alliance, however, boycotted the Conference as not being representative of the wishes of the people but only of a privileged group.[23]

On the face of it, it would appear to be a powerful and perhaps irresistible representative gathering, especially as the plans of the National Conference fitted in very well with the non-communal and more gradual approach to self-government that Templer (and MacDonald) had in mind.

At a meeting with Raja Uda, Nik Kamil and Thuraisingham at King's House, Kuala Lumpur, Templer expressed his concern at what he perceived to be a lack of political unity among the Malays towards self-government, and he told them that Dato' Panglima Bukit Gantang's approach was the right one and all loyal Malays should support him.[24]

The first reaction to the holding of a National Conference was quite favourable but the UMNO-MCA Alliance played down its significance and said it did not represent the people. As the date of the Conference approached, Tunku Abdul Rahman and Dato Tan Cheng Lock, who had not yet been approached by the Panglima and had first heard about the Conference second-hand in the press, attacked it for being "undemocratic" and "dominated by high government officers and persons who did not represent any section of the people".[25] In his memoirs, Tunku Abdul Rahman commented that if the National Conference's programme had been accepted then bureaucratic rule would have become more "firmly entrenched in the hands of a favoured few who would be perpetuating white supremacy with local 'yes-men' and stooges acting as their spokesmen."[26]

Tunku Abdul Rahman was summoned by General Templer at the time and warned to talk less about British misrule and to exercise a little restraint on what he had to say about the British Raj. As the Tunku relates in his book, *Contemporary Issues in Malayan Politics*:

If I were to eulogise British rule, I might as well give up the struggle for Independence because the first thing the people would ask me would be if the British were so good, why then fight for independence? In fact, that was the opinion of many people at the time.

The Tunku continued:

I was prepared to face the consequences, even to the point of going to prison. I would not be muzzled. It was then that Templer said that "he could send me to prison for what I had been saying but that would make a martyr of me".[27]

In regard to the National Conference, the General Assembly of UMNO decided that UMNO would only participate in the Conference on the condition that "recognized political organisations" alone would have the right to vote on any resolutions passed, which was a restriction not likely to find favour with the sponsors. The Peninsular Malays Union, the Pan-Malayan Labour Party, and the Malayan Trades Union Congress, yielded to the Tunku's pressure and decided not to attend the Conference.[28]

In his report on the National Conference which the Australian High Commissioner sent to the Minister for External Affairs, Canberra, he reported that every seat in the public gallery at the Conference was filled, and there was a lot of interest and curiosity in what was going on, and many people had to be turned away.[29]

The correspondent of *The Economist* (London) described the National Conference as largely representing "senior Malay officials in the administration", and went on to say that its unofficial leader behind the scenes was Dato' Onn, who had apparently "stopped trying to blow life into the IMP".[30]

S. (Sinnathamby) Rajaratnam in his "I Write as I Please" column for the *Singapore Standard*, however, was even less complimentary and summed it up as follows:

Although the hall was packed to capacity, the meeting was about as exciting and inspiring as a frozen fish on a marble slab. The sponsors who decorated the platform did not look like men who were going to oust the British Raj and take over the running of this country ... there was little evidence in the speeches of the turbulence of strong emotions that carry political movements forward ....[31]

The Conference resolved that Federal elections should be held towards the end of 1956 and the Federal Legislative Council should be expanded from seventy-five to ninety members with less than half of them elected members, with nine appointed members forming an inner Cabinet led by Templer.[32]

UMNO-MCA ALLIANCE: NATIONAL CONGRESS

In the meantime, UMNO-MCA held a number of meetings to discuss the holding of a round-table conference based on its own road map for self-government and independence for Malaya. On 16 March 1953, to forestall the possibility of the Dato' Panglima Bukit Gantang's non-ethnic group taking the lead, Tunku Abdul Rahman pulled the mat from under its feet and issued a communiqué in favour of holding general elections for the Federal Legislature by November 1954, which was much earlier than the date suggested by Dato' Panglima Bukit Gantang's group, and proposed that a UMNO-MCA National Congress should be convened on 23 August 1953 to discuss "all shades of political opinion to discuss election procedures and methods of representation".[33]

At the opening of the UMNO-MCA National Congress at the Majestic Hotel, Kuala Lumpur, on 23 August 1953, the Tunku put into words the mood of the people in his opening address:

> The people feel that it is time that they are given bigger roles to play in the political affairs of the country…. I believe that the independence of Malaya can only be brought about by constitutional changes and such constitutional changes can only be affected by a change in the Federal Legislature. There is no option but for us to demand an early election.[34]

The aims of the UMNO-MCA National Congress were contained in the following principal resolution:

> We, the representatives of all the democratic Malayan parties, pledge that we shall work for the attainment by peaceful and constitutional means of a sovereign State comprising all the States and Settlements now known as the Federation of Malaya within the British Commonwealth and that as a step towards such attainment we demand that there shall be held elections to the Federal Legislature in 1954.[35]

The delegates pledged themselves to uphold the position of the Malay Sultans, whose approval was necessary if there was to be any change to the Constitution, and to protect the rights of the minorities. A second resolution appointed a committee of ten delegates to "consider and recommend constitutional reforms in the Federation of Malaya" and report back to the Convention not later than 30 November 1953.[36]

The committee recommended that Federal Legislative Council elections with a minimum of three-fifths elected seats should be held not later than 1954 and that the Council should consist of seventy-five members, forty-four of whom would be elected and thirty-one nominated, sixteen by the High Commissioner and fifteen by commercial and agricultural interests. This would mean for the first time that elected members would have a clear majority.

The speeding up of Federal elections for self-government and eventually independence was no doubt helped by the winds of political change that were taking place at this time in other parts of Asia and Africa where the former colonial territories of India, Pakistan, Burma and Ceylon had already been granted independence, and in Africa the demand for self-government was increasing in momentum. It was a time of great political activity in Malaya, too, during which the UMNO-MCA Alliance and IMP had emerged as the main political parties.

Dato' Onn, however, dissolved IMP in 1953, having by then abandoned his vision of a non-communal party, as it failed to obtain the support from the Malay electorate that he had expected. He then directed his attention and energies to forming a new party, Parti Negara or National Party, which he hoped would fare better than IMP, undermine UMNO, and gain the political lead but this new party, too, was not successful in obtaining the support he had expected.[37]

The UMNO-MCA Alliance's plans were in direct opposition to General Templer's plans. He had throughout stressed that the war against the CPM should be won before the question of self-government could be pursued and, of course, in doing so he was adhering strictly to the Directive he had been given by the British Government:

> It will be your duty ... to promote such political progress of the country as will, without prejudicing the campaign against the terrorists, further our democratic aims in Malaya ... His Majesty's Government will not lay aside their responsibilities in Malaya until they are satisfied that Communist terrorism has been defeated and that the partnership of all communities, which alone can lead to true and stable self-government, has been firmly established.[38]

General Templer's plans were to establish an all-nominated Legislative Council for three years with no popularly elected members when the term of the current standing Legislative Council expired in January 1954, which would leave the High Commissioner in full charge of the administration from 1954 to 1956, and that there would only be an elected element to the

Federal Legislative Council after State and Settlement elections had taken place and were working towards this end.[39]

As already mentioned, the records indicate that Templer was firmly of the view that training for elected government should begin at the bottom and develop over several years and that 1960 was the earliest possible date for self-government. In his opinion, the Malayan people were "politically backward".

This process of moving forward towards an elected government had, in fact, already begun in 1952 with the UMNO-MCA success in winning the Kuala Lumpur municipal elections, and had continued since then, at "parish pump" level, with the election of a number of councils in medium-size towns and *kampungs* in Malaya. But beyond this General Templer did not intend to hold elections either in the Malay States or Settlements before the beginning of 1954, and he did not envisage the completion of State and Settlements elections until the end of 1955 with elections to the Federal Legislature to be held in 1956–58.

At a Colonial Office meeting as early as 3 December 1952, Templer had said: "… there was no real desire for independence among any community in Malaya. The country lacked political leaders and there were no political parties of the type required to operate successfully a parliamentary system," and he referred to the "political ineptitude" of the Malays, and said he was worried about the extremist pro-Indonesian trends in UMNO. He felt there was a need for a strong Malayan centre party with a non-communal platform, and "the only hope for leadership was from a handful of Malays now in senior Government positions."[40] Templer expanded on his comments in a candid interview he gave Ian Hamilton, the Public Relations Officer of the Australian Commission in Kuala Lumpur on 9 October 1953 in which he gave his views on political developments and comments on some local politicians, which are invaluable as they provide an idea of the way he was thinking. For instance, he did not consider either the MCA or UMNO "worth a damn as real political parties". All they could do was "call for early Federal elections and "neither had a fiscal or general policy." He said:

> it was difficult to organize local elections in the villages, town or city level — a necessary step along the path leading to State and Federal elections. In Kuala Lumpur only about 7,000 had bothered to vote as electors; the proportion was about the same in the colony of Singapore, which in time would have to become an integral part of a United Malaya. The Federation could not manage without Singapore and Singapore was dependent equally on the Federation.

Of the local politicians, he still considered Dato' Onn "outstanding" and he agreed with his view that 85 per cent of the population of Malaya, that is, Chinese, Malay and Indian, "completely lacked political consciousness". The appointment of Colonel H.S. Lee and Dr Ismail bin Dato Abdul Rahman as Members for Railways and Ports and Communication respectively "would give the men a chance to prove their worth and bring home to them that it was much easier to criticize than to run a Government". Dato Nik Kamil "appeared to be shaping fairly well". He was "doubtful about Heah Joo Seang, Chairman of the IMP Penang Branch, President of the Penang Straits Chinese British Association, and a leading (and wealthy) businessman mainly because of his wartime activities (he had served more or less in the capacity of a Resident Commissioner of Penang during the Japanese Occupation)".[41] However, he did "agree with Heah that Singapore should be linked with the Federation, and had explained his views forcibly on this subject to leaders of the Chinese community at a private meeting recently in Penang".[42]

The tentative timetable for political developments leading to self-government proposed by General Templer at his meeting at the Colonial Office on 3 December 1952 was: (a) elections to town/local councils in 1953; (b) State elections to be held in Johor in 1954, with elections in the remaining States/Settlements to follow in 1955; and (c) "2 years consolidation" before Legislative Council elections were held in 1956–58, with 1960 being the earliest possible date for self-government.[43]

Meanwhile, the *Manchester Guardian* criticized Templer's speech at the press conference following the Colonial Office meeting by saying:

> ...so far no elections [have been held] above village level in the whole peninsula [Malaya] — and this with a literacy rate as high as any in Asia ... this is still a "colonial" territory where the Government has no responsibility to elected representatives.... There are still no elected members in the Federal Legislature or any of the States or Settlements.... The argument that the masses in Malaya are disinterested and unwilling to register as voters is not impressive either.[44]

By 18 May 1953, however, in discussions at the Colonial Office, General Templer had somewhat changed his mind about the timing of Legislative Council elections and doubted "whether it would be possible to delay Federal elections for so long, and was concerned about the likelihood that we should be forced to hold them earlier". He also seemed to have changed his mind about Dato' Onn, too, and commented that the "older political leaders such as Dato' Onn were so unpopular that they might well fail to secure seats in an election". At a press conference on the same day, he went as far as to say: "It is impossible to forecast a date for self-government.... The transfer of power from a colonial or protective authority always produces a difficult situation."[45]

Meanwhile, T.C. Jerrom (Principal Secretary, Colonial Office) advised him to amend the draft of a speech he intended to give at the press conference on 18 May which included reference to 60 per cent of the population in Malaya over the age of fifteen being illiterate, and said: "I think it is as well to avoid [mention of] 'illiteracy', since Communist propaganda used to make a good deal of the alleged comparison between the success of the Soviet Government in eliminating illiteracy and the failure of the Western Governments to do so." Fortunately, Templer took his advice and amended his speech accordingly.[46]

M.J. HOGAN: GOVERNMENT WORKING COMMITTEE

On 15 July 1953, a month before the proposed UMNO-MCA Alliance National Congress, General Templer announced, in a move that was most likely calculated to head off the various political manoeuvrings that were taking place, that he had appointed a Working Committee chaired by the Attorney General M.J. Hogan, to examine the possibility of constitutional development and the holding of State and Federal elections.[47] He perhaps thought this would pre-empt the UMNO-MCA National Congress. However, there was some delay in setting up the Hogan Working Committee which was partly due to the reluctance of the Malay Sultans to countenance proposals that were likely to affect their position if independence was granted, as well as the constitutional need before proceeding further to present the Sultans' views to Lyttelton, Secretary of State for the Colonies. When the names of the members of the Working Committee were published, Tunku Abdul Rahman drily observed that the majority were Onn's supporters who were known to be favourably regarded by General Templer, and that "instead of leading popular demand they [the Colonial Government] decided on tactics, a political ploy, that taxed the patience of the people, and in particular the Alliance."[48]

The report of the Working Committee was published by the Government on 21 January 1954. It was a conservative document which, not surprisingly, followed closely the Government's own timetable. It was not in favour of hastening elections.[49] Its key points were that local/

State elections should be completed by the end of 1955 with elections to the Federal Council to be held in the latter part of 1956. The Working Committee urged the establishment of a special committee to draft a new Constitution for a self-governing Malaya, and recommended that membership of the Federal Legislative Council should be increased from seventy-five to ninety by increasing the number of unofficial members from thirty-nine to sixty-four, who were to be selected on an ethnic basis, and the extension of the "Member System" to provide for a Cabinet of fourteen persons.[50]

The Government's Working Committee's report was criticized by Rajaratnam, the leader writer of the *Singapore Standard*, who wrote rather scathingly in his column:

> [This] is not the work of men who believe in either self-government for Malaya or a democratic constitution but is the product of men who are in a blue funk as to what their fate would be in a self-governing and democratic Malaya.[51]

The eighteen UMNO-MCA members forming a minority in the Working Committee appointed by Templer disagreed with the majority recommendation made by the remaining twenty-nine members, which predictably supported the more conservative Government approach that it would be premature to indicate a precise date on which elections should be held. The minority group, on the other hand, supported the UMNO-MCA line and pressed for federal elections to be held not later than November 1954.[52]

The UMNO-MCA Alliance was especially critical of the Working Committees' report which was published a day or so before it was due to hold its own National Congress, and stood firm in its demand for early Federal elections and a three-fifths elected majority in the new Legislative Council.[53]

At this stage, Templer summed up the situation as he saw it in a message dated 30 September 1953 to Lyttelton:

> ... Certainly, judging by the results of recent Municipal Council elections in various big towns over the countryside, the UMNO-MCA Alliance is at least getting a lot of people to vote for it. No other party can even say that. They have openly declared that they want Federal elections by the end of 1954. And that if they do not get them they will resign from the Legislative Council. The more conservative party, organized largely by the Mentri Besars [i.e, the Panglima Bukit Gantang's National Conference],

has now put in its so-called blueprint, stating that elections should be held in 1956 ...

In the meantime, a nice handy little committee [sic] appointed by myself, consisting of forty-six members of the Legislative Council, have appointed their Working Party (which is really what I was getting at) and under the Chairmanship of the Attorney General [Hogan], to produce proposals on the whole matter...

They will at least be sensible and practical ones. Whether they will be acceptable is a different thing. All parties and interests are of course represented on the Working Party, including the extremists who may well put in a minority report ...[54]

It was clear, however, that neither the Government nor the UMNO-MCA Alliance would give way. As a way out of the dilemma, General Templer proposed a compromise of an elected majority of fifty-two seats out of a total of ninety-eight seats in the Federal Legislative Council but this too did not find favour in the eyes of the UMNO-MCA Alliance, although it was accepted by Lyttelton and rather reluctantly by the Malay Sultans, who were concerned about their own position under an elected majority.[55]

UMNO-MCA DELEGATION TO LONDON

The Alliance reiterated its demand for an elected majority and as it appeared that matters were at a political impasse, with neither side willing to budge, it decided to take the matter out of the hands of the local colonial Government and send a three-man team to London to deal directly with the Secretary of State for the Colonies. As Tan Cheng Lock was unable to accompany them for health reasons, the Tunku and T.H. Tan, the MCA Secretary, left by air on 21 April 1954 to argue their case before Lyttelton, the Colonial Secretary. Dato Abdul Razak, who was then visiting the United States, later joined the Tunku and T.H. Tan in London.[56]

Lyttelton was in Uganda at the time but he reluctantly agreed to meet the delegation on his return from Africa after the intercession of Lord Ogmore, an old friend of the Tunku, who was sympathetic to the UMNO-MCA's cause. The Tunku had known him since he had practised law in Penang many years previously as William David Rees, before he had been ennobled, and in the meantime he had returned to England where he had become Parliamentary Under-Secretary of State for the Colonies from 1947–50 under the Labour Government, and was well known in parliamentary circles in London.[57] With his help, the Tunku met and spoke to several influential MPs on both sides of the Houses of Parliament about the Alliance's plans. These included Tom Proctor, former Parliamentary Secretary to Prime Minister Clement Attlee, James Griffiths (London Whip, House of Commons), and other influential persons in the Conservative, Labour, Liberal Parties, and the Independents. The Tunku hosted a dinner in the House of Lords on 8 May to key persons in the Labour Parliamentary Group.

Before the delegation met Lyttelton, T.H. Tan wrote on 30 April to Tan Cheng Lock in Malacca, summarizing the situation in London, and said it was clear that the Labour Party would support in Parliament the Alliance's stand to press for an elected three-fifths majority in the Legislative Council, though James Griffiths had entered a caveat that Lyttelton would not be willing "to lose face" by making any drastic changes to the published federal elections proposals. However, Griffiths and Proctor felt that the solution lay in the "nominated reserve", which would necessitate the Secretary of State agreeing to authorize General Templer to use the reserve seats to strengthen the majority of the party which won the election and, if it was the Alliance, they should be given the right by the High Commissioner to select who should be nominated as the reserve.[58]

T.H. Tan said that he and Dato Razak, who had by then joined the Tunku and himself in London, had not committed themselves entirely to this solution as Griffiths, Proctor, and Lord Ogmore wanted to "test the waters" in the Colonial Office and the Labour Party before pressing for this solution. T.H. Tan considered that if they stuck to the three-fifths majority when they met Lyttelton, he would agree to the Alliance's proposals.

In conclusion, T.H. Tan said that if necessary the Tunku would tell Lyttelton that the Alliance had done its utmost to reach a satisfactory solution through constitutional means and if the British Government still refused to accede to the Alliance's proposals "the Alliance could not be blamed for the consequences". Presumably he had in mind the Alliance's threat to boycott the Government.

However, although Lyttelton had agreed to meet the Tunku, T.H. Tan and Dato Razak on an informal basis after his return from Africa on 14 May, the small delegation was unable to prevail upon him to budge from his support of the Malayan Government which had rejected the UMNO-MCA Alliance's demand for a two-fifths' elected majority in the Federal Legislative Council and the holding of Federal elections by the end of 1954.[59] Meanwhile, it seemed that Lyttelton was not entirely convinced that the Alliance would carry out its threat to withdraw from government if their demands were not met.[60] As the Tunku and T.H. Tan prepared to return to Malaya, he gave the Tunku a letter to deliver in person to General Templer. While the letter explained at some length why he could not agree with the UMNO-MCA's demands for a three-fifths elected majority in the Federal Legislative Council and the holding of federal elections by the end of 1954, he added that "if in practice it was found that the ability of the majority-elected party to function effectively was being frustrated by a deliberately destructive minority, then the High Commissioner must take steps to remedy it."[61]

The Tunku and T.H. Tan returned to Kuala Lumpur and reported the outcome of their meeting with Lyttelton to the Alliance at a round-table conference in Kuala Lumpur on 24 May 1954. After due deliberation, a resolution was drafted rejecting the British Government's and Templer's proposals and requesting the appointment of a Royal Commission from outside Malaya to report on constitutional reforms. If the Government proceeded with its plans, it confirmed that in accordance with what the UMNO-MCA delegation had told Lyttelton in London, the UMNO-MCA Alliance would have no option but to withdraw its members from working with the Government. *The Times* (London) reflected the seriousness of the situation by reporting on 15 June 1954: "The political dangers in Malaya are now serious. The powerful Alliance of the United Malays National Organisation and the Malayan Chinese Association has decided to withdraw its members from Administrative Councils at all levels before June 23."[62]

As Fernando relates, the resolution read:

That the White Paper [based on the Hogan report] to introduce national elections in the Federation of Malaya is not acceptable to the Alliance and, therefore, the Alliance strongly opposes its implementation by the Federal Government. In order to get an unbiased assessment of the country's progress towards self-government, the Alliance requests that a special independent commission, consisting entirely of members from outside Malaya, be sent immediately to the Federation with the concurrence of their Majesties and Their Highnesses to report on constitutional reforms of the Federation. The Alliance believes the appointment of such a commission will have the support of all who believe in democracy. On the other hand, if the authorities insist on implementation of the White Paper, the Alliance with great regret will have no choice but to withdraw its members from participating in the Government.'[63]

It was estimated that the boycott of all Government administrative bodies would involve over 1,000 persons.[64]

The resolution was handed over to General Templer by the Tunku, Colonel H.S. Lee and Leong Yew Koh, the MCA's Secretary General, on 25 May.

It was clear the gauntlet had been thrown down by the Alliance and it was clear, too, that if the Government's proposals were implemented, Alliance Party members would resign from the Executive and Legislative Councils as well as Municipal and Town Councils throughout the country, and boycott the federal elections.

When Templer received and read the document, he commented: "The pistols are out", and requested that the release of the resolution to the press should be delayed while he telegraphed a copy to Lyttelton and informed the Malay Sultans.[65] But Louis Heren, *The Times* (London) correspondent, who had already seen a copy of the Alliance's resolution, telegraphed a copy to London and it was published in *The Times* (London) on the next day.[66] The timing of the imbroglio could not have been worse as it came only a few days before General Templer's departure from Malaya on 31 May 1954 at the end of his two-year proconsulship.

In an attempt to break the political impasse, Templer suggested at the last moment a compromise solution that UMNO-MCA members of the Legislative Council should withdraw from the Legislative Council when the elections issue was debated and return later for Executive Council business. But this did not suit the Alliance and on 13 June 1954, two weeks after Templer's departure from Malaya at the end of his two-year proconsulship, the Alliance went ahead to boycott all Government proceedings. It is estimated that about 1,000 Alliance members withdrew from Government at all levels and organized demonstrations throughout the country to back their demands.[67]

Templer's biographer reports that the Alliance leaders attended General Templer's last Executive Council meeting on 25 May, when Templer presented the Council with a Georgian ink-stand inscribed "Given in friendship ...". One can only imagine what was going on in their minds at this time, but they attended the farewell cocktail party he gave for the Legislative Council on 30 May and saw him off at Kuala Lumpur airport when he left on his way to London the following day.[68]

One wonders too what must have been in General Templer's mind at this time as he was already aware that his appointment to rejoin the

Army — to assume the most senior command in the field for the British
Army, that of the Northern Army Group, Allied Forces, Central Europe,
and Commander-in-Chief of the BAOR (British Army on the Rhine) — had
been vetoed by the West German Chancellor Konrad Adenauer, whom
he had summarily dismissed as Mayor of Cologne in October 1945 for
incompetence, as will be related in the final chapter. However, the news of
this dramatic turn in events was not made public at Templer's request and
was only known to his immediate family. Even his ADC, Lord Wynford,
and MacGillivray, who became High Commissioner after his departure,
were not aware of it until they received the note he had left for them after
seeing him off at the airport which read: "I have been living a lie for the
last 2–3 months."

SIR DONALD MACGILLIVRAY, HIGH COMMISSIONER, 1 JUNE 1954

Sir Donald MacGillivray, who took over as High Commissioner after
Templer's departure from Malaya on 1 June 1954, was thus faced with
a tense and potentially dangerous situation in the first week of his
governorship, and fearing a breakdown of law and order and the effects
it would have on the ongoing counterinsurgency campaign, he decided
after much thought that he had no option but to agree to consult the
UMNO-MCA leaders if the Alliance won the Federal elections regarding
the appointment of the five nominated members for the reserved seats.
This would in effect be close to their demands for a three-fifths majority
in the Legislative Council.

The outcome was that MacGillivray informed Colonel H.S. Lee
and Hogan, representing the UMNO-MCA Alliance and Government
respectively that he would be agreeable to a compromise, and at a dramatic
meeting with Tunku Abdul Rahman, Colonel H.S. Lee and Dr Ismail on
2 July 1954 on board the British warship HMS *Alert* which was anchored
at the Seletar naval base in Singapore, he informed them that he would be
agreeable to consulting the UMNO-MCA Alliance if the Alliance won the
federal elections regarding the appointment of five nominated members
for the reserve seats. He was just about to depart on the British warship
on a two weeks' tour of Malaya's East Coast although, perhaps wisely,
he did not inform them that the purpose of his tour had been to consult
Malay leaders on Malaya's East Coast about the elections and win them
over to the Government's side.[69]

In his excellent description of the course of the dramatic events that enfolded, political scientist Karl von Vorys, however, errs in saying that the Tunku, Colonel H.S. Lee and Dr Ismail were met on board HMS *Alert* by "General Templer, with whiskey and soda in front of him" [sic] as by then Templer had already departed from Malaya on 1 June and MacGillivray had taken over as High Commissioner.[70]

MacGillivray sailed for the East Coast but when he got there he flew immediately back to Kuala Lumpur to attend an Emergency Executive Council meeting to inform members of the agreement that had been arrived at aboard HMS *Alert*. MacGillivray sent the Federal Executive Council's decision to the Tunku:

> It is therefore my intention to consult the leader or leaders of the majority amongst the elected members before making appointments to these seats [nominated members for the reserve seats]. I hope that with this statement of intention you will find yourself able to cooperate in the establishment of the new constitutional arrangements and to give your support to Legislative Council members.

The Tunku consulted his colleagues and sent a reply to MacGillivray that the Alliance agreed to cooperate with the Government on these terms.[71] The Alliance members who had withdrawn were reappointed and resumed their positions.

Nonetheless, the Alliance continued to press for a commission of legal experts drawn from the Commonwealth as they believed that further constitutional reforms were necessary to bring Malaya to self-government.

The way was now clear for the first Malayan General Election and on 18 August 1954, some two-and-a-half tumultuous months after General Templer's departure, the Federal Legislative Council passed a bill unanimously to amend the Federation of Malaya Agreement Act to allow for the introduction of Federal Elections.

To sum up, and bring this chapter to a fitting conclusion though it lies beyond the time-frame of this book, the first Federal Elections were held on 27 July 1955, and the UMNO-MCA-MIC Alliance (the Alliance had agreed to MIC joining it in 1954 to represent the Indian community) won fifty-one out of fifty-two seats and 79.6 per cent of the vote.[72] MacGillivray announced the composition of a new Executive Council composed of himself as High Commissioner, ten elected members from the Legislative Council together with three ex-officio and two nominated members. All of the ten elected members of the Executive Council became ministers and were assigned portfolios. The Tunku as the leader of the National Alliance became the first Chief Minister of Malaya.[73]

In August 1955 an agreement was reached between the Secretary of State for the Colonies, the Malay Sultans, and the new Alliance Ministers, to hold a conference in London early in 1956 to discuss the road to self-government. As a result of the agreements reached at this conference, Malaya achieved self-government thus enabling arrangements to be put in hand for the achievement of full self-government and *Merdeka* (independence) within the British Commonwealth by August 1957.[74]

By this time, however, General Templer had long since departed from the scene to return to the Army, and the final chapter will deal with the events surrounding his departure from Malaya which cast a long shadow over his military career.

Notes

1. Nilanjana Sengupta, *A Gentleman's Word: The Legacy of Subhas Chandra Bose in Southeast Asia* (Singapore: Institute of Southeast Asian Studies, 2012), pp. 179, 188.
2. See P.G. Lim, *Kaleidoscope,* op. cit., p. 162; T.N. Harper, *The End of Empire and the Making of Malaya* (Cambridge: Cambridge University Press, 1999), pp. 159, 210–14; and Verinder Grover, ed., *Malaysia. Government and Politics* (New Delhi: Deep & Deep Publications Pty Ltd., 2000), pp. 185–98.
3. *Federation of Malaya Annual Report 1953* (Kuala Lumpur: Government Printer, 1954), p. 66.
4. MSS (Malayan Security Service), Secret. *Political Intelligence Journal,* Singapore: No. 10/1948, 31 May 1958, p. 346.
5. See paper "Union of Discord" by P. Ramasamy, Political Science Department, Universiti Kebangsaan Malaysia (n.d.).
6. See National Archives of Australia, NAA: A816, 19/321/18, Confidential, "Singapore. Plans to Improve the Position of the Tamil Community", Australian Commissioner Singapore to Department of External Affairs, Canberra, ACT, 3 June 1952.
7. <www.malayahistory.net> (accessed 25 April 2012).
8. P.P. Narayanan volunteered to join the INA during the Japanese Occupation and was one of the first batch of recruits from Selangor selected by the Japanese to be sent to Singapore for officer training. After being commissioned, he served as a lieutenant quartermaster in an INA camp in Negri Sembilan under Captain Karnail Singh, a former British Indian Army

officer, who had defected to the Japanese after the fall of Malaya. See J. Victor Morais, *P.P. Narayanan: The Asian Trade Union Leader* (Petaling Jaya: National Union of Plantation Workers Sports Club, 1975), pp. 15, 61. The author is grateful to Associate Professor Kevin Blackburn, NIE (National Institute of Education), Singapore, for his e-mail dated 24 October 2012, and Nilanjana Sengupta for her e-mail dated 10 November 2012, for providing information about Narayanan. See also "As I remember It" in *Netaji Subhas Chandra Bose, A Malayan Perspective* (Kuala Lumpur: Netaji Centre, 1992), pp. 66–69, and Michael Stenson, *Class, Race, and Colonialism in West Malaysia: The Indian Case* (Brisbane: University of Queensland Press, 1980), p. 135.

9. *Straits Times*, 27 March 1952.
10. National Archives of Australia, NAA: A816, 19/321/18, op. cit.
11. National Archives of Australia, NAA: A816, 19/321/18, Secret, "The Communal Situation in Malaya", Australian Commissioner in Singapore to Minister for External Affairs, Canberra, 19 May 1952. See also Richard Stubbs, "The UMNO, the MCA, and the early years of the Malayan Emergency, 1948–1955", *Journal of Southeast Asian Studies* 10, no. 1 (March 1979), pp. 37–88.

    Dato' Panglima Bukit Gantang, literally the "Leader of Bukit Gantang", one of the forty-eight principal Malay chiefs of Perak, was commonly referred to in this fashion in official records, but his actual name was Haji Abdul Wahab bin Toh Muda Abdul Aziz. He was a barrister, and had been employed as a judge by the Japanese during the Japanese Occupation. He was an important political figure, and a Malay nationalist of some standing. He had held several important positions such as Secretary General of UMNO (1946–47), Mentri Besar Perak (1948–57), Legco member (1948), CLC member (1949–50), and Leader of the Malay Rulers delegation to London for a Constitutional Conference (1956–57). (See A.J. Stockwell, *Malaya, Part III: The Alliance Path to Independence, 1953–57* (London: HMSO, 1995), p. 422 and Harper, op. cit., p. 259.)
12. Margaret Shennan, *Our Man in Malaya* (Singapore: Monsoon Books, 2014), p. 223.
13. Harper, op. cit., p. 259.
14. Joseph M. Fernando, "Elite Intercommunal Bargaining and Conflict Resolution: the Role of the CLC in Malaya 1949–1951", *Journal of Souheast Asian Studies* 43, no. 2 (2 June 2012), pp. 280–301.
15. Malcolm MacDonald was based in Singapore as British Commissioner General for South East Asia, 1948–55, with joint responsibilities to both the Colonial Office and the Foreign Office. He was the most senior British representative in Southeast Asia and in his long and distinguished career held high offices of state both in England and overseas. His father, Ramsey MacDonald, had been British Prime Minister twice.
16. Clyde Sanger, *Malcolm MacDonald: Bringing an End to Empire* (Montreal: McGill-Queen's University Press, 1995), pp. 302, 313–20.

17. *Straits Times,* 29 February 1952.
18. Ibid.
19. Sanger, op. cit., pp. 302, 313–20.
20. Author's notes.
21. National Archives of Australia, NAA: A816,19/321/18, Secret, "The Communal Situation in Malaya", 19 May 1953, Australian Commissioner's Office, Singapore, to Minister for External Affairs, Canberra. W.N. McLeod had been a chartered accountant with Messrs. Neill & Bell, Kuala Lumpur since 1946. He was a member of the Federal Legislative Council (1953–55), and had joined the Parti Negara, the party formed by Dato' Onn after he wound up IMP. During World War II McLeod had served as a British officer with an Indian Army mountain artillery unit in India and Burma (author's notes).
22. Tunku Abdul Rahman Putra al-Haj, *Looking Back: Monday Musings and Memories* (Kuala Lumpur: Pustaka Antara, 1977), p. 17, and National Archives of Australia, NAA: A816, 19/321/18, Secret, "Movement towards Self-Government in Malaya", op. cit.
23. Joseph M. Fernando, *The Alliance Road to Independence* (Kuala Lumpur: University of Malaya Press, 2009), p. 41.
24. Uda bin Raja Mohammed was Mentri Besar, Selangor (1949–55), Speaker of the Federal Legislative Council (1955–57), and Governor of Penang (1957); Dato Nik Kamil was a barrister, Mentri Besar, Kelantan (1948–53), and Member of the Federal Legislative Council (1948–55); and Dato Ernest Thuraisingham, was a barrister, President of the Ceylon Federation of Malaya, the former Chairman of the Communities Liaison Committee (1949–50), a founder member of Dato' Onn's IMP (1951) and Parti Negara (1954), and a Member of the Federal Legislative Council (1948–55). (See Stockwell, op. cit., pp. 428–32.)
25. Tunku Abdul Rahman Putra al-Haj, *Looking Back: Monday Musings and Memories,* op. cit.
26. Ibid., p. 19.
27. Tunku Abdul Rahman, *Contemporary Issues in Malayan Politics* (Kuala Lumpur: Pelandok Publications, 1984), pp. 217–18.
28. National Archives of Australia, NAA: A816, 19/321/18, Secret, "The Communal Situation in Malaya", op. cit.
29. Ibid.
30. *The Economist,* 10 October 1953.
31. Ibid. National Archives of Australia, NAA: A816, 19/321/18, Secret, "The Communal Situation in Malaya", op. cit.
32. Fernando, op. cit.; "Malaya's New Nationalists" (by a Correspondent, *The Economist,* 10 October 1953); and National Archives of Australia, NAA: A816, 19/321/18, Secret, "The Communal Situation in Malaya", op. cit., 19 May 1953.
33. Ibid.

34. Fernando, op. cit., p, 41.

35. Tunku Abdul Rahman, *Looking Back*, op. cit., pp. 17–19.

36. ISEAS Library, Singapore: Tun Sir Henry H.S. Lee, SMN, KBE, JP, Private Papers Collection, HSL.NC.1.017 "National Convention of UMNO/MCA Alliance for early independence and Federal Elections 1954", 24 August 1953.

37. Sheppard, op. cit., p. 86.

38. Directive to General Sir Gerald Walter Robert Templer, KCB, KBE, CMG, DSO, ADC, High Commissioner in and for the Federation of Malaya, by the Secretary of State for the Colonies on behalf of His Majesty's Government in the U.K., 1 February 1952.

39. Fernando, op. cit., pp. 39–42.

40. CO 1922/86, no. 3, "Political Talks with General Templer. CO minute of discussion with General Templer on political advance", op. cit. According to the influential Malay-language newspaper *Utusan Melayu* dated 3 June 1953, there were not more than 1,000 senior Malay officials in the country.

41. In the turbulent days following the Japanese surrender in Penang, Heah Joo Seang was accused by members of the Penang Chinese community of being a Japanese collaborator — perhaps Templer had this in mind in referring to Heah's "wartime activities" — and during an altercation with demonstrators which got out of hand, his wife's hand was chopped off in attempting to ward off a blow aimed at her husband (author's notes).

42. National Archives of Australia, NAA: A816/58, 19/321/18, Confidential, PR/891/53, "Interview with General Sir Gerald Templer", Ian Hamilton, Public Relations officer, Australian Commission for Malaya to Secretary, Department of External Affairs, Canberra, 9 October 1953.

43. CO 1022/86. No. 3, "Political Talks with General Templer. CO Minute of discussion with Templer on political advance, 3 December 1952". See also CO 1020/493, "General Templer's Speech at Press Conference at Colonial Office, 4 December 1952"; CO 1022/86, no. 35, 18 May 1953; and CO 1022/494, Secret (Closed until 1984), "Visit of General Templer to London May/June 1953". During his visit to London, General Templer attended the Coronation of Queen Elizabeth II in London as Aide-de-Camp General to the Queen.

44. *Manchester Guardian*, 5 December 1952.

45. Ibid.

46. CO 1022/494, Secret (Closed until 1984), "Visit of General Templer to London May/June 1953", op. cit.

47. *Federation of Malaya. Report of the Committee appointed to examine the question of Elections to the Federal Legislative Council* (Kuala Lumpur: Government Printer, 1954), *passim*. Hogan headed the Working Committee of this Report.

48. Tunku Abdul Rahman, *Looking Back*, op. cit., p. 17.

49. Fernando, op. cit., p. 44.

50. National Archives of Australia, NAA: A816: 19/321/18, Secret, "Movement towards Self-Government in Malaya", L.R. McIntyre, Australian Commissioner in Singapore to Minister for External Affairs, Canberra, 23 September 1953.

51. National Archives of Australia, NAA: A816, 19/321/18, op. cit.

52. *Federation of Malaya. Report of the Committee appointed to examine the question of Elections to the Federal Legislative Council*, op. cit., p. 23.

53. Harper, op. cit., pp. 341–42.

54. Cloake, op. cit., p. 312.

55. Ibid., pp. 44–45.

56. Tan Sri Mohammed Tahir Tan Tong Hye (known as T.H. Tan) (b. 1914) was educated at St. Joseph's Institution and Raffles Institution, Singapore. He was formerly Editor of the Singapore *Tiger Standard*. and had invited S. Rajaratnam to join the newspaper as a columnist in April 1950. He became the Secretary General of the Malayan Chinese Association and the UMNO-MCA Alliance, and was the author of *The Prince and I* (1979) about Tunku Abdul Rahman and himself. He was converted to Islam by Dato Abdul Razak.

57. P.G. Lim, op. cit., p. 127.

58. ISEAS Library, Singapore: Tan Cheng Lock Private Archives, TCL.8.36.1, Letter dated 30 April 1954 from T.H. Tan to Tan Cheng Lock (Malacca). See also Fernando, op. cit., p. 48.

59. Wikipedia, "Tunku Abdul Rahman", p. 17.

60. Fernando, op. cit., p. 77.

61. Tunku Abdul Rahman, *Looking Back*, op. cit., p. 22; Fernando, op. cit., pp. 25–27, 47.

62. Ibid.

63. CO 1030/310 (72), "Templer to Secretary of State, 26 May 1954" and Fernando, op. cit., pp. 46–50.

64. Tunku Abdul Rahman, *Looking Back*, op. cit., pp. 26–27.

65. Cloake, op. cit., p. 315.

66. Ibid., p. 313.

67. Sheppard, op. cit., p. 90, and Fernando, op. cit., p. 52.

68. Cloake, op. cit., p. 315.

69. See Ooi, op. cit., p. 67 and CO 1030/311, no. 130, "[Agreement with the Alliance on federal elections]: Inward telegram from Sir D. MacGillivray to Mr Lyttelton transmitting his exchange of letters with Tunku Abdul Rahman, 7 July 1954."

70. Karl von Vorys, op. cit., p. 120.

71. Tunku Abdul Rahman, *Looking Back*, op. cit., p. 30.

72. Harper, op. cit., p. 345.

73. Fernando, op. cit., pp. 89–113.

74. *Malaya: The Making of a Nation* (London: Central Office of Information Reference Pamphlet No. 27, HMSO, 1957), p. 44.

8

CONCLUSION:
General Templer's Departure

When Templer's proconsulship in Malaya was coming to an end, the Colonial Office and War Office made arrangements for his succession, and it was proposed that he should remain in Malaya until the end of May 1954 when the Deputy High Commissioner, Sir Donald MacGillivray, would take over from him. As MacGillivray was a career colonial civil servant and not a soldier, Lieutenant General Sir Geoffrey Bourne would take over as Director of Operations.[1]

It was then planned that Templer would take leave until he assumed in October 1954 his new appointment in Germany as Commander of the Northern Army Group, Allied Forces, Western Europe, a post combined with that of Commander-in-Chief of the 80,000-strong British Army of the Rhine, one of the most important appointments in the British Army.[2]

When the time came for his departure from Malaya on 1 June 1954, Templer was given a grand send-off at Kuala Lumpur International Airport befitting his high position, cheered by thousands of spectators and farewelled officially by a wide array of Malayan dignitaries, including MacGillivray, members of the Federal Executive and Legislative Councils,

Tunku Abdul Rahman, Colonel H.S. Lee, Dato' Onn bin Ja'afar, as well as the Malay Sultans or their representatives, service and police chiefs, and high-ranking civil servants. General Templer, resplendent in his white tropical General's full-dress uniform and wearing all his decorations and the coloured sash of the GCMG, inspected the four guards of honour from the Army, Navy, Air Force and Police that had been drawn up on the tarmac of the airfield. The RAF Band played the Royal Salute followed by *Auld Lang Syne*. It was a most poignant and moving occasion and according to the *Malay Mail*, Lady Templer was in tears and Templer was visibly affected too, when they boarded the VIP aircraft that was to take them to Singapore on the first stage of their journey home.[3]

Everybody assumed, as had been announced, that Templer was on his way to take up what was one of the top appointments in the British Army, and only Templer himself and a very few sworn confidantes knew that his appointment had in fact been cancelled.[4] Dr Konrad Adenauer, the first Chancellor of the Federal Republic of Germany, had vetoed it as he had never forgiven Templer for summarily dismissing him as Mayor of Cologne at the end of World War II when Templer had been Director of Civil Affairs in the British military sector of occupied Germany.

Although the information about the cancellation of Templer's appointment in Germany was withheld from the public at Templer's request, there had been a short reference in the *Straits Times* on 27 February 1954 to his disagreement with Adenauer which seems to have escaped public attention.[5]

Templer himself had been aware that his appointment in Germany was likely to become an issue as early on as 17 April 1954 when Field Marshal Lord Montgomery, under whom he had served in Germany towards the end of World War II, had written to him privately to ask him for an account of his disagreement with Adenauer, as apparently the matter had been raised with him in London by Prime Minister Winston Churchill. Templer had replied rather obliquely that:

> I do not intend to say a word about the affair during my lifetime, or indeed allow anything to be published about it until all the principal characters on the stage of those days have departed. You probably do not agree with this point of view but there we are.[6]

Aside from this rather unusual reply, not long before Templer's departure from Malaya, the Chief of the Imperial General Staff (CIGS), Field Marshal

Sir John Harding, had written a personal letter to him to inform him that Prime Minister Winston Churchill had cancelled his posting to Germany and that the change in plan was connected with an article written by Sefton Delmer regarding Templer's time in Germany at the end of the war as Director of Civil Affairs in the British military sector of occupied Germany which had been published in the London *Daily Express*. In his article Delmer had referred to the most awkward and embarrassing situation that would arise when General Templer met Chancellor Adenauer when he assumed his new appointment in Germany in October as Adenauer had never forgiven him for summarily dismissing him for "incompetence and obstruction".[7]

Harding, however, confirmed in his letter that it had been decided that Templer would take over from him as CIGS in November 1955 as originally planned and said that meanwhile the Secretary of State for War had agreed that in the circumstances he should take "long leave until receipt of further orders". In replying, Templer requested Harding not to announce what had happened until after he had left Malaya.[8]

There the matter remained until a terse announcement from the War Office on 7 June 1954, several days after Templer's departure from Malaya, that "General Templer has been granted long leave and his new appointment will be announced later." Reports then began to spread quickly that his appointment in Germany had been blocked by the West German Chancellor Adenauer.

Time magazine took up the story and on 14 June 1954 reported: "Great Britain: The Templer Mystery. Templer would not get his promised command of the 80,000-strong British Army of the Rhine and an important new appointment will be announced later. General Templer has been granted long leave." In the view of Terence Prittie, who was the London *The Guardian's* correspondent in Germany for seventeen years from October 1946 to June 1963, and was highly regarded as a political commentator, Adenauer always regarded his dismissal as an affront and it had left a mental scar which never healed and he had never forgiven Templer for the role he had played in it nor the British for what they had done.[9]

There were no further official announcements and Templer remained unemployed on full pay leave until October 1954. After the expiry of his leave, as he had still not received a new appointment, he was placed on full pay leave "pending further instructions". It was a sad ending to his two-year proconsulship in Malaya as High Commissioner and Director of Operations, where he had been a towering figure, although perhaps sometimes polarizing as has been brought out in this account.

Templer had to wait until the following year when on 17 January 1955 he was instructed to prepare a report for the Cabinet Counter Subversion Committee on the colonial security services, and on 8 March the Ministry of Defence announced that he had been appointed to conduct an enquiry at the request of the War Office and the Cabinet Office into the "organisation and nature of colonial military forces". Templer duly completed his report ("Security in the Colonies") on 23 April 1955, and at the same time the opportunity was taken to announce officially that he would succeed Field Marshal Sir John Harding as CIGS in November.[10] Although the colonial security services report that he prepared was thorough and valuable in many ways it does not appear to have been given much publicity.[11] However, as a result, two additional MI5 officers were attached to the Colonial Office and in 1955 the Colonial Office established its own secret "Intelligence Security Department", the records of which remained classified until they were released from the British archives in 2008.[12] Templer was, in fact, well qualified to write this report as he had helped to re-establish the Intelligence Corps (IC) of the British Army at the beginning of World War II, for which he had been commended, and he had been appointed later in his career Director of Military Intelligence (DMI) at the War Office, and for two years from 1946 he had been an ex-officio member of the Joint Intelligence Committee (JIC), the leading intelligence body in the United Kingdom. But his assignment to write the report was a "holding appointment" only and it must have been something of a come-down after the cancellation of his top appointment in Germany. The effect of what had happened and the serious setback to his military career was probably only finally mitigated by the official announcement after he had completed his report in April 1955 that he would become Chief of the Imperial General Staff (CIGS) in November 1955, the top post in the British Army, which he had long been promised. Once his appointment as CIGS designate was announced, Templer started on a round of overseas visits to familiarize himself with his new responsibilities, although when he arrived at Australia as CIGS designate, it was clear that the *Sydney Morning Herald* had not forgotten his Malayan days when it commented that "he would have to show more tact than he did in June 1953 when he summoned an Asian journalist who was also a Councillor of the FMS [sic] to his office and called him a rat and a rotten journalist whose name stinks in South East Asia." The newspaper continued: "The Asian journalist had written childishly and spitefully about the Queen's coronation but a Singapore paper mirrored much of the popular feeling when it claimed it was not Templer's place to criticise or make unsuitable and irrelevant references to birds, beasts or rodents."[13]

TEMPLER AND THE KONRAD ADENAUER AFFAIR

As for the Konrad Adenauer affair, how had it come about?

In March 1945 towards the end of World War II, American forces had occupied Cologne and had established a military administration there. Dr Konrad Adenauer was then appointed Mayor of Cologne (*Oberbürgermeister*). In June 1945, the military administration of Cologne was transferred to the British occupying power and General Templer, who was then Director of Civil Affairs and Military Government (British Zone) of the 21st Army Group, assumed control of Cologne and its surrounding region.

Adenauer had already had a long and distinguished political career in Germany which spanned many decades of Germany's history. He had been a leading Catholic Party politician in the Weimar Republic and had served previously as Mayor of Cologne (1917–33) for a long period, and had been President of the Prussian State Council (1922–33). In 1933, he was dismissed by the Nazis as Mayor of Cologne, and in 1944 during World War II he had been detained by them on suspicion of being involved in a failed assassination attempt on Hitler, and imprisoned for three months. In May, after Germany's unconditional surrender, he had been reappointed Mayor of Cologne.

After the war, he devoted his efforts to restoring the economy of Germany and reinstating it to its former position as a world power, and in the post-war 1949 German Federal Elections, he became the first Chancellor of the Federal Republic of (West) Germany, a position he held from 1949 to 1963. As such, he was the supreme commander of the new German Army which would form part of the North Atlantic Treaty Organization (NATO) force.[14]

On 6 October 1945, when Cologne was under British military administration, according to Adenauer's own account, he was summarily summoned to see Brigadier John Barraclough, commanding the North

Rhine Province of the British military sector in which Cologne was situated. He was stopped at a British army checkpoint while he was on his way to Bonn and escorted back to Cologne to see Barraclough. Adenauer thought Barraclough wanted to see him about his disagreement with the British military administration over the British proposal to cut down trees in Cologne's green belt to be used as fuel in the coming winter months and his alleged delay in cleaning up Cologne which had been badly damaged by Allied bombing. About three-quarters of all the houses had been destroyed by Allied bombing together with all bridges across the Rhine and the population had been reduced from a pre-war total of 750,000 to 35,000. Gas, electricity and water supplies had been disrupted, and the sewage system lay in ruins.[15]

A contemporary eye-witness account of the extent of the destruction of Cologne describes it as follow:

> First, the extent of the destruction. Every window was shattered, every church had been hit, and every side street was blocked with rubble. The magnificent cathedral in the centre of the town had been damaged but survived.
>
> The giant statue of Bismarck on a horse was still standing but Bismarck's sword, pointing toward France, had been cut off by flying shrapnel.[16]

When Adenauer arrived at Barraclough's office, he was greeted in a brusque manner by Barraclough and not even offered a chair to sit on. By all accounts, it was an unpleasant meeting, which Adenauer regarded as "grossly insulting". Without more ado, he was handed a letter that Barraclough had prepared which was read out to him by an interpreter, and he was curtly told that he was being summarily dismissed as Mayor of Cologne for incompetence and inefficiency for not taking action on previous warnings he had been given by the British military administration to repair Cologne's damaged buildings and generally clean up the city and prepare it for winter.

Aside from his dismissal, three restrictions were placed on his movements and activities which he found particularly objectionable. They were: (1) that he should leave Cologne as soon as possible and not later than 14 October; (2) after handing over his duties to his successor, he would not be permitted to take part in any way with the administration of Cologne or any other part of the North Rhine Province; and (3) he would not be allowed to participate directly or indirectly in any form of political activity in Germany.

On being handed the letter, Barraclough asked him whether he had anything to say. Adenauer replied in the negative, signed a copy of Barraclough's letter, and left his office. A request he made a day or so later to be allowed to accompany his wife who was seriously ill to Cologne for urgent medical treatment was rejected.

The records indicate that General Templer was not very impressed with Adenauer. For his part Adenauer did not think very highly of him either and he felt that Templer had failed to recognize Cologne's unique problems and the gigantic task with which he was faced single-handed with a complete lack of equipment and supplies. Moreover, he considered the British military administration of Cologne which Templer headed did not compare favourably with what he remembered of the British military administration of Cologne in 1918 at the end of World War I when he had been Mayor of Cologne. However, there is no doubt that the situation in 1945 was quite different from what it was in 1918 when Cologne had not suffered any war damage and the German administration of the city remained intact. By the end of World War II, Cologne had virtually been reduced to rubble by Allied bombing, its civil administration had been devastated and had to be built up again from scratch, and Adenauer had to work under the tight control of the British military administration, which he considered did not understand the part played by Cologne in Germany's history.

When Templer visited Cologne in the previous month, he had thought the cleaning up and repair of the extensive bomb damage the city had suffered and the provision of emergency housing for its population had not progressed as fast as he demanded and he had formed the impression that Adenauer, as Mayor, was not up to his job and the two men had a serious disagreement over what had to be done. On Templer's return on this occasion to Lübbecke where he was based, he stopped off at Barraclough's office to discuss the situation in Cologne and to tell him that "a younger and more energetic man was needed as Mayor".[17] Adenauer was then sixty-nine years old. It was evidently at this meeting that a decision was made to dismiss Adenauer. What remains in doubt, however, is who actually made the decision. Templer himself had always maintained that he made the decision which he had instructed Barraclough to carry out. However, based on Barraclough's own recollection of Templer's words, Templer had said: "*If* the old man [i.e. Adenauer] is no good, you must get rid of him" [emphasis added by the author]. Barraclough had understood this to mean that he had been given the authority to dismiss Adenauer if he wished.[18]

However, whichever interpretation is correct, there seems to be little doubt that Templer had formed a poor opinion of Adenauer and had arrived at the decision that he should be dismissed, and had issued orders accordingly.

Meanwhile, the dismissal of Adenauer and the way in which it had been carried out was not well received by the British Foreign Office in London or the Political Affairs Department of the Allied Control Commission in Berlin, who regarded Adenauer as one of the potential leaders of a rehabilitated Germany, and steps were taken to improve relations between Adenauer and the British. As a result, the restrictions on his movements and political activities were removed although he was not reinstated as Mayor.[19]

Ironically, his dismissal as Mayor of Cologne provided Adenauer with the opportunity to devote his time to national politics and create a new German political party, the Christlich Demokratische Union (CDU) or Christian Democratic Movement, which was to lead to his eventual election in 1949 as Chancellor of the new Federal Republic of West Germany, the post that he held when Templer left Malaya in 1954. During the interim period, Adenauer is credited with rebuilding the post-war German Army and coming to terms with France, thus making possible the reunification of Western Europe, and for Germany to join the North Atlantic Treaty Organization (NATO) and become a firm ally of the United States of America.[20]

CONCLUDING OBSERVATIONS

During his two-year proconsulship, there is no doubt that General Templer did his utmost as High Commissioner and Director of Operations in Malaya to deal with the two-pronged task he had been given by the British Government to subdue the Communist uprising and lead Malaya on the path to self-government. But his task in taking over his appointment could not have been made any easier by the winds of change blowing in many other parts of Asia, such as the successes of the Chinese Communist Party which had led to the recognition of the Chinese People's Republic by the British Government on 6 January 1950; the Korean War in which British and Commonwealth troops were involved in fighting North Korean and

Chinese Communist armies; the uneasy situation in French Indo-China (Vietnam) where the French colonial forces were having a hard task in containing the Vietcong; and the Communist insurgencies in Thailand and Burma, where if the situation in any of them had spun out of control the security situation in Malaya would have been seriously affected.[21]

It was a time of change, too, in neighbouring Singapore with which Malaya had traditionally maintained close ties, where a new Governor (Sir) John Nicoll had been installed on 21 April 1952 after Sir Franklin Gimson retired, and it seemed likely that Malcolm MacDonald's term of office as British Commissioner General for South East Asia would end in May 1952 (it was subsequently extended to 1955).

During Templer's time in Malaya, although asked by the Colonial Office to look into the possibilities of a fusion with Singapore, he does not appear to have formed a close relationship with either Gimson or Nicoll who succeeded Gimson as Governor. On the contrary, he seems to have made it clear that he had little regard for the Singapore Government and especially the Singapore Special Branch. His view of Malcolm MacDonald, the Commissioner General for South East Asia, was well known, too, as has been remarked on in this book.[22]

There is no doubt, however, that Templer worked himself almost to the point of exhaustion in Malaya and expected his subordinates to do the same, but in a strict sense he did not achieve either of the targets he had been set by the British Government. The first Malayan Emergency was not brought to an end until 1960 some six years after he left Malaya, and the political policy he followed was seriously at odds with that of the UMNO-MCA-MIC National Alliance, the leading political force in Malaya, which came to power after the first Federal Elections held in 1955.

The continuing serious security situation in Malaya in December a few months after Templer's departure was succinctly summed up by R.W Furlonger, First Secretary of the Australian Commissioner's Office, Singapore, as follows:

M.R.L.A. [Malayan Races Liberation Army] platoons are coming to notice more and more in Johore, Negri Sembilan, and Perak, [their] organisation and adjustment may not be complete, but there is little doubt that the MRLA platoons, freed from their responsibility for the protection of the Party District and Branch Organisations, now provide the Party with a striking force capable of carrying out well planned attacks on selected targets... . While there has been no increase in the number of terrorist incidents in the last year, and while the Security Forces could probably contain, without undue difficulty (unless the latter receive external aid), the security situation in Malaya, it has nevertheless become more complicated in recent months, and the determination of the Emergency is still not yet in sight.[23]

Further, a few months later in January 1955, Sir Donald MacGillivray who had taken over as High Commissioner from General Templer on the latter's departure from Malaya, confirmed in a report to the Secretary of State, that the CPM still had no less than 5,000 men under arms in the Malayan jungle and it could obtain as many reinforcements from the civilian population as it wished, and "the Emergency remains much more than a nuisance and it would be a grave mistake to think that its end is in sight".[24]

Part of the problem, however, which was always unsaid in the background throughout Templer's proconsulship, though it was brought up by his detractors early on when his appointment was first announced by the British Government, was that he did not have a good understanding of the complex political problems with which he was faced in order to bring about political change in Malaya's multi-ethnic society, and he would perforce have to learn on the spot as he went along. However, it is rather surprising that the imbroglio of the "Adenauer affair" and what had happened in Germany at the end of World War II in which Templer had been involved was not brought up by Lyttelton, then Secretary of State for the Colonies, when the latter interviewed him for his proconsulship in Malaya, especially as it must have been clear that his appointment as High Commissioner in Malaya would involve his working closely with local politicians. If it was, there is no mention of it in Lyttelton's biography or the public records.

In this connection, it is perhaps worth reflecting on Lord Ogmore's pertinent remarks about Templer's appointment in Malaya in the debate in the House of Lords on 27 February 1952, when he said that General Templer did not have a great deal of experience in political matters and certainly nothing like the experience he had in military matters, which should have rung a bell of caution. In his view, Templer was a good professional soldier but he was not a diplomat or a good politician.[25] It did not help, too, that on Templer's part, he had a poor opinion of local politicians and their political parties which is clearly brought out by Cloake, his biographer, and supported, too, by the candid interview Templer gave to Ian Hamilton, the Australian Mission's Public Relations Officer in Kuala Lumpur in October 1953, when he described UMNO and the MCA as "not worth a damn [sic] as real political parties".[26] The alliance of UMNO-MCA in those early days struck General Templer as being fundamentally flawed, and he did not form a high opinion of either Tan Cheng Lock or Tunku Abdul Rahman. In fact, Templer and MacDonald held secret talks with a number of Malay notables to oust the Tunku from the UMNO presidency and establish an alternative party to the UMNO-MCA Alliance.[27]

He thought of Tan, President of the MCA and leader of the Malayan Chinese community, who was a dedicated Malayan nationalist, as an "old dodderer". He perhaps found it easier to understand the Malays with whom he came into contact although even then he disliked the Tunku and his UMNO-MCA Alliance and distrusted his policies, and he roundly abused Aziz Ishak, a leading Malay journalist and member of the Federal Legislative Council, a brother of the first President of Singapore (Yusof bin Ishak), for his criticism of British notables attending the coronation of Queen Elizabeth II in London.

Many other persons experienced the sharp edge of his tongue including Victor Purcell, the noted British sinologist and honorary adviser to the MCA, who was then a Cambridge don who had pre-war occupied many senior positions in the Malayan Chinese Secretariat, and the Singapore journalist, S. Rajaratnam, who subsequently became one of the founding members of the People's Action Party (PAP), Singapore, and a colleague of Singapore's first Prime Minister Lee Kuan Yew. He tried, too, to have Louis Heren, the foreign correspondent of the *London Times* who was based in Singapore, dismissed or transferred for writing critically about him but the Editor of the *London Times,* Sir William Haley, refused to do so, and he attempted unsuccessfully to have the doctor/novelist Han Suyin's novel about Malaya, *...And the Rain My Drink,* banned for its alleged anti-British bias.

General Templer's well-known short temper and rough tongue must have placed him at a considerable disadvantage in his political activities. It was unfortunate too that he did not display much understanding of the background to Malaya's history and the subtleties that are inherent in its culture and way of life, which would have enabled him to arrive at a better understanding of the situation. He was often quite irascible, difficult, and perhaps even brutal, especially in the harsh punishments he inflicted on New Villagers for failing to cooperate with the authorities. For example, the punishments he imposed for failing to provide information about Communist activities on the towns of Sungei Pelek, Pekan Jabi, Tanjong Malim; Permatang Tinggi (where the villagers' houses and shop houses were demolished); and Kulai (Johore) where Templer called the villagers "a lot of bastards", and so on.[28] As the records indicate, questions were asked about this in the House of Commons but no one dared talk about it while he was in Malaya (except perhaps Victor Purcell).

As the historian Karl Hack has observed, it was fortunate that Templer arrived with the turning tide when the security situation was beginning to show signs of improvement.[29] However, the improvement that became apparent then was not due to Templer's arrival in Malaya but to the effects of the brilliant Briggs Plan that had been prepared and implemented by General Briggs earlier which had brought about the withdrawal of the Communists deep into the jungle and a diminution of their terrorist activities in order to concentrate on building up their own resources and temporarily placing less emphasis on terrorism. Templer's own input, for which he should be given credit, was the vigour and military drive he infused into the campaign against the Communists.[30]

General Templer's proconsulship in Malaya has been the subject over the years of both praise and criticism and the truth probably lies somewhere in between. The academic debates that are relevant to this question are advanced by the historians Karl Hack and Kumar Ramakrishna, which were discussed by Simon Smith too, with Hack arguing that in the long run it was the Briggs Plan and not Templer that brought about the defeat of the Communist uprising whereas Ramakrishna adopted the opposite view.[31]

General Templer left Malaya in 1954 in a blaze of glory and he is remembered nowadays as the man who saved Malaysia from Communism and led the way to self-rule and eventually *Merdeka*. This is, however, not entirely correct. As this preliminary study of his political proconsulship in Malaya has attempted to show, using wherever possible primary sources, first-hand experiences, and other relevant records, there were many aspects of his proconsulship in Malaya which if they had been more widely known at the time, would not have placed him in such a favourable light, and would have affected the historical consensus of him that has hitherto been accepted.

Field Marshal Lord Carver, a prominent British General, who wrote Templer's official biography for the *Oxford Dictionary of National Biography*, described him as a "martinet in manner and appearance", and this is probably an accurate and fair portrayal of him and provides some idea of his manner and style.[32] The Australian official historian of the Malayan Emergency was less kind to him and referred to him as a "dictator",[33] and the same description was used by Professor Cheah Boon Kheng, the eminent Malaysian historian, who commented that "Templer was a feared man who became notorious for his violent temper and intemperate language".[34] In the end, when all is said and done, while no doubt he was an outstanding general skilled in the profession of arms and fitting the description of what the French call *un beau Sabreur*, as a politician he was not served at all well by his well-known abrasiveness and use of barrack room language when diplomacy would have served him in better stead, and perhaps one is left with the feeling that he was an old-world imperialist rather out of touch with the times who regarded with extreme distaste the abandonment of Britain's imperial responsibilities.[35]

The author has not set out to create havoc even in a mild way by this preliminary study spread over more than three-and-a-half years of the political and socio-economic role that Templer played in those turbulent days in Malaya. However it is hoped that it will help to contribute to a better understanding of the man and his time and encourage further studies of his proconsulship in Malaya to add to the historical conclusions that have so far been reached about it and perhaps add a more rounded picture of the part he played in it. It was undoubtedly a critical moment in Malaya's history leading to Malaya's self-government and eventual independence and a period of great historical importance.

Notes

1. CO 1022/98, Paskin to Lloyd, 16 June 1953. After leaving Malaya in October 1956, Lieutenant General Sir Geoffrey Bourne became Commander, British Middle East Land Forces.
2. CO 1022/98, Lloyd to Lascelles, 18 December 1953.
3. Cloake, op. cit., p. 326. The *Federation of Malaya Annual Report 1954* (London: HMSO, 1955), pp. 7–8, described Templer's departure as a "memorable occasion marked by a spontaneous recognition by the public of the outstanding services he had rendered to the Federation during a period when the dark clouds of armed Communism hang menacingly over the country at large.... The farewell

accorded to him on the day of his departure by people from all walks of life was an occasion which will find its place in the annals of the Federation."

4. According to Cloake (op. cit., p. 328), Templer's biographer, Lord Wynford, Templer's ADC, and MacGillivray who was the new High Commissioner, only knew that Templer's appointment in Germany had been cancelled when they returned from seeing him off at Kuala Lumpur airport and they received the letters which he had left to be delivered to them in which he had written: "I have been living a lie for the last 2–3 months.'

5. *The Age* (31 May 1954) reported that "Templer leaves for Singapore on his way back to become G.O.C. Commanding the British Forces on the Rhine."

6. Cloake, op. cit., p. 161.

7. Ibid., p. 329.

8. Ibid. Templer was promoted to Field Marshal, the highest rank in the British Army, on 27 November 1956.

9. "How it Really Was. Konrad Adenauer and his dismissal as Mayor of Cologne by the British in 1945", <http://howitreallywas.typepad.com/how_it_really_was/2008/03/konrad-adenauer.html> (accessed 4 November 2012).

10. T 220/1395, "Ministerial Committee to Review Organisation of Armed Forces, Police and Security Services in the Colonies (including investigation undertaken by General Sir Gerald Templer into Colonial security problems)." See CAB 21/2925 General Sir Gerald Templer, "Report on colonial security" (April 1955).

11. Cloake, op. cit., p. 332. See also CO 1030 1030/16, "Committee of Ministers to Consider Security and Intelligence Services in Malaya during the Emergency and pre-Emergency Period"; CAB 134/2544, "Report on Colonial Security 1955"; and Richard J. Aldridge, *Espionage, Security and Intelligence in Britain 1945–1970* (Manchester: Manchester University Press, 1998).

12. Calder Walton, *Empire of Secrets: British Intelligence, the Cold War and the Twilight of Empire* (New York: The Overlook Press, 2013), pp. 140–41.

13. National Archives of Australia, NAA: A5954, 2198/6, *Sydney Morning Herald,* 11 March 1955 and *The Argus,* 14 July 1955. Not long after he became CIGS, Templer played a leading role in the British, French and Israeli invasion of Egypt following the arbitrary nationalization of the Suez Canal by Egypt, although it was unfortunate that he had a serious disagreement with Admiral Lord Louis Mountbatten over the strategy to be followed (see Anthony Gorst "A Modern Major General; General Sir Gerald Templer, CIGS", in Sall Kelly and Anthony Gorst, eds., *Whitehall and the Suez Crisis* (London: Frank Cass, 2000), pp. 29–45 and Adrian Smith, "Resignation of a First Sea Lord: Mountbatten and the Suez Crisis", *History* 98, Issue 329 (January 2013): 105–34).

14. Michael W. Krekel, *Konrad Adenauer: Profiles of the Man and the Politician,* Stiftung Bundereskanzler-denhaus-Haus (Konrad Adenauer Memorial Foundation),

Federal Republic of Germany, 1999, pp. 28–31; Charles Williams, *Adenauer: The Father of the New Germany* (London: Little, Brown & Co. Ltd., 2000), pp. 295–303; and Beate Ruhm von Oppen, translator, *Konrad Adenauer, Memoirs 1945–53* (London: Weidenfeld & Nicolson, 1965), pp. 31–35.

15. Ibid. See also Ronald Irving, *Adenauer* (London: Longman, 2002).

16. Stephen E. Ambrose, *Band of Brothers* (London: Simon & Schuster UK Ltd., 2001), p. 258.

17. Noel Annan, *Changing Enemies: The Defeat and Regeneration of Germany* (Cornell University Press, 1997), p. 167. See also "World Spotlight. Adenauer as Tough as Churchill", 13 September 1953 (Colin Bingham writing from Bonn, where he was observing the West German elections) <http://trove.nla.gov.au/ndpo/del/article/18506663> (accessed 4 November 2012).

18. Charles Williams, op. cit., pp. 302–303; Hans-Peter Schwarz, *Konrad Adenauer: From the German Empire to the Federal Republic, 1876–1952* (Oxford: Berghahn Books Ltd. (English language edition), 1995), pp. 90 and 308; and Cloake, op. cit., pp. 158–62.

19. Cloake, op. cit., p. 304.

20. See Charles Williams, op. cit., and Hans-Peter Schwarz, op. cit.

21. CO 1022/200, Secret. "Potential Effects that deterioration in the situation in Indo-China might have in British colonial and protected territories" (closed until 1984).

22. At a meeting of British Governors attending the Malaya-Borneo Defence Committee held in Singapore in 1952, Templer made what he described himself as a "bloody-minded attack on Singapore" which in his opinion was inhabited by "a selfish lot of coots", and he singled out the Singapore Special Branch for inefficiency. He called MacDonald "the master of the waffling word". See Cloake, op. cit., pp. 298–99.

23. National Archives of Australian, NAA, A7133, Top Secret. "Australian Secret Service Records on Singapore and Malaya (1953–1955). Malaya: The Emergency", 4 December 1954, p. 7. The Combined Intelligence Staff estimate of the CPM's armed strength in April 1954 was a maximum figure of 6,100 and a minimum of 4,400 (See ISEAS Library, Tun Sir Henry H.S. Lee Private Papers, HSL. 18.010. Secret. Director of Operations Committee Meeting in Executive Council Chamber Estimate of Current Armed Terrorists' Strength, No. 8/55, 16 May 1955 (DEF.Y.37/51).

   See also Map of Malaya (1956): Locations of Communist Terrorists by State (p. xvi), which shows the number of Communist terrorists remaining in each State two years after Templer's departure.

   The Emergency was estimated to be costing M$150 million p.a. which was one quarter of the National Income, and the building of hospitals, schools, and roads was being held up by lack of funds (See ISEAS Library, Tun Sir Henry

H.S. Lee Private Papers, HSL. 18.026, Secret. 14 March 1955 "The Chinese fight against Communism in Malaya").

24. CO 1030/174, No. 11, 26 January 1955. "Despatch No. 94/55 from Sir D. MacGillivray to Mr Lennox-Boyd on conduct of the Emergency."

25. See Lord Ogmore's comment in House of Lords debate (27 February 1952) on "The Situation in Malaya", *The Parliamentary Debates (Hansard)*, 5th Series, Vol. CLXXV, House of Lords Official Report, Second Volume of Series 1951–52 (19 February 1952–4 April 1952) (London: HMSO, 1952), p. 300.

26. National Archives of Australia, NAA: PR/891/53, Confidential, Ian Hamilton, Public Relations Officer, to Australian Mission in Kuala Lumpur, "Off-the-Record Interview with General Sir Gerald Templer", 9 October 1953. Cloake, too, said that Templer "could never stand politicians" (Cloake, op. cit., p. 455).

27. See A.J. Stockwell, ed., *Malaya, Part 1: The Malayan Union Experiment 1942–1948* (London: HMSO, 1995), p. lxxi.

28. See S. Smith, "General Templer and counterinsurgency in Malaya: Hearts and minds, intelligence and propaganda". *Intelligence and National Security* (London) 16, no. 3 (2001), pp. 60–78.

29. Karl Hack, "Iron Claws on Malaya: The Historiography of the Malayan Emergency", *Journal of Southeast Asian Studies* 30, no. 1 (March 1999), pp. 99–125.

30. Eric Jardine, "Why Time Works against a Counter-Insurgency", *Journal of Military and Strategic Studies* 11, no. 4 (Spring 2009): 24, and C.C. Chin and Karl Hack, *Dialogues with Chin Peng: New Light on the Malayan Communist Party* (Singapore: Singapore University Press, 2004), p. 295.

31. See Karl Hack, "Screwing Down the People. The Malayan Emergency: The Malayan Emergency. Decolonisation, and Ethnicity", in Hans Antlov and Stein Tonnesson, eds., *Imperial Policy and South East Asian Nationalism 1950–1957* (Richmond, Surrey: Curzon Press, 1995), pp. 803–109; Karl Hack, "British Intelligence and Counter-insurgency in the Era of Decolonisation: The Example of Malaya", *Intelligence and National Security* 14, no. 2 (Summer 1999), pp. 124–55; Karl Hack, "Corpses, Prisoners of War and Captured Documents: British and Communist Narratives of the Malayan Emergency, and the Dynamics of Intelligence Transformation", *Intelligence and National Security* 14, no. 4 (Winter 1999), pp. 211–41; Karl Hack, *Defence and Decolonisation in Southeast Asia: Britain, Malaya and Singapore, 1941–1968* (Richmond, Surrey: Curzon Press, 2001), pp. 113–31; Kumar Ramakrishna, "Transmogrifying Malaya: The Impact of Sir Gerald Templer (1952–1954)", *Journal of Southeast Asian Studies* 32, no. 1 (2001), pp. 79–92; Kumar Ramakrishna, *Emergency Propaganda: The Winning of Malayan Hearts and Minds, 1948–1958* (London: Routledge Curzon, 2002); Simon C. Smith, "General Templer and Counter-Insurgency in Malaya: Hearts

and Minds, Intelligence and Propaganda", *Intelligence and National Security* 16, no. 3 (Autumn 2001), pp. 60–78; Comber, *Malaya's Secret Police 1945–60,* op. cit., p. 287; Short, "Criticism of Templer", op. cit., pp. 379–87.

32. Michael Carver, "Templer, Sir Gerald Walter Robert (1898–1979)", *Oxford Dictionary of National Biography* (London: Oxford University Press, 2004). Field Marshal Lord Richard Michael Carver, GCB, CBE, DSO and Bar, MC, was General Officer Commanding, Far East Land Forces in 1966, and was made a Life Peer in 1977. He served subsequently as Chief of the Imperial General Staff.

33. "The Australian Official History of the Malayan Emergency", <se-asia commemoration.gov.au/> (accessed 19 December 2013).

34. Cheah Boon Kheng, "The Communist Insurgency in Malaysia, 1948–90, Contesting the Nation-State and Social Change", *New Zealand Journal of Asian Studies* 11, no. 1 (June 2009), pp. 132–52.

35. <http://www.oxforddnb.com/templates/article.jsp?articleid=31747&back> (accessed 12 December 2013).

APPENDIX A

DIRECTIVE TO GENERAL SIR GERALD WALTER ROBERT TEMPLER, KCB, KBE, CMG, DSO, ADC, HIGH COMMISSIONER IN AND FOR THE FEDERATION OF MALAYA, BY THE SECRETARY OF STATE FOR THE COLONIES ON BEHALF OF HIS MAJESTY'S GOVERNMENT IN THE U.K., 1 FEBRUARY 1952

The policy of His Majesty's Government in the United Kingdom is that Malaya should in due course become a fully self-governing nation. His Majesty's Government confidently hope that that nation will be within the British Commonwealth.

2. In assisting the peoples of Malaya to achieve that object, you will at all times be guided by the declaration of policy expressed in the preamble of the Federation of Malaya Agreement and by the statement of the special responsibilities of the High Commissioner contained in Section 19 of that Agreement.

3. To achieve a united Malayan nation there must be a common form of citizenship for all who regard the Federation or any part of it as their real home and the object of their loyalty.

4. It will be your duty to guide the peoples of Malaya towards the attainment of these objectives and to promote such political progress of the country as will, without prejudicing the campaign against the terrorists, further our democratic aims in Malaya.

5. The ideal of a united Malayan nation does not involve the sacrifice by any community of its traditional culture and customs, but before it can be fully realized the Malays must be encouraged and assisted to play a

full part in the economic life of the country, so that the present uneven economic balance may be redressed. It will be your duty to foster this process to the best of your ability.

6. His Majesty's Government believe that the British have a mission to fulfil in the achievement of these objects, and that, even after self-government has been attained, the British in Malaya will have a worthy and continuing part to play in the life of the country.

7. Communist terrorism is retarding the political advancement and economic development of the country and the welfare of its peoples. Your primary task in Malaya must, therefore, be the restoration of law and order, so that this barrier to progress may be removed. Without victory and the state of law and order which it alone can bring, there can be no freedom from fear, which is the first human liberty.

8. In furtherance of your task, not only will you fulfil the normal functions of High Commissioner, but you will assume complete operational command over all Armed Forces assigned to operations in the Federation and will be empowered to issue operational orders to their Commanders without reference to the Commanders-in-Chief, Far East. You should establish the closest cooperation between yourself and the Commanders-in-Chief, Far East, in matters of common concern.

9. You may assure the Malayan peoples of all communities that they can count on the powerful and continuing assistance of His Majesty's Government not only in the immediate task of defending the terrorists but in the longer term objective of forging a united Malayan nation. His Majesty's Government will not lay aside their responsibilities in Malaya until they are satisfied that Communist terrorism has been defeated and that the partnership of all communities, which alone can lead to true and stable self-government, has been firmly established.[1]

Note

1.   CO 1022/103, Directive to General Sir Gerald Templer, 1 February 1952.

APPENDIX B

GENERAL SIR GERALD TEMPLER: A SHORT BIOGRAPHICAL NOTE

General (later Field Marshal) Sir Gerald Templer, KG, GCB, CB, GCMG, KBE, DSO (1898–1979) had a traditional military education at Wellington College and the Royal Military College (RMC), Sandhurst (1915). He was commissioned as a Second Lieutenant in the Royal Irish Fusiliers on 16 August 1916 and after the war, he served with them in Persia and Mesopotamia until he returned to England in 1922. He attended the British Army's Staff College from January 1928 to December 1929. He then served as a company commander in Egypt and Palestine during the Arab rebellions 1935–36, and was awarded a DSO and Bar and a Mention in Despatches.

At the outbreak of World War II, he was a Major, acting Lieutenant Colonel, at the War Office, London, and in September 1939, he served as an intelligence officer at the headquarters of the British Expeditionary Force in France under Major General Sir F.N. Mason-Macfarlane. After he returned to England, he became Brigadier General Staff under General B.L. Montgomery, then commanding XII Corps, and was thereafter one of Montgomery's most fervent admirers.

In 1942, at the age of forty-four he became the youngest Lieutenant General in the British Army and he served briefly in North Africa and Italy. He reverted to the rank of Major General to command the 56th Infantry Division and then the 6th Armoured Division in Italy, where he was wounded in 1944 when a land mine blew up the army lorry in front of his staff car while travelling in convoy. The looted contents of the lorry fell on top of him and damaged his spine, and he was evacuated to England. He then worked in the War Office until he became Director of Civil Affairs in the British Zone of Germany under Montgomery, who was by then a Field Marshal commanding the British 21st Army Group. He regarded this period as valuable experience for Malaya although his time in Germany was marred by his having been involved in the summary dismissal at the end of World War II of Dr Konrad Adenauer, then Mayor of Cologne, for incompetence and inefficiency.

On his return to the United Kingdom after Germany, General Templer filled several senior posts at the War Office until he became Commander-in-Chief, Eastern Command, England, and in 1952 he was appointed High Commissioner and Director of Operations, Malaya (1952–54).

He became Chief of the Imperial General Staff (CIGS) (1955–58), a post which he had long been promised, and was appointed Field Marshal on 27 November 1956.

According to his official biographer, Field Marshal Lord Carver, who wrote the entry for Templer in the *Oxford Dictionary of National Biography* (2004), Templer's period as CIGS was an "unhappy one", including as it did "the fiasco of Suez and the reductions in the size of the army resulting from the decision of the British Government to work towards the end of conscription", an unpleasant disagreement he had with Admiral Lord Louis Mountbatten over the Suez fiasco, and his extreme distaste at the abandonment of British imperial responsibilities.[1]

Note

1.   See ABC-CLIO *Encyclopedia of WWII Political, Social and Military History*, 2010, and Michael Carver, "Templer, Sir Gerald Walter Robert (1898–1979)", *Oxford Dictionary of National Biography* (Oxford: Oxford University Press, 2004).

BIBLIOGRAPHY

COLONIAL OFFICE RECORDS, UNITED KINGDOM

AIR 20/7777, "Briggs Report 15 May 1950–30 September 1950".

CAB 21/1681, MAL C (50) 23, Appendix, "Federation Plan for the elimination of the Communist Organisation and Armed forces in Malaya (the Briggs Plan) report by COS for Cabinet Malaya Committee."

CAB 21/1681, MAL C (50) 23, Appendix, "The Briggs Plan", 24 May 1950.

CAB 21/1681, MAL C (1950) 1, dated 17 June 1950, "The Military Situation in Malaya: Memorandum by Mr. Strachey for Cabinet Malaya Committee".

CAB 21/1681, MAL C6 (50) 1, dated 19 June 1950, "The Civil Situation in Malaya: Cabinet Malayan Committee Minutes".

CAB 21/2925 General Sir Gerald Templer, "Report on colonial security" (April 1955).

CAB 128/17, CM37 (50) 1, dated 19 June 1950, "Malayan Cabinet Conclusions on Reports by Mr. Griffiths and Mr. Strachey following their Visits to Malaya."

CAB 129/40, CP (50) 125, dated 13 June 1950, "Preliminary Report on a visit to Malaya and Singapore: Cabinet Memorandum by Mr. Griffiths."

CAB 129/48 (C) 51 59, Malaya, Secret. "Lyttelton's Cabinet papers re. Mission to Malaya, Appendix IX, Intelligence Services & Related Counter-Measures."

CAB 129/48 C (51) 59, "Malaya: Cabinet memorandum by Mr Lyttelton, Appendices 1-XV, 21 December 1951."

CAB 129/59, Secret, "Sanders/Lee Exchange. Memorandum by the Minister of State, 11 March 1953; and Sanders/Lee Exchange. Memorandum by the Secretary of State for the Colonies", 13 March 1953; and Telegram dated 13 March 1953 from High Commissioner for the Federation of Malaya to Secretary of State for the Colonies.

CAB 129/76 CP (55) 81, "Federation of Malaya: Constitutional Developments. Cabinet Memorandum by Mr. Lennox-Boyd, 20 July 1955."

CAB 134/898, FE (0) (53) 6, "Political effects that a deterioration of the situation in Indo-China would have in British colonial and protected territories, 13 June 1953."

CAB 134/2544, "Report on Colonial Security 1955".

CO 229, T 220/282, ff. 211–212, "Aid to Malaya. Minute by AH Clough (Treasury) of a meeting between Mr Gaitskell and Mr Griffiths about UK financial assistance", 28 November 1950.

CO 229, T 220/1395, "Ministerial Committee to Review Organisation of Armed Forces, Police and Security Services in the Colonies (including investigation undertaken by General Sir Gerald Templer into Colonial security problems), 1954-55".

CO 537/657A, "Malayan Film Unit Proposed Reorganisation 1949–50".

CO 537/733, No. 10, "Dato Onn and the Independence of Malaya Party: letter from Sir H. Gurney to JD Higham", 13 June 1952.

CO 537/2141, no. 28 [Constitutional proposals] "report by Mr Thomas on his visit to Malaya 9–16 February 1947" dated 22 February 1947.

CO 537/3669, no. 3, "Closer Association with Federation of Malaya and Singapore. Colonial Office meeting with Mr MJ MacDonald on 16 April 1948".

CO 537/3741, no. 76, letter dated 5 December 1949, from Secretary of State for the Colonies to Sir Henry Gurney, High Commissioner, Federation of Malaya, deals with the points raised in Slim's report.

CO 537/4374, no. 3, "Notes on Tour of South-East Asia, October 1949. Report by Field Marshal Sir William Slim on the Importance of Civil Action in Counterinsurgency."

CO 537/4741, no. 78, 2 April 1949.

CO 537/4741, no. 78. "Letter from Sir Henry Gurney to JJ Paskin, Colonial Office", 2 December 1949.

CO 537/4741, no. 78, 28 December 1949.

CO 537/4751, no. 80, 11 April 1949, "Gurney to Creech Jones, enclosing joint paper by Lt Col Gray and Major General Boucher."

CO 825/74/3, "Monthly Political Reports from Federation of Malaya", minute dated 30 August 1949.

CO 825/74/5, Secret. "Political Developments. The Appointment of a Malay as Deputy High Commissioner. Letter dated 23 December 1948 from Creech Jones to Sir Henry Gurney, High Commissioner, Federation of Malaya".

CO 967/84, no. 70, "Brief for Mr. Rees Williams Tour of Hong Kong, Singapore and Malaya, Oct/Nov 1949".

CO 1022/3/146, File SEA 75/02.

CO 1022/3, "Representations Against Sentence of Death Passed on Lee Ten Tai (Lee Meng) in Federation of Malaya".

CO 1022/6, Top Secret, "Representations against Sentence of Death Passed on Lee Tien Tai (Lee Meng) in Federation of Malaya".

CO 1022/22 No. 1, "Reorganisation of government: memorandum by Mr Fraser to Mr Lyttelton, 16 January 1952."

CO 1022/35, "Home Guard", minute dated 19 February 1952 by PF Jerrom (Colonial Office).

CO 1022/35, "Home Guard. Organisation and Training", Extract from Lord Munster's Brief. House of Lords Debate, 27 February 1952.

CO 1022/35, "Extract from Malayan Federal Executive Council Minutes", 25 March 1952.

CO 1022/35, Federal Government Press Statement D.INF.3/52/264 (DEF), 30 March 1952, "Reorganisation of Home Guard".

CO 1022/35, Malayan Home Guard Reorganisation. ("Best Use of Force", *Glasgow Herald*, 31 March 1952).

CO 1022/35, Minutes of the Federal Executive Council, 25 November 1953.

CO 1022/36, "Chinese Organize Malaya Army Unit. Anti-Reds Forming New Force to Combat Communism in Tin-Rich Kinta Valley", *New York Times*, 30 July 1952.

CO 1022/36, "General Templer's Visit to Kinta Valley", Federal Government Press Statement, Kuala Lumpur, (D. INF. 8/52/ 99 (HG), 9 August 1952.

CO 1022/36, "The Kinta Valley Home Guard", Extract from *Chinese Affairs Review*, September 1952.

CO 1022/37. Secret. "Note on Discussions with Gen. Templer and Lt. Gen. Phao Sriyanond, Director-General of Police, Thailand, at King's House, Kuala Lumpur, on 10 April 1953."

CO 1022/37. "Situation on Malayan-Siamese Border, Memo from Lyttelton to Major Niall Macpherson, MP, 11 June 1953."

CO 1022/51, "Meeting with General Templer", Extract from JIC (52) 15 itrg Directors dated 31 January 1951.

CO 1022/51, See "Extract from Memorandum on Cabinet Paper C (51) 59, 21 December 1951" (Original on SEA/1/03).

CO 1022/51, Secret, "Meeting with General Templer re. Appt of Director of Intelligence, 29 January 1952."

CO 1022/51, Confidential, Templer to Secretary of State for the Colonies, "Director of Intelligence, 13 February 1952."

CO 1022/54, Jerrom to Higham, 21 May 1952.

CO 1022/56, no. 35, 10 December 1952, [Collective punishment]: Letter from Mr. Lyttelton to Mr. Grimmond in support of Templer's methods.

CO 1022/60, Secret. "Merging of Federal War Council and Executive Council of Malaya" (closed until 1983), 29 February 1952.

CO 1022/61, Secret, 29 January 1952. (Closed until 1984). "Closer Association between Federation of Malaya and Singapore."

CO 1022/61, 5 March 1952, Minute by JJ Paskin, Asst. Under-Secretary of State, Colonial Office.

CO 1022/61, Secret, 10 March 1952.

CO 1022/61, no. 15, Inward telegram no. 73. "Closer Association of British territories", from Mr MJ MacDonald to the CO. Minutes by JD Higham and Sir T. Lloyd, 10 June 1952.

CO 1022/61, no. 19, "Closer Association of British territories. Minute by JP Higham to JJ Paskins".

CO 1022/61, No. 40, "Closer association between Federation of Malaya and Singapore. Colonial Office note of meeting with Sir G. Templer and Sir J. Nicoll, 18 May 1953."

CO 1022/81, Dispatch No. 12 of 23/10, registered on 52849/100, "Political Background to the Situation in Malaya."

CO 1022/81. Top Secret. "Report on Recent Political Developments by the Officer Administering the Government, 23 October 1951."

CO 1022/85, no. 36, 18 November 1953, "Protection of Malayan Students from Undesirable Influences".

CO 1022/86. No. 3, "Political Talks with General Templer at Colonial Office. CO Minute of discussion with Templer on political advance, 3 December 1952."

CO 1022/86, "Closer association of British territories. Minute by JJ Paskin to Sir T. Lloyd on discussions with Sir G. Templer and Chiefs of Staff, 10 December 1952."

CO 1022/86 "Minute by JJ Paskin to Sir T. Lloyd re. Discussions with General Templer and the Chiefs of Staff, 10 December 1952."

CO 1022/86, No. 35, 18 May 1953.

CO 1022/87, Confidential, "Review of Field Operations of a Mobile Information Unit in South Thailand, Dispatch No. 49, 16 March 1953."

CO 1022/98, Paskin to Lloyd, 16 June 1953. After leaving Malaya in October 1956, Lieutenant General Sir Geoffrey Bourne became Commander, British Middle East Land Forces.

CO 1022/98, Lloyd to Lascelles, 18 December 1953.

CO 1022/100, "Budget Address", 21 November 1951.

CO 1022/100, Confidential, "General Templer's Address to the Legislative Council, 19 March 1952."

CO 1022/100, No. 5977, *Observer Foreign News Service*, London, "From Michael Davidson by cable from Kuala Lumpur, 19 March 1952."

CO 1022/100, "Gen. Templer's Programme for Malaya. Federation Regiment Planned"; and Denis Warner, *The Scotsman*, 20 March 1952.

CO 1022/100, "General Templer's Speech from the Chair, 19 November 1952."

CO 1022/103, Top Secret. Minute by Sir G. Templer to Mr. Churchill, 12 January 1952.

CO 1022/103, Directive to General Sir Gerald Walter Robert Templer, KCB, KBE, CMG, DSO, ADC, High Commissioner in and for the Federation of Malaya, by the Secretary of State for the Colonies on behalf of His Majesty's Government in the U.K., 1 February 1952.

CO 1022/103, Directive to General Sir Gerald Templer, 1 February 1952.

CO 1022/103. Directive to General Sir Gerald Templer, 12 February 1952.

CO 1022/148, The Organisation of Chinese Resistance to Communism in Malaya.

CO 1022/165, *The Scotsman*, 16 February 1952.

CO 1022/165, extracted from letter reference INF.No. 360/49/110, 3 March 1952, from JN McHugh, Director Information Services, Federation of Malaya, to the Colonial Office.

CO 1022/165, "Police Recruits in Malaya. Sir G. Templer's Call to Chinese, 31 March 1952".

CO 1022/165, *The Times* (London), "Police Recruits in Malaya, 1 April 1952."

CO 1022/165, extract from *The Straits Budget*, 17 April 1952.

CO 1022/187, Secret, "Paper by Combined General Staff Intelligence on CPM's Finance, 27 November 1953."

CO 1022/198. "Secret letter dated 2 September 1952 from Sir JF Nicoll to General Templer."

CO 1022/200, Secret. "Potential Effects that deterioration in the situation in Indo-China might have in British colonial and protected territories" (closed until 1984).

CO 1022/205 CIS (52) (2), Final. Top Secret, "The Situation on the Thai-Malayan Frontier as at 15 April 1953".

CO 1022/298, Confidential. Inward Telegram no. 348, "Gen. Sir G. Templer to Secretary of State, 12 March 1952," indicating the lines Templer proposed to take on elections in his forthcoming speech to the Legislative Council.

CO 1022/298, no. 30, 18 October 1952. "[Elections]: letter from DC MacGillivray to JD Higham on current plans. Minutes by AS Gann, TC Jerrom and JD Higham."

CO 1022/461, "Extract from press statement by General Templer in London, 14 June 1952."

CO 1022/485, no. 2, 9 May 1952, "Letter from OA Spencer to JD Higham suggesting a World Bank Mission to Malaya."

CO 1022/485, "World Bank Mission to Malaya: Revision of Development Plan for Federation of Malaya: Malayan Section of Colombo Plan for end 1944 – mid 1950, 9 May 1952."

CO 1022/492, "Federal Press Statement D.INF.7/52/20 (HC), 4 July 1952."

CO 1022/493, "General Templer's Speech at Press Conference at Colonial Office, 4 December 1952".

CO 1022/494, Secret (Closed until 1984), "Visit of General Templer to London May/June 1953". During his visit to London, General Templer attended the Coronation of Queen Elizabeth II in London as Aide-de-Camp General to the Queen.

CO 1030/16, "Committee of Ministers to Consider Security and Intelligence Services in Malaya during the Emergency and pre-Emergency Period".

CO 1030/163, no. 1, "Closer association of British territories: Despatch no. 3 from Mr MJ MacDonald to Mr Lennox-Boyd, 2 April 1955".

CO 1030/163, no. 2, "Closer association of British territories: Despatch (reply) no. 150 from Mr Lennox-Boyd to Mr MJ MacDonald, 2 June 1955".

CO 1030/174, No. 11, 26 January 1955. Secret. "Security in Malaya: Despatch No. 94/55 from Sir D. MacGillivray to Mr Lennox-Boyd on Conduct of the Emergency".

CO 1030/310, no, 72, "Templer to Secretary of State, 26 May 1954".

CO 1030/311, no. 130, "[Agreement with the Alliance on federal elections]: Inward telegram from Sir D. MacGillivray to Mr Lyttelton transmitting his exchange of letters with Tunku Abdul Rahman, 7 July 1954."

CO 1045/484, "Papers including Communist Influence in Chinese Schools in Malaya 1959".

DEF 7/421, Commissioner General to Colonial Secretary, J. Griffiths, 9 August 1950.

FO 371/1169, no. 14, "Inward telegram from Mr. MJ MacDonald to Sir T. Lloyd", 5 November 1951.

PREM 8/1406/23, "The Malayan Situation and the Far East, Minute by Mr. Strachey to Mr. Atlee urging the appointment of a regional Supremo".

PREM 11/113,"Personal and Confidential letter dated 12 March 1952, Templer to Secretary of State for the Colonies".

PREM 11/639, f.51, Inward telegram from Mr Lyttelton to Mr Churchill, 8 December 1951.

PREM 11/639, Telegram no. T6/52 from Mr Lyttelton to Mr Churchill, 4 January 1952.

WO 216/874, 174831, Secret. "Report by Lt. Gen. Bourne", Appendix "A" to DEF/DO/1, 17 July 1954.

OFFICIAL RECORDS, NATIONAL ARCHIVES OF AUSTRALIA

National Archives of Australia, NAA: A816, 19/321/18, Secret, "Annual Report for the British Territories in Southeast Asia for the year 1951", Australian Commissioner in Singapore to Department of External Affairs, Canberra.

National Archives of Australia, NAA: A816, 19/321/18, Confidential, "Government Changes in the Federation of Malaya and Singapore — Appointment of Templer", Actg. Australian Commissioner in Singapore to Department of External Affairs, Canberra, 4 February 1952.

National Archives of Australia, NAA: A816, 19/321/18, Secret, "The Communal Situation in Malaya", Australian Commissioner in Singapore to Minister for External Affairs, Canberra, 19 May 1952.

National Archives of Australia, NAA: A816, 19/321/18, Confidential, "Singapore. Plans to Improve the Position of the Tamil Community", Australian Commissioner Singapore to Department of External Affairs, Canberra, ACT, 3 June 1952.

National Archives of Australia, NAA: A816, Cablegram, "MCA Plans for the recruitment of Chinese into the Malayan Police", 5 July 1952.

National Archives of Australia, NAA: A816, 19/321/18, Secret, "Singapore: The Federation Regiment", 12 August 1952, Australian Commissioner, Singapore, to Minister for External Affairs, Canberra.

National Archives of Australia, NAA: A816, 19/321/18, Confidential, Memo no. 475, "Singapore. Joint Co-ordination Committee", 2 May 1953.

National Archives of Australia, NAA: A816,19/321/18, Secret, "The Communal Situation in Malaya", 19 May 1953, Australian Commissioner's Office, Singapore, to Minister for External Affairs, Canberra.

National Archives of Australia, NAA: A816, 19/321/18, Secret, "Movement towards Self-Government in Malaya", 19 May 1953, Australian Commissioner's Office, Singapore, to Minister for External Affairs, Canberra.

National Archives of Australia, NAA: A816, 19/321/18, Secret, "Movement towards Self-Government in Malaya", 23 September 1953, "LR McIntyre, Australian Commissioner in Singapore to Minister for External Affairs, Canberra".

National Archives of Australia, NAA: A816, 19/321/18, Malaya File 3, Top Secret, "Malaya: The Emergency", Australian Commissioner's Office, Singapore, to Department of External Affairs, Canberra, 4 December 1954.

National Archives of Australia, NAA: A816, Malaya – File 3, "High Commissioner's Budget Speech", 20 December 1954, from Australian Commissioner, Singapore, to Department of External Affairs, Canberra.

National Archives of Australia, NAA: A816/58, Confidential, Item: 19/321/18PR/891/53, "Off-the-record Interview with General Templer on 3 October 1953", Australian Commissioner, Singapore, to Department of External Affairs, Canberra.

National Archives of Australia, NAA: A816/58, 19/321/18, Confidential, PR/891/53, "Interview with General Sir Gerald Templer", Ian Hamilton, Public Relations officer, Australian Commission for Malaya to Secretary, Department of External Affairs, Canberra, 9 October 1953.

National Archives of Australia: NAA: PR/891/53, Confidential, Ian Hamilton, Public Relations Officer, to Australian Mission in Kuala Lumpur, "Off-the-Record Interview with General Sir Gerald Templer", 9 October 1953.

National Archives of Australia, NAA: A1058, D/L 47/5/8a, Top Secret, "Far East Intelligence Reports from Singapore 1948-50", Australian Commission in Singapore to Department of External Affairs, Canberra, 29 April 1949.

National Archives of Australia, NAA: A5799, 9/1957. Top Secret. Report of the

Australian, New Zealand, and Malaya Intelligence Meeting, Singapore, November 1956, attaching a copy of the JIC Report No. 6/1957 "Threat to Malaya from Communist dominated Thailand."

National Archives of Australia, NAA: A5954, 2198/6, *The Sydney Morning Herald,* 11 March 1955 and *The Argus,* 14 July 1955.

National Archives of Australia, NAA: A5954/1, 2292/5, Confidential, "Interview with Dato Sir Onn on 5 October 1953", Ian Hamilton, Public Relations Officer, Australian Commission in Singapore, to Department of External Affairs, Canberra, 15 October 1953.

National Archives of Australia, NAA, A7133, Top Secret. "Australian Secret Service Records on Singapore and Malaya (1953-1955). Malaya: The Emergency", 4 December 1954.

OFFICIAL RECORDS, NATIONAL ARCHIVES OF MALAYSIA

Federal Government Press Statement, D.INF. 3/52/264 (DEF), 31 March 1952, "Reorganisation of the Home Guard and Appointment of Major General EP de Fonblanque, CB, CBE, DSO as Inspector-General of 246,978 Home Guards."

Arkib Negara, Kuala Lumpur, SP/13/A/41, "Malayan Chinese Association. Scheme on Recruiting of Chinese into the Police Force for Submission to H.E. the High Commissioner; Malacca. Chinese Police Recruiting Campaign. Questions and Answers; and Recruitment of Chinese into the Police Force. Memorandum for the consideration of the Delegation to the Conference at King's House on Monday, 21 April 1952".

OFFICIAL RECORDS, NATIONAL ARCHIVES OF SINGAPORE

Malayan Security Service (MSS), Secret, *Political Intelligence Journal,* Serial No. 14/1947, 1 September 1947.

Malayan Security Service (MSS), Secret, *Political Intelligence Journal* 1/1948, Supplement no. 1, "The 1947 Muslim Pilgrimage Season and the Pan-Islamic Movement", 15 January 1948.

Malayan Security Service (MSS), Secret. *Political Intelligence Journal, Who's Who,* Serial No. 38, P.F. No. 1/430.

Malayan Security Service (MSS), Secret. *Political Intelligence Journal,* Singapore: No. 10/1948, 31 May 1958.

COUNCIL AND WHITE PAPERS

The Parliamentary Debates (Hansard), Fifth Series, Vol. CLXXV, House of Lords Official Report, "The Situation in Malaya", Second Volume of Series in 1951–52, 19 February – 4 April 1952, London: HMSO,1952.

Proceedings of the Legislative Council of the Federation of Malaya, 19 March 1952, Kuala Lumpur: Government Printer, 1953.

Minutes of the Legislative Council with Council Papers for the Period (Sixth Session), March 1953 to January 1954, Kuala Lumpur, Government Printer, 1954, pp. 1–18.

Minutes of the Legislative Council of the Federation of Malaya with Council Papers for the Period (Sixth Session) March 1953 to January 1954, Kuala Lumpur: Government Press, 1954, "Petition re. Criminal Procedure Code", pp. 1087–91.

Minutes of the Legislative Council of the Federation of Malaya with Council Papers for the Period (Sixth Session) March 1953 to January 1954, Kuala Lumpur: Government Press, 1954, "Petition re. Criminal Procedure Code", pp. 1163–71.

Minutes of the Legislative Council of the Federation of Malaya with Council Papers for the Period (Sixth Session) March 1953 to January 1954, Kuala Lumpur: Government Press, 1954, "Petition re. Criminal Procedure Code" p. 1238.

The Criminal Procedure Code (Amendment) Bill 1957, Federal Legislative Council, 5th Meeting of the 2nd Session, 14 November 1957 ("Trial by Jury").

GOVERNMENT PUBLICATIONS

Chinese Schools and the Education of Chinese Malayans: The Report of a Mission Invited by the Federation Government to Study the Problem of the Education of Chinese in Malaya, Kuala Lumpur: Government Press, 1951.

Education Ordinance, No. 63 of 1952, Kuala Lumpur: Government Printer, 1952.

Federation of Malaya Annual Report 1952, Kuala Lumpur, Government Printer, 1953.

Federation of Malaya Annual Report 1953, Kuala Lumpur: Government Printer, 1954.

Federation of Malaya Annual Report 1954, Kuala Lumpur: Government Printer, 1955.

Federation of Malaya Annual Report 1954, London: HMSO, 1955.

Federation of Malaya. Report of the Committee appointed to examine the question of Elections to the Federal Legislative Council, Kuala Lumpur: Government Printer, 1954.

Lee Kuan Yew, Prime Minister of Singapore, *The Battle for Merger*, Singapore: Government Printing Office, 1961.

Malaya: The Making of a Nation, London: Central Office of Information Reference Pamphlet No. 2, HMSO, 1957.

Report of The Federation of Malaya Constitutional Commission 1957 (Lord Reid, WJ KcKell, B Malik, Abdul Hamid, and Ivor Jennings), Kuala Lumpur: Government Printer, 1957.

"Report on the Special Committee appointed on the 20th September 1951 to

Recommend Legislation to cover all aspects of Educational Policy for the Federation of Malaya", Kuala Lumpur: Government Printer, 1952.
Report of the Police Mission to Malaya, Kuala Lumpur: Government Printer, 1950.
The Economic Development of Malaya. Report of a Mission organized by the International Bank for Reconstruction and Development at the request of the Government of the Federation of Malaya, the Crown Colony of Singapore and the United Kingdom, Singapore: Government Printer, 1955.

PRIVATE PAPERS

ISEAS Library, Singapore, Tan Sri Phair Gan Lim (P.G. Lim) Private Papers Archives Collection, Folios 5 & 14.

ISEAS Library, Singapore, Tan Cheng Lock Private Papers Collection, TCL 1.7a, Strictly Confidential, "Tan Cheng Lock to Oakley" (undated).

ISEAS Library, Singapore, Tan Cheng Lock Private Papers Collection, TCL 3.274, 21 April 1952, "Meeting of MCA Reps. at Federal Executive Council Meeting Room".

ISEAS Library, Singapore, Tan Cheng Lock Private Papers Collection, TCL 3.274, "Letter from General Templer to Sir Cheng Lock Tan, 24 April 1952".

ISEAS Library, Singapore, Tan Cheng Lock Private Papers Collection, TCL.5.3007, 12 September 1952.

ISEAS Library, Singapore. Tan Cheng Lock Private Papers Collection, TCL.6.1.1, "Report on Visit to Malaya 20 August – 20 September 1952 at invitation of MCA by Victor Purcell and Francis Carnell".

ISEAS Library, Singapore, Tan Cheng Lock Private Papers Collection, TCL.6.2, 21 August 1952, "Letter to Tan Cheng Lock from Tunku Abdul Rahman".

ISEAS Library, Singapore, Tan Cheng Lock Private Papers Collection, TCL.6.3, 25 August 1952. "Tan Cheng Lock to Tunku Abdul Rahman, President UMNO."

ISEAS Library, Singapore, Tun Sir Henry H.S. Lee Private Papers Collection, HSL.8.036, "Letter dated 12 June 1952 from Mrs. BH Oon to Colonel HS Lee."

ISEAS Library, Singapore: Tan Cheng Lock Private Archives, TCL.8.36.1, Letter dated 30 April 1954 from T.H. Tan to Tan Cheng Lock (Malacca).

ISEAS Library, Singapore, Tan Cheng Lock Private Papers Collection, TCL. 8.37.1, "Letter dated (?) May 1954 from Lady Templer to Tan Cheng Lock appealing for funds for the Federation School for the Deaf."

ISEAS Library, Singapore, Tan Cheng Lock Private Papers Collection, TCL. 9.33.1, "Letter 18 February 1952 from Colonel H.S. Lee re. MCA/UMNO co-operation in Kuala Lumpur Municipal Elections.

ISEAS Library, Singapore, Tan Cheng Lock Private Papers Collection, TCL. 9.35.1, "Letter 22 February 1952 from Colonel HS Lee to Tan Cheng Lock."

ISEAS Library, Singapore, Tan Cheng Lock Private Papers Collection, TCL. 10.1, "Purcell to Tan Cheng Lock, 7 October 1952."

ISEAS Library, Singapore, Tan Cheng Lock Private Papers Collection, TCL. 10.4, Secret, "Letter from Acting Secretary of Chinese Affairs (RH Oakley) to Tan Cheng Lock dated 5 January 1953."

ISEAS Library, Singapore, Tan Cheng Lock Private Papers Collection, TCL. 10.6.1 Strictly Secret, "Letter from HS Lee to Tan Cheng Lock, 9 January 1953."

ISEAS Library, Singapore, Tan Cheng Lock Private Papers Collection, TCL. 10.14.1, "From Purcell to Tan Cheng Lock, 8 February 1953.

ISEAS Library, Singapore, Tan Cheng Lock Private Papers Collection, TCL. 10.14, August 1954, "Memo on Education Ordinance 1953, Federation of Malaya", addressed to Madame Vijavalakshmi Pandit, President, UN General Assembly.

ISEAS Library, Singapore, Tan Cheng Lock Private Papers Collection, TCL. 10.15, "Letter dated 9 February 1953 from Oakley to Tan Cheng Lock."

ISEAS Library, Singapore, Tan Cheng Lock Private Papers Collection, TCL. 10.17, "Letter from Tan Cheng Lock to Oakley."

ISEAS Library, Singapore, Tan Cheng Lock Private Papers Collection, TCL.10.17.1, "Undated handwritten letter from Purcell to Tan Cheng Lock."

ISEAS Library, Singapore, Tan Cheng Lock Private Papers, TCL. 10.19/1, "Letter dated 11 February 1953 from Tan Cheng Lock to Templer."

ISEAS Library, Singapore, Tan Cheng Lock Private Papers Collection, TCL. 10.23a, "Letter from Purcell to Tan Cheng Lock dated 19 February 1953."

ISEAS Library, Singapore, Tan Cheng Lock Private Papers, TCL. 10.23, "Templer's reply to Tan Cheng Lock, 25 February 1953."

ISEAS Library, Singapore, Tan Cheng Lock Private Papers Collection, TCL. 10.24.1, "Letter from Tan Cheng Lock to Purcell dated 3 March 1953."

ISEAS Library, Singapore, Tan Cheng Lock Private Papers Collection, TCL. 058, Speech by Tan Cheng Lock at the Conference of Chinese School Committees and Teachers, Chinese Assembly Hall, Birch Road, Kuala Lumpur, on 20 April 1953.

ISEAS Library, Singapore, Tan Cheng Lock Private Papers Collection, TCL. 14.460/1-5, "Confidential letter dated 15 May 1953 from Tan Cheng Lock to General Templer".

ISEAS Library, Singapore, Tan Cheng Lock Private Papers Collection, TCL. 065, MCA President's Speech, 6th General Meeting, 27th December 1953.

ISEAS Library, Singapore, Tan Cheng Lock Private Papers Collection, TCL. 70, 21 August 1954, Speech on "The Future of Chinese Education" by Dato Sir Cheng Lock Tan at MCA Chinese Education Central Committee Meeting.

ISEAS Library, Singapore, Tan Cheng Lock Private Papers Collection, TCL. 190.13, "Secret letter dated 29 December 1952 from Tan Cheng Lock to Director-General of Information Services, Kuala Lumpur."

ISEAS Library, Singapore, Tun Sir Henry H.S. Lee Private Papers Collection, HSL.NC.1.017 "National Convention of UMNO/MCA Alliance for early independence and Federal Elections 1954", 24 August 1953.

ISEAS Library, Singapore, Tun Sir Henry H.S. Lee Private Papers Collection, HSL. 2.039, 29 November 1951, extract of letter to the Hon'ble JT Chappel.

ISEAS Library, Singapore, Tun Sir Henry H.S. Lee Private Papers Collection, HSL. 2.045, Secret, "Memo on the Chinese Community in Malaya in July 1952."

ISEAS Library, Singapore, Tun Sir Henry H.S. Lee, Private Papers Collection, HSL. 4.009, "MCA Supports General Templer's Call for Chinese Youths to join Police, 2 April 1952."

ISEAS Library, Singapore, Tun Sir Henry H.S. Lee Private Papers Collection, HSL. 4.022/10, quoting The Malay Mail, 26 August 1952.

ISEAS Library, Singapore, Tun Sir Henry H.S. Lee Private Papers Collection, HSL. 4.022/10, quoting The Singapore Standard, 26 August 1952.

ISEAS Library, Singapore, Tun Sir Henry H.S. Lee Private Papers Collection, HSL. 4.024/1, quoting The Malay Mail, 25 October 1952.

ISEAS Library, Singapore, Tun Sir Henry H.S. Lee Private Papers Collection, HSL. 7.058, "Fortnightly Press Digest, Department of Information Services, Federation of Malaya, No. 4/52 for period 16 February – 29 February 1952, English Language Press".

ISEAS Library, Singapore, Tun Sir Henry H.S. Lee, Private Papers Collection, HSL. 11.099/1, "Secret & Personal letter, 8 March 1954, from the Malayan Colonial Secretary to Colonel HS Lee."

ISEAS Library, Singapore, Tun Sir Henry H.S. Lee, Private Papers Collection. HSL. 15.24, Secret. "MCA HQ Kuala Lumpur, 5th Cabinet Meeting, 3 October 1952."

ISEAS Library, Singapore, Tun Sir Henry H.S. Lee, Private Papers Collection, HSL. 15.24. "Minutes MCA HQ 5th Cabinet Meeting. 5 October 1952".

ISEAS Library, Singapore, Tun Sir Henry H.S. Lee, Private Papers Collection, HSL. 18.007 (undated), "Mining Representative, Selangor State War Executive Committee".

ISEAS Library, Singapore, Tun Sir Henry H.S. Lee, Private Papers Collection, HSL 18.007, "Selangor War Executive Committee".

ISEAS Library, Singapore, Tun Sir Henry H.S. Lee Private Papers, HSL. 18.010, Secret. "Director of Operations Committee Meeting in Executive Council Chamber Estimate of Current Armed Terrorists Strength", No. 8/55, 16 May 1955 (DEF.Y.37/51).

ISEAS Library, Singapore, Tun Sir Henry H.S. Lee Private Papers, HSL. 18.026, Secret. 14 March 1955 "The Chinese fight against Communism in Malaya".

ISEAS Library, Singapore, Tun Sir Henry H.S. Lee Private Papers Collection, HSL. 20.040c, Secret, "Home Guard in 1954".

ISEAS Library, Singapore, Tun Sir Henry H.S. Lee, Private Papers Collection. HSL. 20.042, Confidential. "Letter dated 29 October 1954 from JGH Brett, Force Commander, Kinta Valley Home Guard, Perak, to Colonel HS Lee, enclosing a copy of the Malayan Government draft budget for 1955, together with his report on the KVHG which he had prepared for a meeting of the Perak State War Advisory Council."

ISEAS Library, Singapore, Tun Sir Henry H.S. Lee, Private Papers Collection, HSL. 20.042, Confidential, "Report on Kinta Valley Home Guard, J.G.H. Brett, Force Commander, KVHG, to Colonel HS Lee, CBE, JP, 29 October 1954."

ISEAS Library, Singapore, Tun Sir Henry H.S. Lee, Private Papers Collection, HSL 20.042a, Confidential, "Report on Kinta Valley Home Guard" by JCH Brett, Force Commander, KVHG, to Colonel H.S. Lee, CBE, JP.

ISEAS Library, Singapore, Tun Sir Henry H.S. Lee, Private Papers Collection, HSL. 20.046C, Secret, "Director of Operations Combined Emergency Planning Staff Paper 49, The Home Guard in 1954."

ISEAS Library, Singapore, Tun Sir Henry H.S. Lee, Private Papers Collection HSL. 20.046C, Secret, "Home Guard in 1954", Director of Operations Combined Emergency Planning Staff Paper No. 49, 6 October 1954.

ISEAS Library, Singapore, Tun Sir Henry H.S. Lee, Private Papers Collection, HSL. 20.046C/1, Secret. "The Home Guard in 1955, Director of Operations Combined Emergency Planning Staff Paper 49, Appendix A to Director of Operations Committee Meeting 38/54".

ISEAS Library, Singapore, Tun Sir Henry H.S. Lee, Private Papers Collection, HSL. 21.041, "Colonel HS Lee, Member Federation of Malaya War Council, 1952".

ISEAS Library, Singapore, Tun Sir Henry H.S. Lee Private Papers Collection, HSL. 24.018a, "MCA Plan to recruit 2.000 Police Recruits".

ISEAS Library, Singapore, Tun Sir Henry H.S. Lee Private Papers Collection, HSL.029/1, "Statement on Communal Relations in Malaya, 8 November 1952".

ISEAS Library, Singapore, Tun Sir Henry H.S. Lee Private Papers Collection, HSL. 031.023, "Singapore Standard, 5 February 1952.

ISEAS Library, Singapore, Tun Sir Henry H.S. Lee Private Papers Collection, HSL. 031.057, 3 March 1952.

ISEAS Library, Singapore, Tun Sir Henry H.S. Lee, Private Papers Collection, HSL. 031.057, "Templer scraps Federal War Council", *Malay Mail*, 3 March 1952.

ISEAS Library, Singapore, Tun Sir Henry H.S. Lee, Private Papers Collection, HSL. 031.069, "US Backs Policy in Malaya, 7 March 1952".

ISEAS Library, Singapore, Tun Sir Henry H.S. Lee, Private Papers Collection, HSL. 031.085, "The Templer Plan", *Malay Mail*, 21 March 1952.

National Army Museum, Chelsea, ACC: 8011-132-2, "Documents relating to General Templer's Period as High Commissioner, Malaya, 1952-4", General Templer's letter dated 5 January 1977 to Major General JM Gow, Ministry of Defence.

National Army Museum, Chelsea, ACC: 8011-132-3, Major General Lloyd Owen's letter dated 30 June 1976 to Major General JM Gow, Director, Army Training, Ministry of Defence.

National Army Museum, Chelsea, ACC: 8301-6, "Correspondence of Major DL Lloyd Owen as Military Assistant to High Commissioner, Malaya, March 1952-September 1953, Secret and Personal letter to Lieutenant General Nevil Brownjohn, KBE, CB, CMG, CBE, dated 9 June 1952."

BOOKS AND ARTICLES

ABC-CLIO *Encyclopedia of WWII Political, Social and Military History*, USA: California, 2010.

Abdul Muthalib. "The End of Empire: The Films of the MFU in 1950's British Malaya". In *End of Empire: Cultural Histories of Cinema*, edited by Lee Grieveson and Colin McCabe. London: British Film Institute, 2011, pp. 69–89.

Aldridge, Richard J. *Espionage, Security and Intelligence in Britain 1945–1970*, Manchester: Manchester University Press, 1998.

Ambrose, Stephen E. *Band of Brothers*, London: Simon & Schuster U.K. Ltd., 2001.

Andaya, Barbara Watson and Leonard Y. Andaya. *A History of Malaysia*. London: Macmillan Press, 1982.

Annan, Noel. *Changing Enemies: The Defeat and Regeneration of Germany*. Ithaca: Cornell University Press, 1997.

Barber, Noel. *The War of the Running Dogs: The Malayan Emergency 1948–1960*. London: Fontana Books, 1973 (3rd impression).

Bartlett, Vernon. *Report from Malaya*. London: Derek Verschoyle, 1954.

Benest, David. *British Leadership and Irregular Warfare*. London: British Army Review, Defence Academy of the United Kingdom, 2007.

Blythe, W. *The Impact of Chinese Secret Societies in Malaya*. Kuala Lumpur: Oxford University Press, 1969.

Boyce, Peter. "Australian Diplomacy in Malaya". *Journal of Southeast Asian Studies* 4, no. 2 (September 1963), pp. 65–100.

Bruce CE. *Waziristan 1936–1937*. New Delhi: Gyan Publishers, 1996 (reprint).

Campbell, Arthur. *Jungle Green*. Boston: Little Brown & Co., 1953.

Carruthers, Susan L. *Winning Hearts and Minds. British Government, the Media and Colonial Counter-Insurgency, 1944–1960*. Leicester University Press, 1998.

Carver, Michael. "Templer, Sir Gerald Walter Robert (1898-1979)". *Oxford Dictionary of National Biography*. Oxford: Oxford University Press, 2004.

Cheah Boon Kheng. *Malaysia: The Making of a Nation*. Singapore: Institute of Southeast Asian Studies, 2002.

———. "The Communist Insurgency in Malaysia, 1948–90, Contesting the Nation-

State and Social Change". *New Zealand Journal of Asian Studies* 11, no. 1 (June 2009), pp. 132–52.

Chin, C.C. and Karl Hack. *Dialogues with Chin Peng: New Light on the Malayan Communist Party*. Singapore: Singapore University Press, 2004.

Chin Peng. *Alias Chin Peng: My Side of History* (as told to Ian Ward & Norma Miraflor). Singapore: Media Publishers, 2003.

Cloake, John. *Templer, Tiger of Malaya: The Life of Field Marshal Sir Gerald Templer*. London: Harrap, 1985.

Clutterbuck, Richard. *The Long Long War: The Emergency in Malaya 1948–1960*. London: Cassell, 1967.

Coates, John. *Suppressing Insurgency: An Analysis of the Malayan Emergency, 1948–1954*. Boulder, CO: Westview Press, 1992.

Comber, Leon. *13 May 1969: A Historical Survey of Sino-Malay Relations*. Singapore: Heinemann Asia, 1983.

———. "The Weather has been Horrible: Malayan Communist Communications during the Emergency (1948–1960)". *Asian Studies Review* 19, no. 2 (1995), pp. 37–57.

———. "Review of *Alias Chin Peng: My Side of History*". *Intelligence and National Security* 19, Pt 1 (2004), pp. 125-9.

———. *Malaya's Secret Police 1945-60: The Role of the Special Branch in the Malayan Emergency*. Singapore: Institute of Southeast Asian Studies / Monash University Press, 2008 (reprint 2009).

———. *The Triads: Chinese Secret Societies in 1950's Malaya and Singapore*. Singapore: Talisman Publishing and Singapore Heritage Society, 2009.

———. *Singapore Correspondent. Political Dispatches from Singapore (1958–1962)*. Singapore: Marshall Cavendish International (Asia), 2012.

———. "The Malayan Emergency: General Templer and the Kinta Valley Home Guard 1952-1954". *Journal of the Malaysian Branch of the Royal Asiatic Society* 85, Pt. 1, no. 302 (June 2012), pp. 45-62.

Curriculum Development Institute of Singapore, *Social and Economic History of Modern Singapore*. Singapore: Curriculum Development Institute of Singapore / Longman Singapore Publishers, 1985.

Dixon, Paul. "Hearts and Minds? British Counterinsurgency from Malaya to Iraq". *Journal of Strategic Studies* 32, no. 3 (June 2009), pp. 353–81.

Durdin, Frank Tillman. "Chinese Organise Malayan Army Unit in Tin-Rich Kinta Valley". *New York Times*, 28 July 1952.

Emerson, Rupert. *Malaysia: A Study in Direct and Indirect Rule*. Kuala Lumpur: University of Malaya Press, 1966 (reprint).

"Federation of Malaya Information Services. An Authoritative Survey". *Journal of Association of British Malaya*, February 1953.

Fernando, Joseph M. *The Alliance Road to Independence*. Kuala Lumpur: University of Malaya Press, 2009.

———. "Elite Intercommunal Bargaining and Conflict Resolution: the Role of the CLC in Malaya 1949-1951". *Journal of Southeast Asian Studies* 43, no. 2 (2 June 2012), pp. 280-301.

Fifield, Russell F. *The Diplomacy of Southeast Asia*. Hamden, Conneticut: Archon Books, 1958.

Galula, David (Lieutenant-Colonel). *Counterinsurgency Warfare: Theory and Practice*. Westport, CT: Praeger, 1994 (reprint 2006).

Ginsburg, Norton and Chester F. Roberts, Jr. *Malaya*. Seattle: University of Washington Press, 1958.

Grieveson, Lee and Colin McCabe, eds. *End of Empire: Cultural Histories of Cinema*. London: British Film Institute, 2011.

Grover, Verinder, ed. *Malaysia: Government and Politics*. New Delhi: Deep & Deep Publications, 2000.

Hack, Karl. "Screwing Down the People: The Malayan Emergency: the Malayan Emergency. Decolonisation, and Ethnicity". In *Imperial Policy and South East Asian Nationalism 1950–1957*, edited by Hans Antlov and Stein Tonnesson. Richmond, Surrey: Curzon Press, 1995, pp. 803–909.

———. "Iron Claws on Malaya: The Historiography of the Malayan Emergency". *Journal of Southeast Asian Studies* 30, no. 1 (March 1999), pp. 99-125.

———. "British Intelligence and Counter-insurgency in the Era of Decolonisation: The Example of Malaya". *Intelligence and National Security* 14, no. 2 (Summer 1999), pp. 124–55.

———. "Corpses, Prisoners of War and Captured Documents: British and Communist Narratives of the Malayan Emergency, and the Dynamics of Intelligence Transformation". *Intelligence and National Security* 14, no. 4 (Winter 1999), pp. 211–41.

———. *Defence and Decolonisation in Southeast Asia: Britain, Malaya and Singapore 1941–68*. Richmond, Surrey: Curzon Press, 2001.

Han Suyin. *And the Rain My Drink*. Singapore: Monsoon Books, 1956 (reprint 2013).

Harper, T.N. *The End of Empire and the Making of Malaya*. Cambridge: Cambridge University Press, 1999.

Hembry, Boris. *Malayan Spymaster, Memoirs of a Rubber Planter, Bandit Fighter and Spy*. Singapore: Monsoon Books, 2011.

Heng Pek Khoon. *Chinese Politics in Malaysia: A History of the Malaysian Chinese Association*. Singapore: Oxford University Press, 1988.

Heren, Louis. *Growing Up on the Times*. London: Hamish Hamilton, 1978.

Heussler, Robert. *British Rule in Malaya 1942-1957*. Kuala Lumpur: Heinemann Educational Books (Asia), 1983.

Hickey, Pennell J. *Counterinsurgency Operations in Malaya, 1948–1960: The Role of Regular Forces*. Pennsylvania: U.S. War College, 1971.

Hickling, R.H. *An Introduction to the Federal Constitution*. Kuala Lumpur: Federation of Malaya Information Services, 1960.

Hill, R.D. *Rice in Malaya: A Study in Historical Geography*. Kuala Lumpur: Oxford University Press, 1977.

International Bank for Reconstruction and Development. *The Economic Development of Malaya*. Washington, D.C.: International Bank for Reconstruction and Development, September 1955.

Irving, Ronald. *Adenauer*. London: Longman, 2002.

Ishak bin Tadin. "Dato Onn and Malay Nationalism, 1946–1951: The Birth of the UMNO". *Journal of Southeast Asian History* 1 (1960), pp. 62–99.

Jardine, Eric. "Why Time Works against a Counter-Insurgency". *Journal of Military and Strategic Studies* 11, no. 4 (Spring 2009), pp. 1–34.

Jeffery, Keith. *Mi6: The History of the Secret Intelligence Service, 1909–1949*. U.K.: Bloomsbury, 2011.

Jones, R.V. *Reflections on Intelligence*. London: Mandarin Publishers, 1990.

Kelly, Saul and Anthony Gorst, eds. *Whitehall and the Suez Crisis*. London: Frank Cass, 2000.

Khoo, Salma Nasution and Abdul-Razzaq Lubis. *Kinta Valley: Pioneering Malaya's Modern Development*. Ipoh: Perak Academy, 2005.

Komer, R.W. *The Malayan Emergency in Retrospect: Organisation of a Successful Counterinsurgency Effort*. Santa Monica: Rand Corporation, 1972.

Krekel, Michael W. *Konrad Adenauer: Profiles of the Man and the Politician*. Federal Republic of Germany: Stiftung Bundereskanzler-denhaus-Haus (Konrad Adenauer Memorial Foundation), 1999.

Kwok Kian-Woon, Kwa Chong Guan, Lily Kong and Brenda Yeoh, eds. *Our Place in Time*. Singapore: Singapore Heritage Society, 1999.

Lee Su Yin. *Rock Solid: The Corporate Career of Tan Chin Tuan*. Singapore: Landmark Books, 2006.

——. *British Policy and the Chinese in Singapore, 1939 to 1955: The Public Service Career of Tan Chin Tuan*. Singapore: Talisman Publishing, 2011.

Lee Ting Hui. *Chinese Schools in Peninsular Malaysia: The Struggle for Survival*. Singapore: Institute of Southeast Asian Studies, 2011.

Lim, Phair Gan. *Kaleidoscope: The Memoirs of P.G. Lim*. Petaling Jaya: Strategic Information & Research Development Centre, 2012.

Lyttelton, Oliver (Viscount Chandos). *The Memoirs of Lord Chandos*. London: The Bodley Head, 1962.

McIntosh, Amy. *Journey into Malaya*. London: China Inland Mission, 1956.

Miller, Harry. *Jungle War in Malaya: The Campaign against Communism 1948–1960*. London: Arthur Barker, 1972.

Milne, R.S. and Diane K. Mauzy. *Politics and Government in Malaysia*. Singapore: Federal Publications, 1977.

Mohamed Amin and Malcolm Caldwell, eds. *Malaya: The Making of a Neo-Colony*. London: Spokesman Books, 1965.

Mohamed Noordin Sopiee. *From Malayan Union to Singapore Separation: Political Unification in the Malaysia Region, 1945–65*. Kuala Lumpur: Universiti Malaya, 1974.

Morais, Victor, J. *P.P. Narayanan: The Asian Trade Union Leader*. Petaling Jaya: National Union of Plantation Workers Sports Club, 1975.

Netaji Centre. *Netaji Subhas Chandra Bose, A Malayan Perspective*. Kuala Lumpur: Netaji Centre, 1992.

Ng, Irene. *The Singapore Lion: A Biography of S. Rajaratnam*. Singapore: Institute of Southeast Asian Studies, 2010.

Nicolson, Nigel. *The Life of Field Marshal Alexander of Tunis*. London: Weidenfeld and Nicolson, 1973.

O'Ballance, Edgar, *Malaya: The Communist War, 1948–1960*. London: Faber & Faber, 1996.

Ooi Kee Beng. *The Reluctant Politician: Tun Dr Ismail and His Time*. Singapore: Institute of Southeast Asian Studies, 2007 (2nd reprint).

Osipov, V. "Templer Loses His Temper". *Soviet Press Translations* 8, no. 3 (1953).

Parkinson, C. Northcote. *Templer in Malaya*. Singapore: Donald Moore, 1954.

Purcell, Victor. *Malaya: Communist or Free*? Published under the auspices of the Institute of Public Relations. Stanford: Stanford University Press, 1955.

———. *The Chinese in South East Asia*. London: Oxford University Press, 1965.

———. *The Chinese in Malaya*. Kuala Lumpur: Oxford University Press, 1967 and 1978.

Ramakrishna, Kumar. "'Transmogrifying' Malaya: The Impact of Sir Gerald Templer (1952–1954)". *Journal of Southeast Asian Studies* 32, no. 1 (2001), pp. 79–92.

———. *Emergency Propaganda: The Winning of Malayan Hearts and Minds, 1948–1958*, London: Routledge Curzon, 2002.

Roff, Margaret. "The Malayan Chinese Association, 1949–65". *Journal of Southeast Asian History* 6, no. 2 (September 1965).

Roff, W.R. *The Origins of Malay Nationalism*. Kuala Lumpur: University of Malaya Press, 1967.

Rooney, David. *Mad Mike: A Life of Brigadier Michael Calvert*. London: Pen and Swords Books, 1997.

Rudner, Martin. "The Structure of Government in the Colonial Federation of Malaya". *South East Asian Studies* 13, no. 4 (March 1976), pp. 495–512.

Sandhu, Kernial Singh. "The Saga of the New Villages". *Journal of Southeast Asian History* 5, no. 1 (March 1964), pp. 143–77.

Sanger, Clyde. *Malcolm MacDonald: Bringing an End to Empire*. Montreal: McGill-Queen's University Press, 1995.

Schwarz, Hans-Peter. *Konrad Adenauer: From the German Empire to the Federal Republic, 1876–1952*. Oxford: Berghahn Books (English language ed.), 1995.

Scurr, John. *The Malayan Campaign 1948–60*. Oxford: Osprey Publishing, 1982.

Sengupta, Nilanjana. *A Gentleman's Word: The Legacy of Subhas Chandra Bose in Southeast Asia*. Singapore: Institute of Southeast Asian Studies, 2012.

Shahrom Md. Ariffin. "Malay Reservation Land — Unleashing a Century of Trust". *International Surveying Research Journal* 3, no. 2 (2013), pp. 1–28.

Shennan, Margaret. *Our Man in Malaya: John Davis (CBE, DSO), SOE Force 136 and Postwar Counter-Insurgency*. Singapore: Monsoon Books, 2014.

Sheppard, Mubin. *Tunku, His Life and Times: The Authorized Biography of Tunku Abdul Rahman Putra al-Haj*. Petaling Jaya: Pelanduk Publications, 1995.

Short, Anthony. *The Communist Insurrection in Malaya 1948–60*. London: Frederick Muller, 1975 (reprinted in 2000 by Cultural Lotus Press, Singapore, under the title *In Pursuit of Mountain Rats*).

Smith, Adrian. "Resignation of a First Sea Lord: Mountbatten and the Suez Crisis". *History* 98, issue 329 (January 2013), pp. 105–34.

Smith, Simon C. "General Templer and Counter-Insurgency in Malaya: Hearts and Minds, Intelligence and Propaganda". *Intelligence and National Security* 16, no. 3 (Autumn 2001), pp. 60–78.

Stenson, Michael. *Class, Race, and Colonialism in West Malaysia: The Indian Case*. Brisbane: University of Queensland Press, 1980.

Stockwell, A.J. "Insurgency and Decolonization during the Malayan Emergency". *Journal of Commonwealth and Comparative Politics* 25, no. 1 (1987), pp. 71–81.

———, ed. *Malaya, Part 1: The Malayan Union Experiment 1942–1948*. London: HMSO, 1995.

———, ed. *Malaya, Part II: The Communist Insurrection 1948–1953*. London: HMSO, 1995.

———, ed. *Malaya, Part III: The Alliance Path to Independence, 1953–1957*. London: HMSO, 1995.

———, ed. *British Documents on the End of Empire*, Series B, Vol. 4, *Malaya. The Communist Insurrection 1948–1953*, "Principal Members of Office 1948–1953", Pt. II. London: HMSO, 1995.

Stubbs, Richard. "Counter-insurgency: The Impact of the Korean War Prices Boom on the Malayan Emergency". Occasional Paper No. 19. Singapore: Institute of Southeast Asian Studies, February 1974.

———. "UMNO, MCA and Early Years of the Malayan Emergency, 1948–55". Paper presented at the Annual Conference of Canadian Society for Asian Studies, Laval University, Quebec, 28/29 May 1976.

———. "The UMNO, the MCA, and the early years of the Malayan Emergency, 1948–1955", *Journal of Southeast Asian Studies* 10, no. 1 (March 1979), pp. 37–88.

———. *Hearts and Minds in Guerilla Warfare: The Malayan Emergency 1948–60*, Singapore: Oxford University Press, 1989.

Tan Cheng Lock. *Malayan Problems: From a Chinese Point of View*. Singapore: Tannsco, 1947.

Tan Kim Lwi, Agnes. *A Son of Malacca: Tun Dato' Sir Cheng Lock Tan, SMN, DPMJ (Johore), CBE, KBE, JP*. 2nd ed. Singapore: Lithographic Print House, 2006.

Tan Liok Ee. *The Politics of Chinese Education*. Oxford: Oxford University Press, 1997.

Tun Sir Henry HS Lee. Muzium Negara, Kuala Lumpur, 19 November 1988.

Tunku Abdul Rahman Putra al-Haj. *Looking Back: Monday Musings and Memories*. Kuala Lumpur: Pustaka Antara, 1977.

————. *Viewpoints*. Kuala Lumpur: Heinemann Asia, 1978.

————. *As a Matter of Interest*. Kuala Lumpur: Heinemann Asia, 1981.

————. *Contemporary Issues in Malayan Politics*. Kuala Lumpur: Pelandok Publications, 1984.

von Oppen, Beate Ruhm, translator. *Konrad Adenauer, Memoirs 1945–53*. London: Weidenfeld & Nicolson, 1965.

von Vorys, Karl. *Democracy without Consensus: Communalism and Political Stability in Malaysia*. Princeton, New Jersey: Princeton University Press, 1975.

Walton, Calder. *Empire of Secrets: British Intelligence, the Cold War and the Twilight of Empire*. New York: The Overlook Press, 2013.

White, Nicholas J. *Business, Government, and the End of Empire: Malaya 1942–1957*. Kuala Lumpur: Oxford University Press, 1996.

————. *Business, Government and the End of Empire: 1952–7*, London: Oxford University Press, 1996.

Williams, Charles. *Adenauer: The Father of the New Germany*. London: Little, Brown & Co. Ltd., 2000.

Winstedt, Richard. "Obituary: Victor Purcell". *Journal of the Royal Asiatic Society* (London) 97, Issue no. 1 (January 1965), p. 39.

Wong Hoi Kee, Francis and Ee Tiang Hong. *Education in Malaya*. Hong Kong: Heinemann Educational Books (Asia), 1971.

Yap Yook Foo. "The Assessors. Precursors to the Jury System". *Berita Malaysia*, 11 March 2003.

Yuen Yuet Leng. *Operation Ginger*. Kuala Lumpur: Vinpress Press, 1988.

Zainah Anwar. *Three Who Built Malaysia, Legacy of Honour*: Kuala Lumpur: Yayasan Mohamad Noah, 2011.

Zhèng Zhào Xián. *Ma Gung qi nü zi. Chen Tian fu ren. Li Ming kou su li shi* [A Woman of the Communist Party of Malaya. Mdm. Chen Tian. An Oral history of Lee Meng]. Petaling Jaya: Strategic Information & Research Development Zhèng Zhào Xián Centre, 2007.

THESES AND ACADEMIC EXERCISES

Hawkins, Lewis James. "British Administration of Malaya during the Emergency, 1948–1957". MA History thesis, University of Delaware, June 1970.

Threlfall, Adrian. "The Malayan Emergency. A Historiographic Analysis". BA honours thesis, School of Social Science, Victoria University, 2003.

NEWSPAPERS AND PERIODICALS

Age, The (Melbourne), 31 May 1954.
Berita Harian, 11 March 2003.
Daily Telegraph, The (London), 16 January 1952.
————, 20 March 1952.
*Economist, The,*10 October 1953.
Independent, The, 28 January 1995.
Malay Mail, 21 March 1952.
Manchester Guardian, 5 December 1952.
Nanyang Siang Pau (Singapore), 1 December 1952.
Nation, The, 17 January 1953.
New Statesmen, The, 17 January 1953.
New York Times, 28 July 1952.
Observer, The (London), 22 June 1952.
Scotsman, The, 20 March 1952.
————, 19 August 1952.
Singapore Standard, 12 December 1951.
————, 30 January 1952.
————, 21 March 1952.
Spectator, The 5 February 1953.
Star ePaper, The (Malaysia), 21 February 2014.
Straits Times, 17 January 1952.
————, 30 January 1952.
————, 31 January 1952.
————, 29 February 1952.
————, 3 March 1952.
————, 27 March 1952.
————, 17 April 1952.
————, 30 August 1952.
————, 19 February 1953.
————, 20 February 1953.
————, 5 March 1956.
————, 3 January 2009.
————, 27 April 2012.
Times, The (London), 14 December 1950.
————, 14 January 1952.
————, 15 January 1952.
————, 10 March 1952.
————, 19 July 1952.
————, 3 September 1952.
————, 15 November 1952.

————, 15 December 1952.
————, 22 December 1952.
————, 18 February 1953.
————, 20 February 1953.
————, 2 March 1953.
————, 10 March 1953.
————, 12 March 1953.
————, 13 March 1953.
————, 19 March 1953.
————, 18 August 1953.
————, 1 October 1953.
————, 2 October 1953.

WEBSITES

Australian Involvement in South-East Asian Conflicts. "The Australian Official History of the Malayan Emergency" <http://se-asia.commemoration.gov.au> (assessed 19 December 2013).

Britain's Wars in Malaya. "The Pretty Communist, and a Hollywood Star", 20 November 2012 <http://malayanwars.blogspot.sg/2012/11/the-pretty-communist-and-hollywood-star.html> (accessed 27 October 2011).

How it Really Was. "Konrad Adenauer and his dismissal as Mayor of Cologne by the British in 1945", 30 March 2008 <http:/howitreallywas.typepad.com/how_it_really_was/2008/03/konrad-adenauer.html> (accessed 4 November 2012).

Malaysian Indian Online. "Union of Discord" by P. Ramasamy, 17 September 2001 <http://www.indianmalaysian.com/union_of_discord.htm> (accessed 25 April 2012).

Malaysia History. <www.malayahistory.net> (accessed 25 April 2012).

Miller, Sergio. "Malaya. The Myth of Hearts and Minds". *Small Wars Journal*, 16 April 2012 <http://smallwarsjournal.com/jrnl/art/malaya-the-myth-of-hearts-and-minds> (accessed 25 April 2012).

Official Portal of Director General of Lands & Mines, Ministry of Natural Resources and Environment. <http://www.nre.gov.my/en-my/Pages/Online-Services.aspx> (accessed 27 October 2011).

Official Portal of the Parliament of Malaya. "Parliamentary Democracy in Malaysia", Kuala Lumpur, 1963 <http://www.parlimen.gov.my/pengenalan.html?&view=236&uweb=p&lang=en> (accessed 27 October 2011).

Pointer — Singapore Ministry of Defence Journal. "Personality File General Templer", Vol. 29, No. 4, 2003 and Ipoh World Archive Records, <http://www.mindef.gov.sg/imindef/publications/pointer/journals/2003/v29n4/personality_profile.html> (accessed 27 October 2011).

Wikipedia. "Henry Lee Hau Sik". <http://en.wikipedia.org/wiki/Henry_Lee_ Hau_Shik> (accessed 1 August 2011).

Wikipedia, "Gerald Templer". <http://en.wikipedia.org/wiki/Gerald_Templer> (accessed 26 March 2012).

Wikipedia. "Tunku Abdul Rahman". <http://en.wikipedia.org/wiki/Tunku_ Abdul_Rahman> (accessed 26 March 2012).

World Spotlight. "Adenauer as Tough as Churchill", 13 September 1953 <http:// trove.nla.gov.au/ndp/del/article/18506663> (accessed 4 November 2012).

INDEX

Note: Pages numbers followed by "n" refer to notes.

ABOUT THE AUTHOR

Dr Leon Comber is a Visiting Senior Research Fellow at the Institute of Southeast Asian Studies (ISEAS), Singapore, and a Research Fellow (Adjunct) at Monash Asia Institute, Monash University, Melbourne. His interest in Malay/sian affairs extends over more than half a century from the time he first landed as a Major with the returning British and Indian forces (as part of "Operation Zipper") at Morib Beach on the west coast of Malaya in September 1945 following the surrender of the Japanese. Thereafter, he served for several years as a Chinese-speaking Special Branch officer in the Malayan Police dealing with political and security intelligence, during the Malayan Emergency. He subsequently had a distinguished career in book publishing. Over the years, his main interest has been Malaysia and Singapore and he has written extensively about them. He holds a BA (Hons) from SOAS, University of London, an MA (Comparative Asian Studies) from the University of Hong Kong, where he was Director and Publisher of the University of Hong Kong Press, an MBA from the University of East Asia, Macau, and a PhD from Monash University, Melbourne. He speaks Malay, Chinese (Cantonese and Mandarin), with some Hindi. He is one of the few European Malaysian citizens.

Among his recent books are:

Singapore Correspondent: Political Dispatches from Singapore (1958–1962);
Malaya's Secret Police 1945–1960: The Role of the Special Branch in the Malayan Emergency;
13 May 1969: The Darkest Day in Malaysian History;
The Strange Cases of Magistrate Pao;
Xun Miao: The Temples of the Chinese in Singapore (in Chinese with Xu Liying).